THE LIGHT ENTRUSTED TO YOU

JOHN R. WOOD

The Light Entrusted to You

Keeping the Flame of Faith Alive

IGNATIUS PRESS   SAN FRANCISCO

RESCRIPT

In accord with canon 827, § 3 of the *Codex Iuris Canonici*,
I hereby grant my permission to publish
The Light Entrusted to You: Keeping the Flame of Faith Alive,
by John R. Wood.

Given at the Chancery of the Diocese of Toledo in America on the
sixth day of June, in the year of our Lord, two-thousand seventeen.

+ Daniel E. Thomas
Bishop of Toledo

Front cover photograph by Kristin Wood

Cover design by Davin Carlson

© 2018 by Ignatius Press, San Francisco
All rights reserved
ISBN 978-1-62164-172-8
Library of Congress Control Number 2017947380
Printed in the United States of America ∞

For my wife and children, the inspiration for this book. My prayer for you is that Christ's light within you may always burn brightly so you reflect the light of the Son. Let us live our lives in such a way that we may be assured of spending eternity together. I love you forever.

CONTENTS

INTRODUCTION

Life holds only one tragedy ... not to have been a saint.

—Leon Bloy

Sharing the Gift

I love the Catholic faith. I have an insatiable hunger to learn more about the faith. There is always more to learn, and the more I learn about the faith, the more I love it. It has brought me an unspeakable joy that I cannot help but want to share with others. I have always had an introverted personality, and growing up, I was a closed book. Sharing my thoughts and speaking in front of others were probably last on my list of things to do. Frankly, they were at the top of the list of things I did not want to do. Reflecting on how God nudged me into the roles of author and speaker, I can relate to the words of Jeremiah the prophet: "Ah, Lord GOD! Behold, I do not know how to speak, for I am only a youth.... O Lord, you have deceived me, and I was deceived; you are stronger than I, and you have prevailed. I have become a laughingstock all the day; every one mocks me.... If I say, 'I will not mention him, or speak any more in his name,' there is in my heart as it were a burning fire shut up in my bones, and I am weary with holding it in, and I cannot" (Jer 1:6; 20:7, 9).[1]

---

[1] Unless otherwise noted, Scripture quotations are from the Revised Standard Version, Second Catholic Edition.

Trying to share the genius of Catholicism with others, I quickly discovered how difficult it was to inspire them. It was often frustrating and disheartening. I desperately wanted to give the gift to others, but nobody seemed to want it. Consumed by pride and the drive to succeed, and seeing myself as a failure, I decided it was not worth it on many occasions. However, with every attempt to quit, that fire inside began to consume me. As Jeremiah described, I grew weary holding it in. We simply cannot keep the faith to ourselves, even though that option often seems easier, or at least safer. Christianity is about evangelization. It is meant to be spread to the ends of the earth. The fire inside is meant to "set the world ablaze", as Saint Catherine of Siena once said.

I recognize now that I cannot *give* the gift to other people. The gift cannot be forced; it must be *chosen*. The Catholic faith is a spiritual North Star. We cannot force people to follow the star, but we can point them to the star— and we must. It is our duty and our obligation to share the faith by our words and our actions. Sharing the faith begins in the domestic church, the family. Saint John Paul II said, "The future of humanity passes by way of the family."[2] Parents are called to be the primary educators of the faith. In the sacrament of marriage, we are asked to make several vows, one of which is our response to the question "Are you prepared to accept children lovingly from God and to bring them up according to the law of Christ and his Church?" If you were married in the Catholic Church, each of you said "I am" to that question. Then, when you lovingly accepted children from God and had them baptized, you were asked by the Church what you wanted

---

[2] *Familiaris Consortio*, 86. Unless otherwise noted, quotations from Church documents are taken from the Holy See website, www.vatican.va.

for your child. Your reply was "Faith" or "Baptism." The Church then asked you to train your child in the practice of the faith, to bring your child up to keep God's commandments by loving God and neighbor, and to see that the divine life in your child is kept safe. In the sacraments of marriage and baptism, you stood before the altar of God and promised to teach your children the faith and protect them from the enemy! We must start keeping our promises because the stakes are very high. It is not about whether your children make the basketball team or get into Harvard. It is about whether we, as parents, and our children spend eternity with God or without Him. It is about heaven and hell, salvation and damnation.

Saint John Paul II said, "Parents must be acknowledged as the first and foremost educators of their children. Their role as educators is so decisive that scarcely anything can compensate for their failure in it."[3] If we fail as parents to pass on the faith to our children, nothing can fully take our place—no religion class, no sermon, no retreat, no book, no CD, no movie, no coach. Nobody has the potential to influence children more than their parents.

Saint John Paul II was certainly not the first to give this advice and warning. Moses made the same point to the Israelites more than three thousand years ago. The book of Deuteronomy in the Bible is Moses' farewell speech to the Israelites. He led the Israelites to freedom from Egypt and guided them through the desert for forty years. When Moses is dying, he tells his people that they are about to go into a land filled with people who are far more advanced in technology and agriculture. It is a wealthy and prosperous land, but the inhabitants worship many false gods, and even sacrifice their own children to those gods. He gives

[3] Ibid., 36.

them a stern warning, cautioning that if they are going to live in a land like that, they must teach the faith to their children. Otherwise, they will be consumed by the culture. "Hear, O Israel! The LORD is our God, the LORD alone! Therefore, you shall love the LORD, your God, with all your heart, and with all your soul, and with all your strength. Take to heart these words which I enjoin on you today. Drill them into your children" (Deut 6:4–7).[4]

If Moses were here today, he would warn us about living in a prosperous and advanced culture and the same temptation to worship our own "false gods" of power, wealth, pleasure, and honor. Since 1973, when abortion was legalized, fifty-five million babies have been killed, sacrificed because they were inconvenient. If we are going to live in this land where it is so easy to be consumed by the culture, we have to teach the faith to our children. If we do not, they will be annihilated by what Saint John Paul II called a "culture of death"—by an enemy who never sleeps. All that is needed for evil to prosper is for good to do nothing. We cannot be silent while negative influences deceive our children and our families. God commanded Adam to guard and protect the garden. Yet Adam, like a coward, did nothing as the serpent deceived his bride.

Adam was the first coward in the story who allowed the serpent to deceive, but not the last. It is a recurring theme in the story. Moses warned his people, but they did not listen. Shortly after the Israelites entered the promised land, Scripture recalls:

> All that generation also were gathered to their fathers; and there arose another generation after them, who did not know the LORD or the work which he had done for Israel.

[4] New American Bible.

> And the sons of Israel did what was evil in the sight of the LORD and served the Baals; and they forsook the LORD, the God of their fathers, who had brought them out of the land of Egypt; they went after other gods, from among the gods of the peoples who were round about them, and bowed down to them; and they provoked the LORD to anger. (Judg 2:10–12)

It took just one generation for the Israelites to lose their story and their faith. They failed to teach it to their children, and their children were consumed by false gods. We must learn from their mistakes. I fear that our children do not know the Lord. We must start a revival.

Worth Fighting For

To teach the faith, we must know the faith and we must live the faith, but that does not mean we have to know *everything* before we can teach *anything*. I would argue that the best way to know the faith is to teach it, most especially to our own children. Once again, the sacrament of baptism comes to mind. During our baptism, we receive a candle that represents the light of Christ. The parents, godparents, and the whole Church community vow to help the child keep the light of Christ always burning in his heart. The words the Church uses are beautiful. As the child's candle is lit from the Easter candle, the priest or deacon says, "Parents and godparents, this light is entrusted to you to be kept burning brightly. This child of yours has been enlightened by Christ. He is to walk always as a child of the light. May he keep the flame of faith alive in his heart. When the Lord comes, may he go out to meet him with all the saints in the heavenly kingdom."

These words show how we are all connected through baptism. We are all one family with one mission—to share the fire of God's love with the whole world so that we may spend eternity together in heaven. Like love, fire is not divided or diminished when it is shared; it only multiplies. This is why it is so essential to share our faith with others. Sharing our faith does not just help others; it helps us. We do not just learn our faith so we can teach others; we teach others so we can learn our faith. That is why children often help us on our spiritual journey as much as we help them. That is part of the genius of Catholicism.

This book is a guide to help you rediscover the genius of Catholicism, live an authentic Catholic life, and share Catholicism with your family and friends. It is a boot camp to prepare us for the spiritual warfare spoken of in the Scriptures, Church tradition, and the writings of almost all the saints.

Unfortunately, many Catholics have quit fighting for Christ and His Church. I have spoken to many engaged couples and Catholic high school students at events where they are forced to be there. Most of them are not angry at the Church, just indifferent. The reality is that the number of Catholics who have stopped practicing their faith over the last fifteen years is alarming. According to the Georgetown University Center for Applied Research in the Apostolate (CARA), since the year 2000, sacramental Catholic marriages have dropped by 43 percent, baptisms of adults have dropped by 45 percent, baptisms of infants have dropped by 43 percent, Catholic school enrollment has dropped by 21 percent, and parish religious education enrollment has dropped by 25 percent.[5] According to the

[5] "Frequently Requested Church Statistics", Center for Applied Research in the Apostolate (CARA), accessed October 18, 2017, http://cara.georgetown.edu/frequently-requested-church-statistics/.

research of the Dynamic Catholic Institute, less than 7 percent of Catholics in any give parish contribute 80 percent of the volunteer hours, and less than 7 percent donate 80 percent of the financial contributions. There is an 84 percent overlap between those two groups, so it is mostly the same people![6] And perhaps the most staggering statistic, 85 percent of young adults leave their faith within ten years of being confirmed.[7]

By the numbers, Catholicism is by far still the largest religious denomination in the United States (68 million), and fallen-away Catholics are ranked second (25 million). Quite frankly, most Catholics do not realize deeply enough how relevant their faith is for their own lives and the culture around them. Little do they realize that Catholicism will make them better parents, better spouses, better businesspeople, better doctors, better athletes, better teachers, and better Americans. Our culture and our world are soaked in Catholic influences and origins; these roots have just been masked by a secular society.

Many of our great cities are named after Catholic saints, such as Saint Francis (San Francisco), Saint Louis, Saint Paul, Saint Monica (Santa Monica), Saint Barbara (Santa Barbara), and Saint Diego (San Diego). The holidays we celebrate have many Christian influences as well, although we have turned them into secular traditions. Every New Year's Day we turn the calendar another year, measured by the number of years since the birth of Christ. We celebrate Saint Valentine's Day, which is not about Cupid but about a Catholic martyr, who, like all the martyrs, teaches us that "greater love has no man than this, that a man lay down

[6] Matthew Kelly, *The Four Signs of a Dynamic Catholic* (Cincinnati, Ohio: Beacon Publishing, 2012), 12.

[7] Matthew Kelly, *DECISION POINT Leader Guide* (Hebron, Ky.: Beacon Publishing, 2014), 9.

his life for his friends" (Jn 15:13). In March, we celebrate Saint Patrick's Day, which is not about shamrocks and leprechauns but about a Catholic bishop who converted an entire nation. We celebrate Easter, not because of the bunnies and eggs, but because Jesus Christ was resurrected. "Halloween" means "All Hallows Eve" since it is the eve of All Saints Day, which is November 1. "Thanksgiving" is another word for Eucharist; as Catholics we are a Eucharistic people. At Christmas, we celebrate the birth of Christ, and Santa Claus is not just some jolly fat man with flying reindeer—he is Saint Nicholas, another Catholic bishop known for his extreme generosity and giving in secret. Even the Fourth of July is a celebration as a nation that all men "are endowed by their Creator with certain inalienable rights", among them "life, liberty and the pursuit of happiness". We celebrate the fact that we have no human king. God is our King, and in Him we trust. We are free only inasmuch as we choose to do what is right.

Before the Catholic Church, there were no hospitals or schools for the common man. These kinds of institutions were built in Western civilization because of the Church's belief in the sacredness of every human life. The Catholic Church feeds more people, clothes more of the naked, comforts more of the sick, visits more prisoners, and educates more students than any other institution could ever hope to. The Catholic Church has positively influenced the entire world for the last two thousand years. Hers is a history steeped in tradition and with an unbroken chain of apostolic succession that can be traced all the way back to the first pope, Peter, on whom Christ said He would build His Church.

The Church has remained consistent and steadfast in her teachings, and she has always spoken the truth, no matter how unpopular. If there are teachings of the

Church that you find challenging or unbiblical, I challenge you to research why the Church teaches what she does. If you dig into Church history and read the teachings of the early Church Fathers and early Church councils, you will discover a constant unwavering truth based on sacred Scripture and sacred tradition. Just ask men like Jeff Cavins, Tim Staples, Scott Hahn, Allen Hunt, and Marcus Grodi. These men were Protestant pastors and biblical scholars and were anti-Catholic, each of them setting out on a journey to prove the Catholic Church wrong. Their journey into history led them to embrace a faith they once saw as corrupted. They are now some of the most well-respected Catholic authors and speakers, teaching millions the genius of Catholicism.

However, in the media, we do not often hear about the true teachings of the Church or her overwhelmingly positive influence on the world; instead, we hear about corruption and the sins of Catholic people and leaders. As Pope Francis warned a group of priests, "I once read that priests are like airplanes: they only make news when they crash."[8] We tend to ignore the fact that a huge majority soar in their service and sacrifice for others. Many people have left the Church founded on the rock of Peter because of the sins of a few Judases. This Church has remained strong for two millennia, not always because of the people who are members, but often despite them. While the Church has indeed had her share of corrupt leaders and scandals, her moral truth and doctrine has remained constant, pure, and spotless. Christ promised that

[8] "Address of His Holiness Pope Francis at the Presentation of the Christmas Greetings to the Roman Curia", Clementine Hall, Rome, December 22, 2011, https://w2.vatican.va/content/francesco/en/speeches/2014/december /documents/papa-francesco_20141222_curia-romana.html.

His Church would always be guided by the Holy Spirit, and He has kept His promise.

This Catholic faith is worth dying for. It still thrives today because so many men and women throughout history were willing to give their lives for it. All the apostles were persecuted and most were brutally executed for proclaiming that Christ really did rise from the dead. Saint Peter was crucified upside down, Saint Paul was beheaded, Saint Stephen was stoned to death, and Saint Bartholomew was skinned alive. If the Resurrection of Christ was a lie, don't you think at least one of those men would have confessed while he was being tortured? They, and all the martyrs that followed them, died for a faith they believed to be true with all their hearts, and the faith spread because of their conviction.

I am not asking you to die for the faith. I am asking you to live for it—to open yourself up to receiving a gift that nobody can ever take from you. The goal of our faith is salvation (see 1 Pet 1:9). Salvation means getting to heaven, and leading others to heaven. Getting to heaven means becoming the saints God created us to be, for a saint is simply someone in heaven. As human beings, we are not the sum of our sins, failures, and faults. We are children of God, beloved sons and daughters of the Most High God, and heirs to the kingdom of heaven. By virtue of our baptism, in a sense we are already saints, but we are also saints in the making. So, to accomplish this universal (Catholic) mission, we need a type of "university"—a "saints-in-the-making" university. Is this Saints in the Making University (SIMU) worth your time and energy? I would say that becoming a saint is the *only* thing worth your time and energy. If what you have and do now are not helping you become a saint, then at the very best they are wasting your time.

Become a saint. Nothing else really matters.

The Curriculum

SIMU is made up of six "classes", each with its own unique color. These six classes, explained in the following six chapters, make up the acronym SAINTS:

Saving Grace: This class is green, for new life.

Athletics: This class is blue, for strength.

Instructor's Manual: This class is red, for God's love letter (the Bible) and His blood poured out.

Need to Know Him: This class is purple, for the royalty of God and His kingdom.

Theology of the Body: This class is orange, for health of mind, body, and soul.

Sacrifice and Service: This class is yellow, for brightening somebody's day.

Everything in Catholicism fits into one or more of these six classes. Much like the *Catechism of the Catholic Church*, this book is designed to help you rediscover all aspects of the faith, as too often we do not see the big picture of how everything in our faith fits together. Each of these classes is designed to help you grow in your faith using everyday examples we are all familiar with, including movies, sports, and music. Wherever you can find beauty and truth, you can find God and His Church.

I am convinced that if you open your heart and mind to these lessons, you not only will know and understand your Christian faith better but will fall in love with your faith and want to share it with others. God is after your heart, not just your mind.

Perhaps you do not feel you are qualified to share the faith or have enough education to really understand the faith. I do not have a theology degree. I have discovered the beauty and genius of Catholicism through great authors, priests, videos, audio recordings, speakers, and Catholic radio. There is a wealth of resources for every age and every level. Allow me to share with you the resources I found and how I have successfully used those resources to pass the faith on to my own small children, the teenagers I teach, the engaged couples I speak to, and the adults at our parish. This book will take you on a journey through each of these classes, explaining how they relate to the modern world, and providing detailed suggestions on how and when to implement these classes in your family and parish community.

Inspire, Desire, Fire

We are all at a different stage of our spiritual journey, but I think we all go through a similar process. As you begin this book, I want you to consider these three steps for yourself and for those with whom you share the faith.

1. INSPIRE: *New York Times* best-selling author Matthew Kelly often says that most people will do almost nothing until they are inspired. But once they are inspired, there is almost nothing they will not do. I like to think of inspiration as a "breathing in" of the Holy Spirit and an encounter with the real and living God. First and foremost, I hope you realize that Catholicism is not primarily a religion of rules and regulations but a religion of relationship. Through this book and through the resources I recommend, you will encounter God in a real and personal way and be inspired to want to know Him more.

2. DESIRE: Once we encounter God and fall in love with Him, we will automatically want to do things

to make Him proud. As you will discover in this book, God's dream for you is to be a saint. I pray this desire to be a saint will burn within your heart.

3. FIRE: There is nothing more attractive than holiness. Love of God and desire for sanctity should radiate from each of us. The fire of God's love within is the spark for the fire without—a fire that should set the whole world ablaze. Fire begets fire. This book's ultimate purpose is to make sure the light of Christ, entrusted to each and every one of us, burns brightly for the whole world to see. Be confident that God can do great things through those who trust in Him.

Chapter 1

S: SAVING GRACE

Color: Green, for New Life

*Fairy tales are more than true; not because they tell us
that dragons exist, but because they tell us that dragons
can be beaten.*

—G. K. Chesterton

The Question

I recently came up with the idea to read through all four
Gospels searching for questions that Jesus asked. I simply
started in Matthew and just kept reading each day until I
came to a question. When I would come across a "Jesus
question", I would stop and answer it as if He were talking
to me. I have been doing this for five months almost daily,
and I am still not through the Gospels. As all great teachers
do, Jesus asked a lot of questions. Some questions were
easy to answer, some were challenging, and some were just
confusing. However, there is one question Jesus asked that
I think is the most important question: "But who do you
say that I am?" (Mt 16:15). This is a question that Jesus
is addressing to every one of us, and how we answer this

question determines our whole worldview and influences every decision about the way we live. Some say Jesus was just a nice man with some nice teachings. Some say He is a coping mechanism for certain people. Some say He is a figment of our imagination. Who do you say that He is?

It was Peter who first answered this question correctly. "You are the Christ, the Son of the living God" (Mt 16:16). Peter is kind of childlike in how he wears his heart on his sleeve. One minute he is saying something brilliant such as this response, and the next minute he is saying something not so brilliant. Jesus rewards Peter's profession of faith by declaring that He will build His Church on this rock of Peter, and He gives him the keys to the kingdom of heaven (see Mt 16:19). Receiving the keys to the kingdom of heaven is quite an honor and had to be one of the greatest moments of Peter's life. However, only four verses later, Peter's rebuke of Jesus' talk of His upcoming passion causes Jesus to say to him, "Get behind me, Satan!" (Mt 16:23). Being called "Satan" by Jesus had to be one the worst moments of his life. Peter's roller-coaster ride with Jesus reminds me of what it is like raising my own four small children. One minute I am thinking to myself, "On these rocks I will rebuild the Church", and the very next minute I am thinking, "Get behind me, Satan! What kind of demon is possessing you!" If you are a parent, I am sure you know what I am talking about.

We can learn a lot from our children because we are not so different. Like them (and like Peter in the Gospels), there is a saint inside each of us, and there is a sinner inside each of us. Each day we must struggle to choose the saint. I wrote about this struggle in my first book, *Ordinary Lives, Extraordinary Mission: 5 Steps to Winning the War Within.*[1] I

---

[1] *Ordinary Lives, Extraordinary Mission: 5 Steps to Winning the War Within* (Hebron, Ky.: Beacon Publishing, 2002).

think the internal war is summed up perfectly in *Gaudium et Spes*: "The whole of man's history has been the story of dour combat with the powers of evil, stretching, so our Lord tells us, from the very dawn of history until the last day. Finding himself in the midst of the battlefield man has to struggle to do what is right, and it is at great cost to himself, and aided by God's grace, that he succeeds in achieving his own inner integrity."[2] As Christians, we are all summoned to spiritual warfare, and the battle begins at our baptism. According to the *Catechism of the Catholic Church*, "Baptism, by imparting the life of Christ's grace, erases original sin and turns a man back toward God, but the consequences for nature, weakened and inclined to evil, persist in man and summon him to spiritual battle."[3] As soon as we are adopted into the royal bloodline of Christ, we are meant to fight this spiritual warfare for the sake of the kingdom of heaven.

Christ is our model. After His baptism He does not go to the beach to drink a piña colada. He goes to the desert to fast and do battle with the devil (see Mt 4). We must follow His lead and also teach our children to "do battle". Much of our time parenting is simply training our children to overcome concupiscence, the tendency to do wrong because of original sin. It should be obvious that children often desire to do and have things that are not good for them. Imagine if we simply let our children do everything they wanted to do. They would probably end up either dead or in prison very early in life. We strive to teach them to live lives of virtue, and we all know it is a long journey that each of us continues his whole life.

---

[2] Vatican Council II, *Gaudium et Spes*, 37.2, quoted in *Catechism of the Catholic Church*, 2nd ed. (Vatican City: Libreria Editrice Vaticana; Washington, D.C.: United States Catholic Conference, 2000), 409 (hereafter cited as *CCC*).
[3] *CCC* 405.

A book that has been very helpful for my wife and me with our children is *Dragon Slayers*, by Sir Wyvern Pugilist.[4] The book's genius is how it identifies, names, describes, and gives the reader visual pictures of dragons (sins and temptations) you and your children face each day. Each dragon comes with "symptoms of exposure to stench". My children absolutely love this book. They have every dragon memorized, and they know everything about them. It has also greatly helped me as a parent. If my children are being lazy, not doing their chores, not listening to our requests, or complaining about going to Mass, I simply have to say, "You are letting Slackbottom get you", and they jump to the task. They do not want to let the dragons defeat them. In essence, they are learning the dangers of the deadly sin of sloth. If your children know and understand these dragons and how they work, it opens up endless opportunities to teach your children right from wrong every day, simply by naming the dragons. It also opens up opportunities to teach them the swords (virtues) that can defeat the dragons, and it is grace that gives the children their "superpowers". Very rarely do kids like to be told right and wrong, but I have yet to come across kids who do not like learning how to be great dragon slayers or superheroes. I have used this model of teaching with kids whom I have spoken to all over the country. It works. It is so encouraging and rewarding to receive letters from elementary school kids across the country telling me how they want to be great dragon slayers.

As adults, we can learn something from this model of "training" as well. We too must identify our dragons. This is one of the reasons I was so excited when Pope Francis announced the Year of Mercy from December 8,

---

[4] *Dragon Slayers* (Bewster, Mass.: Paraclete Press, 2011).

2015, to November 20, 2016. Mercy, the pope teaches us, is not about telling people everything is OK. Mercy is about conversion. Mercy is about turning back to God to relieve a suffering heart. Our hearts suffer for many reasons, sometimes from self-inflicted wounds and sometimes from deep hurts. Many people need the message of mercy because they believe they have fallen too far to be worthy of God's mercy. The message of Divine Mercy teaches us that our sins are but a drop of water in the ocean of God's mercy.

However, many people need the message of mercy because they do not believe there is anything wrong. For many years I have tried evangelizing others with the "good news" of the Gospel and often feel frustrated when they do not seem to want it. I could not understand how people just were not interested. Have you ever had really good news that you wanted to share, but nobody seemed to care? I remember when I was a child coming home from school and getting the mail. It had one of those Ed McMahon million-dollar sweepstakes letters with bold words on the front that read, "You have won a million dollars!" My two older brothers convinced me we had actually won. For two hours I thought we were millionaires. When my parents got home I could not wait to tell them. Imagine my disappointment when they did not seem to care. I decided there could be only one of two conclusions. Either my parents did not believe the good news, or they did not think they needed a million dollars.

I think the same two conclusions can be applied to the good news of the Gospel when people are "bored" by it. Either they do not believe Jesus really died for our sins as our Savior (it is too good to be true), or they do not believe they need a Savior. If you do not realize the "bad news", then you will not be attracted to the "good news".

The bad news is this: We are sinners! Many people will say they do not believe in sin and do not see a need for a Savior. You may claim you are fine and have no need for a Savior, but there is an elephant in the room that cannot be ignored. You are dying, and so am I. Any hope you have can be only temporary, and any joy you experience can be only a distraction from the reality that death is imminent for you and the people you love. We have a problem—namely, sin and death. The death problem is because of the sin problem. "The wages of sin is death" (Rom 6:23). God did not intend for us to suffer and die, and He did not create death—we did! Sin brought death into the world. Jesus came to solve the sin problem and the death problem. That is good news!

Identifying our weaknesses (dragons) and understanding our need for a Savior is the first step in the spiritual life. On a recent trip to Texas, an older couple, after learning I was from Ohio, was telling me how Alcoholics Anonymous was started in Ohio and had saved their family. The organization is very successful in helping people overcome addiction with a twelve-step program. Step 1 is recognizing that you have a problem and you need help to overcome it. This should sound familiar to us as Catholics. How do we start every Mass? By admitting our faults and asking for mercy. "I confess to almighty God and to you, my brothers and sisters, that I have greatly sinned ..." "Lord, have mercy. Christ, have mercy. Lord, have mercy."

My name is John, and I am a sinner. In fact, I am even a great sinner because I have broken the greatest of all the commandments: "You shall love the Lord your God with all your heart, and with all your soul, and with all your strength, and with all your mind; and your neighbor as yourself" (Lk 10:27). If you are honest with yourself, you have probably broken that commandment as well, so none of us has reason to boast. We all need help. I cannot "slay my dragons" without help. Step 2 in Alcoholics Anonymous is "Came to believe that a Power greater than ourselves could restore us to sanity." That power is visible in the crucifix. God became man in the person of Jesus Christ to set us free! As we will see in this chapter, it was the blood that stained that Cross that sets us free. His blood was the ransom that paid the wages for our sin. The wounds of Christ were the gateway from which God's saving grace and mercy flowed forth.

"I Do Not Know You"

How we respond to God's love matters. Jesus says some pretty scary things in the Gospels. Perhaps the scariest for me is when He says, "Not every one who says to me, 'Lord, Lord,' shall enter the kingdom of heaven, but he who does the will of my Father who is in heaven. On that day many will say to me, 'Lord, Lord, did we not prophesy in your name, and cast out demons in your name, and do many mighty works in your name?' And then I will declare to them, 'I never knew you; depart from me, you evildoers'" (Mt 7:21).

I always try to put myself in the story, and I wonder what Jesus would say to me. The nightmare is this: I will tell Jesus, "I worked hard to become a track champion and a doctor who helps people. Plus, I was at Mass every Sunday—check your attendance book!" He will look at me and say, "Depart from me; I do not know you." I will further plead my case and say, "Lord, I am a father and a husband. I taught my kids how to ride a bike, how to shoot a basketball, and how to get into a good college." He will reply, "If you did not teach them who I am and how much I love them, then you've taught them nothing. Depart from me; I do not know you." In a final plea I will say, "But, Lord, my mom is a good Catholic. My wife is a good Catholic." He will solemnly declare, "Another person cannot have a relationship with Me for you. Depart from me; I do not know you."

In chapter 4, the most important chapter in this book, we will discuss in great detail the family of God and our need to know Him. In this chapter, the point is understanding that without God's saving grace, we are doomed, and we do not get that grace by earning it—we get it by knowing the Savior. If we want to go to heaven, then we need to know people in high places. Spiritually speaking, our only true need is to know God. We must do the will of the Father not because our religion is about following rules or earning our way to heaven but because rules and deeds are part of being in a family of love.

I do not "need" a state championship. I do not "need" a doctor's degree. I do not "need" wealth, or comfort, or success in this life. These good things are only gifts that can help us experience the fulfillment of God's love. These things are not themselves the fulfillment. We cannot worship the creation and forget the Creator. The reality is—and this may sound harsh—I do not even "need" my wife and children. My wife is the one who taught me this. We will better come to understand this in chapter 5 when we discuss the goal of marriage and every other sacrament as getting to heaven. I need God. Everything else is a gift given to us by God to help draw us closer to Him. Even our relationships should lead us to God. God is the source of love and mercy, and I cannot truly and completely love my wife and children if I do not love God first. My wife and children could be taken from me in an instant. My talents and abilities, my wealth, my home, my freedom, my job, and my earthly life can all be taken away from me in an instant. What then? Without God, there is no hope. I want to be a state champion, a good doctor, a good father, and a good husband and to serve those I encounter because I love *Him*. I do not love God because of the gifts He gives; I love the gifts He gives because they are from Him and lead me back to Him. My foundations of hope and happiness are not the gifts; they are God and heaven. There is only one thing that can never be taken away—the hope of heaven.

My mother wrote me a letter for my confirmation retreat that I have kept all these years. In the letter she explained how life is hard and involves suffering, and true happiness comes from knowing and loving God. She ended that letter with the words, "You can't change fate, but you can change the direction it takes you." Years later I watched my mother and father suffer through the final months of my dad's life. Through all that suffering, and to this day, I never saw my mother lose her joy and her faith. In my years of high school and college I tried finding happiness in all the things of this world, but nothing could truly satisfy me. I want what my mom has. She has something that no person or circumstance—not even death—can take from her. She knows the King of the Universe. She trusts Him.

The Flow of Grace

For the remainder of this chapter, we will focus on nine agents and principles of grace. We need the witness and intercession of the awesome power of grace in the saints and angels, who help us (nos. 1–4); and we need to know where grace comes from (no. 5), what grace is (no. 6), and what it can accomplish in our lives (nos. 7–9).

1. We need not fear the "dragons", because we have **Saint Joseph**, the terror of demons.

2. We have the **Blessed Mother**, whose seed crushes the head of the serpent.

3. We have legions of good **angels** guarding and protecting us.

4. We have the **saints of the past** praying for us and interceding for us.

5. We have the greatest weapon in the world: the **blood of the Cross**.

6. From that blood flows **saving grace**.

7. Grace helps build **virtue**.

8. Virtue breeds **holiness**.

9. Holiness makes **saints**. Saints—and this includes you and me—slay dragons and, in doing so, help get souls to heaven and are agents of grace for others.

1. The Terror of Demons

If you were the enemy, what would you attack? I would choose the things that are most sacred and have the most potential to stand in my way. I would attack God's Church—His universal Church and the domestic church. The Catholic Church is no doubt under attack, and so is the family, which is the building block of society and the foundation of the Church. The Church is the Bride of Christ, and she carries within her a new life—an eternal life. Revelation 12 describes a huge red dragon that stands before a woman about to give birth so it can devour her child. That dragon no doubt wants to devour any life and hope the Church brings to the world. If our Church and our families are under attack, maybe now more than ever, then I think it is time to turn to the patron of the universal Church and the domestic church—Saint Joseph.

Saint Joseph is known as the terror of demons precisely because he is the guardian of the Church. These times call for a renewal in devotion to Saint Joseph. Sometimes Joseph gets forgotten. He is rightly overshadowed by the Son of God and the Mother of God, but his is not an insignificant role just to complete the Holy Family. In fact, after Jesus and the Blessed Mother, nobody deserves more of our devotion.

Until recently, Saint Joseph never caught my attention. You do not read much about Saint Joseph in the Scriptures, and there are no recorded words of his on which to reflect. However, I came to realize that nobody embodies the phrase "actions speak louder than words" more than Saint Joseph. His life was his message. He shows me what it means to be a man. This ordinary man, who was given a seemingly impossible task, shows me what it means to be a husband and a father. He was asked to be the foster father of the God of the universe and to be the spouse of the Immaculate Virgin Mary. There is no way that Joseph felt prepared or worthy for such a task as to be the guardian and protector of the Holy Family. Yet he obeyed and he trusted. He simply did what he was told by God. Obedience and trust can go a long way. Many times God seems to ask us to do impossible tasks, and Saint Joseph can be a great intercessor in helping us to obey and trust.

Speaking from my own experience, I think men have built-in DNA to want to "save the damsel in distress". I remember as a child putting my underwear on over my pants and having Mom safety-pin a towel around my neck for a cape so I could jump off every piece of furniture in the house pretending to be Superman, flying around saving Lois Lane from the bad guys. The Church is certainly a damsel in distress. She carries eternal life within her, and she needs people who are willing to fight for her, to live for her, and if need be, even die for her. The problem is, as Catholic author Jason Evert bluntly says, sometimes we want to look like a knight but do not want to bleed like one. Saint Joseph's love for Jesus and Mary gave him his courage. A knight cannot be brave without love, because his love gives him his courage. We must turn to Saint Joseph at this time in history because it is his love for the Church that terrorizes the dragons who attack us. I want that kind of love because I want that kind of courage.

Saint Teresa of Avila had a strong devotion to Saint Joseph, and she said of him:

> I do not remember to this day ever having asked him for anything that he did not grant me. I am amazed at the great mercies which the Lord has done me through this blessed saint, and from what perils, both of body and soul, he has delivered me. The Lord seems to have given other saints grace to help in some troubles, but I know by experience that this glorious saint helps in all. For His Majesty wishes to teach us that, as He was Himself subject to him on earth—for having the title of father, though only his guardian, St. Joseph could command Him—so in heaven the Lord does what he asks.[5]

Saint Joseph is a powerful intercessor in this time especially. He is the head of the Holy Family. Ultimately it is Jesus we seek, and we gain special access into the life of Jesus through His Immaculate Mother Mary, and in seeking a devotion to Saint Joseph we find it much easier to

[5] Teresa of Avila, *The Life of St. Teresa of Avila by Herself*, trans. J. M. Cohen (New York: Penguin Classics, 1988), 47.

consecrate our lives to Mary, a perfect picture of humility and grace.

2. The Humble Handmaid

If pride is the root of all sin, humility is the root of all virtue. Humility is about doing things God's way instead of our way. It requires us to let go of our plans and embrace God's plan for our life. Sometimes that means letting go of our own plans on how to become a saint. As human beings, we want control. Even when we make a commitment to serve God, we end up setting our own terms on how we will serve Him. This is why humility is so important. It comes from the Latin word *humilitas*, which comes from *humus*, which means "earth" or "ground". To be "grounded" is to remember that we are formed from the dust, and as "humans" we must be submissive and serve our Creator and our fellow man, which is exactly what Satan—lacking all humility—said he would not do.

This is exactly why Satan, filled with pride, is at such odds with Mary, "the woman" (see Gen 3:15). Mary is what Bishop Robert Barron, quoting William Wordsworth, calls in his *Catholicism* series "our tainted nature's solitary boast".[6] She represents the perfect model of humanity because of her perfect humility, and Satan is no match for her. Saint Vincent de Paul once instructed, "The most powerful weapon to conquer the devil is humility. For, as he does not know at all how to employ it, neither does he know how to defend himself from it."[7] True humility is not weakness or self-loathing. True humility

[6] William Wordsworth, "The Virgin", line 4.
[7] Quoted in *A Year with the Saints* (New York: P.J. Kenedy & Sons, 1891), 47.

is understanding that you do not have what it takes to do God's will, but you believe you can do it anyway. Jesus said, "I am the vine, you are the branches" (Jn 15:5). Humility helps us remember that if we separate ourselves from the vine or the "grounded" root, we will wither and die; but as long as we are attached to the vine, we can and should bear much fruit.

Mary is constantly submissive to the will of God, always aligning her will with His. Behind the scenes she is praying, reflecting, and, when the time comes, suffering with her Son, committed to God's will no matter the cost. You will notice that Mary never makes herself the center of attention even though she is sinless and immaculate. Steadfast in her love and devotion to her Son, she is there for his conception, birth, life, death, and Resurrection. A picture of perfect obedience, we hear from her own lips phrases such as "I am the handmaid of the Lord; let it be to me according to your word" (Lk 1:38). Mary teaches us how to pray with humility. Her conduct at the wedding at Cana is a perfect example of prayer. When the celebration runs out of wine, notice what Mary says to Jesus. She does not say, "Go make more wine!" or "If you don't make more wine, their party will be ruined!" No, Mary simply describes the situation to Jesus. She says only a few words to Jesus: "They have no wine." That's it. Then we read her last recorded words in Scripture, and they say it all. She tells the servers, "Do whatever he tells you" (Jn 2:5).

This petition of Mary at the wedding at Cana illustrates her humility and trust. We would do well to model our prayer after hers. I must admit, my prayer usually does not sound like that. I have prayed things like "Jesus, if you don't help me find the right woman to be my wife, I can never be happy"; "Jesus, if you don't heal my father of cancer, it will be too much for me to handle"; and "Jesus, I need to win this race, or I will be a failure." I am always telling Jesus the situation, but I also feel the need to tell Him how to fix it. Would that I could learn to trust and do whatever He tells me, even if it means my prayer may not be answered in the way I desire. Would that I could have the peace of knowing that His will is better than mine. It is great to give God our petitions in prayer, but our prayer should always end with "Thy will be done."

Mary's humility makes her a perfect model for every other virtue. As this quote often attributed to Saint Augustine explains, "Humility is the foundation of all the other virtues; hence, in the soul in which this virtue does not exist, there cannot be any other virtue except in mere appearance." As you travel up "Mount Purgatory" in Bishop Barron's *Seven Deadly Sins, Seven Lively Virtues*, he will cite Dante's Marian counterexample to each of the deadly sins, reaffirming Mary as our model of all virtue.[8]

Joseph and Mary received much aid and guidance in their mission from the same heavenly messengers to whom we have access in our journeys—the angels.

3. Spiritual Guardians

Pope Francis said, "Around us there is the presence of evil, the Devil is at work. But I would say in a loud voice that: 'God is stronger!' "[9] There are many dragons lurking in this world, but I have to believe there are many more

---

[8] *Seven Deadly Sins, Seven Lively Virtues* (Skokie, Ill.: Word on Fire, 2007), DVD.

[9] "'God Is Stronger,' Pope Insists as He Urges Outreach", *Catholic News Agency*, June 12, 2013, http://www.catholicnewsagency.com/news/god-is-stronger-pope-insists-as-he-urges-outreach/.

good angels than demons. Revelation 12 states that the dragon's tail swept away a third of the stars in the sky and hurled them down to the earth. This has been interpreted by theologians as meaning a third of the angels became demons and joined the prince of darkness. That means two-thirds of the angels remained good. Angels were created for our benefit and our protection.

One of the most fascinating talks on angels is Mark Miravalle's "Angels Explained".[10] Miravalle explains the nine choirs of angels, Church teaching and tradition regarding angels, and what angels are and what they are not. Higher-order spiritual beings, they were created at the beginning of time completely filled with the love and knowledge of God. They possess free will and have already undergone their spiritual testing, so no more angels will become demons and no demons will ever become good angels; all the angels' eternal destinies have been determined. Angels do not possess bodies, nor will they ever possess bodies. They do not procreate or multiply. They are just created.

The three most famous angels are archangels Saint Michael, Saint Gabriel, and Saint Raphael, who belong to the eighth choir of angels and often bring messages of great importance. Saint Michael, because of his honor of and obedience to God the Father, was raised up to be the commander of the army of angels. Saint Gabriel seems to be the special angel of God the Son, as his appearance in the Scriptures is often associated with Jesus—the most famous account being his Annunciation to Mary that she would bear the Christ child. Saint Raphael is the angel of healing, and so we could say perhaps he is the special angel

[10] *Angels Explained* (Greenwood Village, Colo.: Lighthouse Talks, Augustine Institute, 2016), CD.

of God the Holy Spirit, since the Holy Spirit brings us grace and healing.

Devotion to Saint Michael is a great way to pray for extra protection for our families and our Church from the forces of evil. I say "extra" protection because each of us has a guardian angel. How many angels God created is unknown, but we do know that every human being who has ever existed has had an angel created just for him. That is a pretty awesome gift.

Tradition tells us that the guardian angels come primarily from the ninth and last choir of angels, which means that the number of angels is so large that a single choir (the ninth) has more angels than the number of human beings who have ever lived or will ever live. That is a lot of angels! Your guardian angel has been infused with the love and knowledge of God the Father, so be assured that your guardian angel loves and knows you better than any human being. We should truly be grateful for and knowledgeable about these wondrous spirits that accompany us on our journey.

One of my favorite prayers and perhaps one of the most important prayers for "slaying dragons" is the Saint Michael prayer. This prayer really should be on the tip of everyone's tongue, and we should teach it to our children from an early age. Its origin goes back to Pope Leo XIII.

Late in the nineteenth century, Pope Leo suddenly went into a trance during a meeting with the cardinals. Those who rushed to his aid thought they had already lost the aging pontiff. However, he suddenly rallied, and upon awakening exclaimed, "Oh, what a horrible picture I was permitted to see!" In his vision, he saw the immense vile activities of the evil spirits and their ravings against the Church. The vision frightened Pope Leo so much that shortly afterward he composed the prayer to Saint Michael to protect the Church, and for many years this prayer was said at the conclusion of every Mass.

We need a revival of this prayer. In 1994 Pope Saint John Paul II reiterated the importance of this prayer when he said:

> May prayer strengthen us for the spiritual battle we are told about in the Letter to the Ephesians: "Draw strength from the Lord and from His mighty power" (Eph 6:10). The Book of Revelation refers to this same battle, recalling before our eyes the image of St. Michael the Archangel (Rev 12:7). Pope Leo XIII certainly had a very vivid recollection of this scene when, at the end of the last century, he introduced a special prayer to St. Michael throughout the Church. Although this prayer is no longer recited at the end of Mass, I ask everyone not to forget it and to recite it to obtain help in the battle against forces of darkness and against the spirit of this world.[11]

Prayer to Saint Michael the Archangel

Saint Michael the Archangel,
defend us in battle.
Be our defense against the wickedness and
    snares of the devil.
May God rebuke him, we humbly pray,
and do thou,
O Prince of the heavenly hosts,
by the power of God,
thrust into hell Satan,
and all the evil spirits,
who prowl about the world
seeking the ruin of souls. Amen.

---

[11] Pope John Paul II, "Regina Caeli", April 24, 1994.

4. Dragon Slayers of Old

While it is comforting to know that the angels surround us and protect us at all times, it may seem difficult to relate to them. They are purely spiritual beings, higher-order creatures. Sometimes you need somebody who has walked the path before you—somebody who has sinned as you have sinned but ultimately overcame those obstacles to slay the dragons you now face.

This is where the saints come in. They are our brothers and sisters. My brothers in my family have always been the ones who have encouraged me and warned me of imminent dangers. They have gone out of their way to help me succeed and avoid pitfalls they encountered along their journeys. When I get myself in trouble or get down on myself, they help me through those situations that they have already experienced. The saints act in the same way. They are siblings, coaches, mentors, and ultimately our greatest fans.

Matthew Kelly, in his best-selling book *Rediscover Catholicism*, points out that to be successful in any endeavor you should study the lives of those who were already successful in that endeavor.[12] If you want to be a great athlete, study great athletes. If you want to be great in business, study great businesspeople. If you want to have a great marriage, study couples who have had great marriages. The same principle applies to our dragon slaying.

If there is a dragon that you struggle with, chances are there are some saints who struggled with the same dragon. Part of the reason we do not utilize the saints' help as we should is that our perception of them is very skewed. In fact, many people actually interchange the words "saints"

---

[12] *Rediscover Catholicism* (Cincinnati, Ohio: Beacon Publishing, 2002).

and "angels", which is very telling. Angels, while they are definitely holy—*sanctus*, "holy", being the root of the word "saint"—have never been human and never will be. The human saints will always be human. They are not God's favored few, and they did not possess some magical talent or ability that you lack. In fact, saints are defined not by what they can or did do but by who they become.

The original title I chose for my first book was not *Ordinary Lives, Extraordinary Mission*. It was *Choosing the Saint Inside*, and it was to be published by Matthew Kelly. For me, this is still hard to believe. Kelly is undeniably one of the greatest spiritual voices of our time—a great inspiration for me for over a decade. You can imagine my excitement talking on the phone with Kelly when he agreed to publish my book. Before hanging up, though, he said there was one thing I needed to work on: the title. I really liked my title. I thought *Choosing the Saint Inside* flowed well, and I had already created a website with that title. His explanation was fascinating: "I don't think your target audience wants to be saints. The book is trying to convince them to be saints, but the title has to convince them to read the book."

My initial response was, "What does Matthew Kelly know? So what if he's sold millions of books and traveled to fifty countries." Of course, Kelly was right, and he is pretty good at keeping his finger on the pulse of his audience. What he said made a lot of sense but really knocked the wind out of me. The idea of becoming a saint had totally captured my interest and motivation. I found it absolutely fascinating that our mission is sainthood and that it is God's dream for every single one us. It broke my heart to admit that the very idea of becoming a saint turns off many people, and perhaps this is why we treat the stories of saints as fairy tales or myths. These were real human beings with real sins. Embellishing their stories as if they were always perfect does them and us a huge injustice. It was precisely their struggles and transformations that made them saints. If we do not want to be saints, we are missing the fact that sainthood is the path to heaven. Everybody in heaven is a saint, for a saint is simply somebody who has become who they were created to be through their journey in life and any needed purification in purgatory (purgatory will be discussed in greater detail in chapters 2 and 6).

If you struggle with anger, find a saint who struggled with anger, perhaps Saint Peter, who cut off a man's ear. If you struggle with lust, find a saint who struggled with lust, perhaps Saint Augustine, who once said, "Make me chaste, Lord, but not yet." If you struggle with pride and arrogance, find a saint who struggled with these things, perhaps Saint Francis of Assisi, who was a spoiled, rich, and arrogant ladies' man before going off to war and encountering God in a near-death experience. If you, or perhaps your child, are whiny, selfish, and overly emotional about the littlest problems, ask for the intercession of Saint Thérèse, as this was her childhood before she discovered her "little way".

The point is that the saints who have gone before us are in heaven praying for us and interceding for us as great allies. This is precisely why we choose a confirmation name. My confirmation saint is Daniel. I wish could tell you a great story about how I had a vision of Saint Daniel or that his story changed my life—but when I picked him I did not have the slightest clue who he was. You see, I did not comprehend the whole saint thing when I was confirmed. I am sure someone probably told me, but I was not listening. I picked the name Daniel because one of my favorite movies at the time was *The Karate Kid*, and Daniel was the lead character in the movie. (If you think that is bad, my friend picked Leonardo, after his favorite Teenage Mutant Ninja Turtle.) The archbishop who confirmed me was named Daniel, and interestingly enough, I remember him telling me he liked the name I chose. I did not know his name was Daniel at the time—I just thought maybe he liked *The Karate Kid* also.

Perhaps, though, *I* did not pick Daniel. Maybe *he* picked *me*. Bert Ghezzi, in his book *Voices of the Saints*, describes Daniel as an "ascetic, an 'athlete' training to win the prize of spiritual perfection. Like all monks, he identified his enemies as the temptations of the flesh and harassments of the devil. Daniel practiced rigorous penitential disciplines.... He literally took a *stand* against these enemies, never sitting or lying down."[13] In other words, he slayed dragons. I am sure my family and friends are smiling at that description of Saint Daniel. I guess Saint Daniel has had his eye on me all these years, even though for the most part I have ignored him. It is important for us to teach confirmation students the great opportunity they have in choosing a "coach" or mentor to help them through life. Pray to your confirmation saint and ask him each day to guide you and intercede for you in your struggles. The saints know what it takes to "win the prize of spiritual perfection".

5. The Greatest Weapon in the World

"Earn this." These are the words spoken to Private Ryan at the climax of the movie *Saving Private Ryan*. All of Private Ryan's brothers have been killed in combat, so the president orders a troop of soldiers to make its new mission to find and

---

[13] *Voices of the Saints* (Chicago: Loyola Press, 2000), 198.

save this man and bring him home to his grieving mother. The soldiers struggle with their orders to risk their lives for this one man, but all of them end up giving their lives for the mission and succeed. Private Ryan is indeed sent home unharmed, but the words of a man who gave everything to save him will forever echo in Ryan's mind.

At the end of the movie, he is shown as an old man with a wife and children and grandchildren, kneeling next to the grave of the soldier who asked him to earn the life he had been given, and he wonders if he is a good man and if he has truly lived his life to the fullest.

I think of this movie often on Memorial Day, that day in America when we remember all those who have risked and given their lives in the armed forces so that we may have the freedom of our country. The purpose of Memorial Day is to remember the sacrifices made, lest we forget that our freedom has a cost. The price was blood.

Just as Memorial Day helps us call to mind the sacrifices of our country's soldiers, the Catholic Mass helps us call to mind the sacrifice of our Savior. Our eternal salvation was a free gift. No matter how much willpower we have and how hard we try, we cannot earn it. However, it is important for us to remember where our freedom comes from to make the most of the life we have been given. This is one of the reasons I think it is so important to attend Mass every Sunday and spend time with Jesus often. The Mass is a memorial of Jesus' suffering and death, but more than that, it is an opportunity to share in His suffering. We are spiritually brought to the real sacrifice of Calvary and given an opportunity to unite our suffering to the suffering of Jesus and receive the life-giving grace that flows from His blood. He did not just save our ancestors through His body and blood; He saved each one of us throughout all of time.

In all the wealth, conveniences, and distractions of a free society, it is easy to forget that even though our salvation is a free gift, it is very expensive. The price is blood. It is the blood of Jesus Christ that set us free from the bondage of sin and death, and without this gift we are doomed. "Do you not know that your body is a temple of the Holy Spirit within you, which you have from God? You are not your own; you were bought with a price. So glorify God in your body" (1 Cor 6:19–20).

God loves us so much that He was willing to take on human flesh and spill every drop of His blood to win our souls. That blood is the "secret weapon". It destroys Satan, it destroys evil, it destroys sin, and it destroys death. I have the following prayer on my bathroom mirror to remind me each morning where our strength and power to destroy dragons comes from:

> O Jesus, in union with your most precious blood
> Poured out on the Cross and offered in every Mass,
> I offer you today my prayers, works, joys, sorrows, and sufferings
> For the praise of your holy name
> And all the desires of your Sacred Heart,
> For reparation of sins,
> The conversion of all sinners,
> The union of all Christians,
> And our final union with you in heaven.
> Amen.

It is from that blood of Jesus Christ, poured out for us, that we receive the grace necessary to become who we were meant to be.

6. Amazing Grace

"But by the grace of God I am what I am, and his grace toward me was not in vain" (1 Cor 15:10). My name, John, means "God is gracious." This quote from the First Letter to the Corinthians is always attached to the name John on those little nameplates and keychains you see in stores, so I had this quote all over my room growing up.

To explain how grace works in our lives, I will use an analogy involving Spider-Man (in chapter 5, I will discuss the many references to Catholicism in the *Spider-Man* movie series). As is the case with all superheroes, Spiderman receives superhuman strength. Bitten by a mutant spider, he wakes up the next morning with a gift and a power he did not have before. That spider bite is like sacramental grace. It gives us the power to do things that we do not have the power to do. It makes us all "superheroes" with the ability to help save souls in distress.

I was a state track champion in high school and college, and I will tell you the secret to my success—I will tell you my "superpower". In high school, my local church was on the way to school. Before every game and track meet, I would stop at that church, sit in front of the tabernacle, and beg God to give me the power to do things that I did not have the power to do. Track season coincided with Lent, and during Lent my mother would take me to Mass every morning before school, so I was receiving the power of the Eucharist pretty much every single day. The result of those prayers and the reception of the body and blood of Christ was not necessarily that I won all the time but that I gained the ability to find and give what I never knew I had. (Steroids are illegal in sports because they give people an unfair and unnatural advantage. One might jokingly suggest that sacramental grace ought to be illegal in sports, since grace builds on nature to direct it toward a supernatural end.)

There is one race in particular I will always remember because I cannot explain what happened during it. I will give you some background. I was a high school sophomore, and it was a breakout season, when I was really starting to develop and see my potential. Still young and inexperienced, I did not expect to make it to the state championship track meet. I knew it would be difficult to make it out of the regional meet, as only the top four finishers from each region qualify, and I was on the bubble. I tried my hardest all season in the sixteen-hundred-meter run but struggled to cut my time by just a second or two each week. The regional race was probably one of the hardest I have ever run. To my surprise, I qualified for the state meet, though barely, taking fourth place at the regional meet. I felt as if there were no way I could have run even a tenth of a second faster; that race took absolutely every ounce of strength I had.

So as I prepared to run in my first-ever state track meet race the following week, I was pretty satisfied with just being there. I was ranked almost last, and expectations were not high. In the previous month, at the peak of my season, I was able to chip away three or four seconds off my time to get down to 4:31. With the pain and tribulation of the previous week's regional race still on my mind, I knew it would take everything I had to repeat that performance, which still would have placed me near the back of the pack of sixteen qualifiers. However, as that race in the state meet progressed, I found myself near the top half of the pack with one lap to go. Panicking a little, I thought to myself, "I don't belong up here, and runners will surely fly by me on the final lap." But something strange happened on the back stretch. I started passing other runners. I felt better instead of worse. It was the only time in my life that the Scripture verse "They shall run and not be weary" (Is 40:31) even came close to making sense. I crossed the finish line, placing fifth in the state, high enough to stand on the podium. But why had all the other runners run so much slower than their qualifying times? They had not. Actually, I ran a 4:23 sixteen-hundred-meter run—a school record—eight seconds faster than I had ever run. Eight seconds faster than I had run one week earlier, when I felt I could not possibly run a tenth of a second faster.

Sure, there are lots of explanations: adrenaline, atmosphere, peak performance, weather. However, looking back after having run competitive races for more than ten years against and with some of the best runners in the nation, I know what I can and cannot do. That time was something I did not have the ability to run as a sophomore in high school, and I never had an experience like that again, at least not anywhere to that degree.

The grace we receive from sacraments is not a magic trick, and we should not use it to try to gain earthly success. Again, the real power I obtained from sacramental grace was not medals and trophies; it was that I found something deep inside and discovered that I was not alone. That one race is a reminder to me that even though God often asks us to do things beyond our ability, we should trust Him and believe in His power. It is not about what we can do; it is about what God can do through us—what we can do by His power—if we simply open ourselves to the grace we are given.

7. The Swords of Virtue

The supernatural power we receive from grace does not give us the power to leap over tall buildings like Spider-Man, fly faster than a speeding bullet like Superman, or

even win trophies and medals most of the time. The power
we receive is an even higher power. The grace we receive
leads not to victory over others but to virtue in ourselves.
The transformation is internal. If we are to be great dragon
slayers, we must master the swords that will defeat the
dragons. Just like everything else, virtue is learned by practice. We are not born with all virtues, although some virtues come more naturally to some people, just as some
people are more prone to certain vices.

If our country hopes to return to its strong moral foundation, we need a revival of virtue. The danger lies in the
attitude of defeat. We have removed God from society,
which means we have removed grace; and if we remove
grace, we cannot attain lives of virtue. This is where the
attitude of defeat arises. You hear excuses like "I'm just
not a patient person. You are just going to have to accept
me for who I am." Virtue starts with humility, and that is
why it is so important to utilize the witness of Jesus, Mary,
and Joseph, the greatest models of humility that we have.
With humility we can change our attitude to "I am not a
patient person, but I know my source of strength is God,
not myself. With God's grace and a training of my will, I
can become a more patient person."

Slaying dragons is about spiritual warfare, and in warfare
you must have a strategy. You must be prepared to defend
against and conquer any dragon that comes your way. Just
as soldiers go through boot camp to prepare for battle, our
boot camp begins at baptism when, as sons and daughters
of the King, we become part of God's spiritual "army",
trained for battle by parents, teachers, and pastors.

I recently witnessed a baptism during Mass, where the
priest explained that the oil of the catechumens used during
baptism is like the oil used by ancient athletes. Olympic
athletes used oil to give suppleness to their muscles as they

prepared for competition. The priest also used the analogy of a wrestler using oil to escape more easily the grasp of the opponent. As Catholics, the *Catechism of the Catholic Church* tells us that at our baptism we are summoned to battle with the forces of evil.[14] Our baptism prepares us not only to let the light of Christ shine through the witness of a virtuous life (as oil is burned in a lamp) but also to escape the enemy's grasp. Remember that through baptism (and all the sacraments) we are given the grace necessary to fight the good fight and run the good race—to live a life of virtue. It is a great power—and with great power comes great responsibility.

Those who train us in the swords of virtue need to have mastered the art of virtue themselves, since virtue is easier "caught than taught". We should remember this when trying to teach virtue to others, especially our own children. We have to model it above all else.

Knowing the dragons is key to mastering the virtues. If we understand the damage that greed can do in our lives and relationships, we will see the value in generosity and be more motivated to attain it. When we know which dragons we struggle with the most, we can identify the virtues to practice the most. Perhaps you struggle with gluttony and an unhealthy attraction to pleasure. Bend the stick the other way. Fast often and practice moderation in everything you do. Consciously think about ways you can train yourself in the virtue of temperance. If you are prone to despair and discouragement, study the virtue of hope. Write out Scripture verses about hope, and tape them where you will see them. Read stories of saints who struggled with these same vices, and discover how they overcame their dragons. If you have trouble trusting God, do

[14] *CCC* 405.

some faith exercises. Try something you feel called to do but have never dared to attempt. Get out of your comfort zone and expand the limits of your faith. Like Bilbo Baggins in J. R. R. Tolkien's *The Hobbit*, sometimes you have to go on an unexpected journey to face the dragons in life. As Bilbo discovers, if you do not get out of your "hobbit hole" and take the journey to defeat the dragon, you end up catching the dragon sickness yourself.

The four cardinal virtues of justice, fortitude (courage), prudence, and temperance and the three theological virtues of faith, hope, and love are the building blocks of a virtuous life. Of course, the greatest of these virtues is love. Without love, all virtue is dead and worthless. (In chapter 5, on Theology of the Body, we will discuss love in great detail.) Above all, God is love. He is the source of all love, and it is through Him that we have the ability to love and be loved. Jesus Christ is our greatest model of love. Love is the source of all virtue. We struggle with virtue and avoid lives of virtue because it requires great sacrifice, effort, suffering, and risk. Much like a dream that a person would chase after, love is a great unknown. Trouble arises when we begin to fear that the cost outweighs the reward. We fear that we might give all that we have, only to lose in the end and gain nothing. But true love does not count the cost.

It is true—love is risky. Making yourself vulnerable to another person is risky. Putting your faith in another person is risky, but love is not *afraid* of those things. Love *is* those things. Love is risky because it requires a free giver and a free receiver, and there is always a chance that what is given will not be received. Love does not remove suffering; it sometimes even causes it, as anyone who has lost a loved one knows. Love simply makes the suffering worth it. Oh, how God's heart must break when, after taking so great a risk to make Himself vulnerable and weak, empty-ing Himself completely, He is rejected by His Bride whom he came to save—us. But the hope of spending eternity with you and me makes it all worth it for Him.

Jesus Christ is our model for love and for every single virtue. He proves that we do not ever have to be afraid that we may love God but He does not love us. Whenever we doubt God's love for us, all we have to do is look at the crucifix. If God is not afraid to love every one of us, then we should not be afraid to love each other. In fact, we are obliged to. Jesus said, "A new commandment I give to you, that you love one another; even as I have loved you, that you also love one another" (Jn 13:34). He did not just recommend it—He commanded it.

When we choose to love, we come to discover who we really are and why we were created. We also open our-selves up to a life of profound virtue. Living a life of virtue leads to the most attractive thing in the universe ...

8. There Is Nothing More Attractive

One of my favorite books is *Words from God* by Matthew Kelly.[15] Many years back, when I had an opportunity to meet Kelly in person after one of his talks, I had him sign my copy. The inscription he wrote was, "There is nothing more attractive than holiness." This statement is extremely countercultural, but it is 100 percent true. It is countercultural because holiness is grossly misunderstood.

I recently drove past a country church with one of those signs out front—you know, the ones with a clever saying or pun about God. This particular sign said, "God

---

[15] *Words from God* (New York: HarperCollins, 1997).

makes you holy, then He makes you happy." I understand the message, but I do not think I would phrase it that way. The problem is that our culture views Christianity as something unattractive. For most people, the message they hear from outspoken Christians is: "Christianity is about being holy. Holiness is about picking up your cross, following Jesus and all His rules, loving people out of obligation, and avoiding pleasure in this life so you can attain your reward of happiness in the next life." That may not be what most Christians are saying, but that is what people are hearing.

People are not attracted to what they assume is holiness, and who can blame them? In that attitude, holiness is an obstacle to happiness. What do most people picture when they hear the word "holiness"? A secluded monk. A celibate priest. Perhaps a missionary in a developing country. These are images of holiness, but they are not everyone's call to holiness, and those called to them are not miserable. God loves variety, and there are as many paths to holiness as there are people. We must seek God's path for our lives so we can become fully alive and allow God to effect change in the world through us.

I assure you, those who discover their true selves are sincerely happy, regardless of what the world may think about them. I would be miserable trying to lead praise and worship songs because that is not my gift. However, leading songs is part of some people's path to holiness, and they have greatly inspired me with their gift. Perhaps you would be miserable as a secluded monk or nun. If that is true, trust that God will not call you to that. God is not going to think up the path that will make you the most miserable and send you down that path just to see if you will jump through His hoops so you can be happy later. With that said, your true path may be very different from what you initially perceive it to be. That is why we must trust God. He designed you, and His plan for you is always best.

"Be miserable now so you can be happy later" is not an attractive philosophy, and that is not holiness. Holiness comes from virtue. Virtue is attractive. Would you rather be around people who are patient or people who are impatient? Would you rather be around people who are selfish or selfless? Would you rather be around people who are greedy or people who are generous? I think we can agree that we are attracted to people who are virtuous. The question becomes, Are we attracted just to being around them, or are we attracted to being like them? Does the practice of virtue lead to holiness? If so, do happiness and holiness go together?

The confusion is created by our warped idea of happiness and what our culture tries to sell as happiness. Everybody wants to be happy, and marketers know that. However, companies do not have happiness to sell—they have pleasure; and they are going to call their pleasure happiness. Every marketing genius knows this. No wonder we confuse pleasure and happiness. If you bring your children to McDonald's, what do they want? A "Happy Meal". Check out Coca-Cola's slogan, "Open happiness." I recently saw a Cracker Barrel billboard that said, "Happiness from scratch". Pepsi's slogan is "Live for now." Why do you think Pepsi wants you to live for now? Because pleasure is all about now! Pleasure is a good thing, but it is not the same thing as happiness. Pleasure is fleeting, and happiness is sustainable. Instant gratification does not equal true happiness.

There is a word in Greek, *eudaimonia*, which has one of its meanings "have a good soul." If we consider that virtues are powers of the soul, then we can quickly see how virtue can be connected to happiness. Happiness and holiness are closely related. You will be happier living a life of virtue despite the storms, trials, and heartaches you encounter, because your happiness is based on who you are, not on what you are doing or experiencing. You do not become happy after you learn to be holy. You become happy by becoming holy. Holiness is sought after by pilgrims—those who are on a journey to a greater destination. Pleasure is sought after by tourists—those who are just taking in the sights and hoping to find something good in their wanderings. If you seek holiness, you will find happiness, *and* you can enjoy the world's sights in the light of God. If you seek only pleasure, you will find that even the pleasure is elusive and unfulfilling.

God wants you to be holy. "This is the will of God, your sanctification" (1 Thess 4:3). God wants you to experience the holiness that causes happiness. God wants you to be a saint.

9. The Saint Who Is Just You

Saint John Paul II has been a huge influence on my life. He is proof to me that there is nothing more attractive than holiness. This man was a model of holiness, and millions of people worldwide flocked to see him, especially young people. So much of what John Paul II said and did inspired me. I already loved JPII and his message of holiness to the world, but after reading the book by Jason Evert called *Saint John Paul the Great: His Five Loves*, I love him even more.[16] Jason Evert was fortunate enough to meet many people who were close to this saint of our times, and so

---

[16] *Saint John Paul the Great: His Five Loves* (Lakewood, Colo.: Totus Tuus Press, 2014).

he shares many stories and qualities about JPII that most people do not know.

After finishing the book, two thoughts came to my mind:

1. I want to be like JPII!
2. I cannot be JPII.

I want JPII's love for the poor. I want his love for young people and his ability to inspire them. I want his love for the Eucharist and his ability to suffer well. I want his relationship with the Mother of God. I want his wisdom.

Although I can do all I can to emulate his virtue and form his good habits, I cannot be JPII. If I try to be JPII, I will fail miserably, and if I compare myself to JPII, I will see myself as a huge failure. This past year, on the last day of class, I gave an anonymous survey to the high school kids I taught in religious education. The first question was "How do you see your Catholic faith?" The four choices were

A. Exciting
B. Boring
C. Confusing
D. I am indifferent about my faith.

Out of seventeen students in the class, only four chose "Exciting". It broke my heart. I want to inspire young people so much. I want them to love their faith and receive the great gift I have been given, and all the joy and happiness that comes with the truth. I thought of how JPII attracted millions of young people to World Youth Days. And here I am—I engaged four out of seventeen. Soon, the enemy started posing questions in my head:

What possible difference can I make? Am I not supposed to be an evangelizer? This is the best I can do? The message amounted to: "What a horrible failure you are. Just give up."

I love John Paul II, but I can only be John Wood. I am thankful for the four students I somehow reached, and if I let go of my pride, I can rest knowing that I do not convert people—God does, in God's time. I cannot make the students love God and His Church. I can only introduce them and point them to God and His Church. I can only plant seeds and trust that in God's time they will grow. The hoe that tills the soil in the early spring may never get to see the seeds begin to sprout.

I recently heard a great homily in which the priest pointed out that the Christian life is a journey from who we are now (point A) to the saint God created us to be (point Z). Everyone has to journey from A to Z. We can help each other on that journey. However, we cannot expect to take everybody to Z. Maybe I took some of those students from A to B, and maybe that was my role. Perhaps somebody else in their journey will help them further.

In my pride, though, four out of seventeen seems quite embarrassing for somebody who is supposed to evangelize, and I honestly did not want even to admit this statistic in a book that is supposed to be about evangelizing. However, numbers can be deceiving, and if we let pride get in the way, we can quickly forget about the ripple effect of doing God's work. Four people can change the world. Receiving letters from students years later helps me realize that my efforts are worthwhile. One of my former students is in the seminary. How many souls will he reach? Two of my former students have traveled the country with me to sing at my events. They have a gift that I truly believe will reach millions of souls, starting with me. I have become a student to them. Four is not a failure—it is just the start of a bountiful harvest. All things in time. I will learn from my mistakes, fix what I can, and keep trying. I will continue to do my best to play John Wood's role, not John Paul II's.

Reading stories of the saints every day, I realize that I cannot be any of them. The saints were the most diverse group of people in history—young and old, rich and poor, black and white, religious and laity, parents and celibates, kings and slaves, mystics, monks, missionaries, and martyrs. No two are the same. I cannot be any of them, but I can be like all of them because I have access to the same path to sanctity. I have the intercession of the angels and the saints who have gone before me. I have access to the same grace, which leads to virtue, which breeds holiness, which makes saints.

The saints capture imaginations of every generation. The saints were "set apart" because they had a peace and joy beyond the confines of birth and death that transcended the greatest hardships, persecutions, and failures. They attracted people because they were authentic witnesses to a greater source—the source of all love and happiness. As the moon reflects the sun, they reflected the Son. While we cannot stare at the sun because of its brightness, we can stare at the moon, which reflects that brightness. We cannot instantly be perfect like Jesus, but we can reflect His perfection as the saints did, so that one day we will be perfected and shine like the Son. The reality is, the world needs saints. The world will always need saints, and not just the saints of the past. The world needs the saints of this generation. The world needs saints who are doctors, lawyers, teachers, musicians, athletes, farmers, architects, scientists, moviemakers, storytellers, businesspeople, factory workers, police officers, electricians, social workers, politicians, and artists. The world needs saints who live on college campuses and in dorm rooms. Saints who are mommies and daddies, grandmas and grandpas, friends, and siblings. The world needs the saint that is you! There are no unimportant roles. You have what it takes to be a saint: a simple response of "Yes, Lord, I will it." Just allow God to work through you. You can be His instrument that plays beautiful music. You can be His tools to rebuild His Church. You can be His paintbrush to reveal Himself to the world. You can be His match that He uses to start a fire, and you can set the world ablaze with His love.

One of my favorite stories of JPII is when he met a U.S. senator traveling with his family to Rome. One of the men traveling with the senator introduced the senator to the pontiff, saying, "Your Holiness, this is a senator from the United States of America." JPII looked at the man and said, "You are a very important person." The man smiled sheepishly, thinking he was referencing his career status. However, JPII then pointed toward his children and told him again, "You are a very important person. You are a father." You are important not because of *what you can do* but because of *who you are*.

Remember, we are children of God, sons and daughters of the Most High King, heirs to the kingdom of heaven. We are saints in the making, and saints slay dragons.

For all the recommended resources for "Saving Grace", go to the website: www.saintsinthemaking.com/saving -grace-resources.html.

Chapter 2

A: ATHLETICS

Color: Blue, for Strength

Every Christian is called to become a strong athlete
of Christ, *that is, a faithful and courageous witness to
his Gospel. But to succeed in this, he must persevere in
prayer, be trained in virtue and follow the divine Master
in everything.*

—Saint John Paul II

Destiny

When I was about ten years old, my brother and I found
an old hockey stick in our basement. I do not know where
the stick came from. My father did not know the first
thing about hockey. I grew up in a small farming town
of about twenty-five hundred people in southwest Ohio,
a place where hockey did not exist. I had never seen the
game played and could not name a single hockey player. I
had never even seen a real ice rink. But there it was in our
basement. And that old stick changed my life.

My brother and I found some old woodwork and nailed
a few pieces together to make more sticks. Then we took

them outside and started playing. I instantly took to the sport. My brother said he would be the Red Wings and I could be the Penguins, since those were the only two professional hockey teams he had heard of. Ever since, I have been a Penguins fan. We gathered my brother's friends and made more sticks. We made hockey goals out of old pipes and cloth, took them to the playground, and started playing every weekend. My older brother was five years older than I (he still is), and so there I was, a ten-year-old playing against a bunch of high schoolers—and winning. Over the next three years, we formed our own little hockey league called the Back Yard Hockey League, or BYHL.

Eventually we received ice skates for Christmas and started playing on ponds during the winter. I remember my brother's friend hammering the goals in place and hearing the ice crack. I was scared, but I wanted to play badly enough that I was willing to risk falling through. After my brother and his friends all graduated from high school, I found some recreational leagues and started playing on real sheets of ice.

Now mind you, I was not built like a hockey player. There was not much meat on my bones, and I did not have much of a physical-contact kind of personality. Hockey is an aggressive and powerful sport, and I was a bit small and tranquil, built more like a runner. The problem was, I hated running and I loved playing hockey. By the time I graduated from high school, I set five school records in track and cross-country and placed first, second, third, fourth, fifth, sixth, and seventh in the state track meet. I could have gone to almost any college or university on a track scholarship, but I turned all the scholarships down. Why? Because when I was ten years old I found an old hockey stick. I chose the college I chose for one reason and one reason alone: I wanted to play hockey.

If I had not found that hockey stick, I would never have met my wife. I probably would not have selected the career I did. I would not be living in the town I live in. I would not be writing this book. That hockey stick changed the direction of my entire life. Was I meant to play hockey for a living? After about twenty seconds on the ice with the NCAA team I tried out for, I discovered that I was not. But I was meant to find that stick. In fact, God's fingerprints were all over that stick.

My passion and desire to play the sport of hockey changed the direction of my life, as did all the sports in which I participated, including track and cross-country. For the first twenty-two years of my life, sports consumed most of my time. God does not want us to be consumed by things of the world. He wants our talents and abilities to be consumed for Him, but He knows how to use what *we* want, to accomplish what *He* wants. I cannot think of any other aspect of my life where I discovered my Catholic faith more than in sports. In the midst of practices, games, successes, and heartbreaks, I discovered what it takes to win the game of life. I discovered the ultimate battle raging inside of me: good versus evil, saint versus sinner. I discovered the ultimate trophy and the ultimate goal—sanctity and sainthood. From the battle cry of "Win, win, win" came the battle cry "Sanctus, sanctus, sanctus".

Sports

You may have noticed by now that I like acronyms. They help me remember information. For this chapter, our Athletics class, I have come up with the acronym SPORTS. There are six life lessons that we can learn from sports that will help us become saints. (Actually, you do not have to apply these lessons only to sports. This chapter can be summed up by the Scripture verse "Whatever you do, do all to the glory of God" [1 Cor 10:31]. I am applying these lessons to sports to give glory to God, but you can apply them to whatever you do.) The six lessons we will focus on in this chapter expand on the discussion of the last chapter, as these are all similar to virtues, or weapons that can defeat the enemy.

1. Self-discipline
2. Perseverance and passion
3. Obedience
4. Repetition and recreation
5. Teamwork
6. Sportsmanship

Self-Discipline

Do you not know that in a race all the runners compete, but only one receives the prize? So run that you may obtain it. Every athlete exercises self-control in all things. They do it to receive a perishable wreath, but we an imperishable. Well, I do not run aimlessly, I do not box as one beating the air; but I pommel my body and subdue it, lest after preaching to others I myself should be disqualified. (1 Cor 9:24–27)

Every serious athlete knows there are certain things he cannot eat or drink during the season to reach maximum potential. Every athlete knows he will need to show up for workouts even when he does not feel like showing up to be successful. In sports, you obviously need self-discipline to be successful, and most people who are "sports crazy" are willing to practice self-discipline to a high degree. News coverage of the Olympics is filled with stories about the individual athletes and what they went through to get where they are, and their stories always involve a tremendous level of self-discipline.

In my own athletic career, self-discipline was something I took very seriously. Many said I took it too seriously, especially during track and cross-country seasons. They often pointed out that I might have enjoyed running more if I had not put so much pressure on myself and had not followed the "rules" so strictly. In some regards, they were right. My self-discipline often bordered on pride. I was determined to complete *every* step of *every* workout. I ran each race in a very predictable way, going straight to the front every time and straddling the line in order to run the shortest distance since every tenth of a second mattered to me. Other people actually loved running against me because I was so predictable and foolish enough to run straight to the front every time, which is the hardest way to win a race. I set the pace for everyone else; it was the only way I knew to run. I was racing against myself. As far as diet, I did not eat or drink for pleasure during the season. Eating was more of a chore, trying to figure out the proper amount of carbohydrates and avoid anything that might decrease my performance.

Perhaps I went overboard on self-discipline, which very well could have hindered my success in terms of what place I got in some races. However, I do not regret the way I trained or the way I ran those races. In my mind, the goal was to cross the finish line with nothing left to give. I saw running as a battle of the will. There is a point in every distance or middle-distance race when a runner has to win an internal battle. The body says to slow down, and the heart says to push on. Self-discipline is telling the body to listen to the heart. This is where courage comes in. The Latin root of the word "courage" is *cor*, "heart" (think "*cor*onary"). Courage is having the heart to do what makes you uncomfortable for the greater good. Everything worthwhile in life requires courage, and courage plays a huge role in self-discipline.

The crises we face in our country today come from the death of self-discipline. Whether it is the health-care crisis, the economic crisis, the vocations crisis, or the sex-abuse crisis, the primary culprit is a lack of self-discipline. We have a war within because we all struggle from the effects of original sin. This war within is what the Church calls concupiscence, or the tendency to do wrong. The Church tells us we have three opponents: the world, the devil, and the flesh. We will discuss these more in our reflections on the Theology of the Body in chapter 5, but I believe the greatest battle lies within—the flesh. The flesh is that unruly part of our inner life that tends toward objective evil at times.

This is why self-discipline is so essential to sanctity. The world cannot force you to do evil. The devil cannot force you to do evil. Your will is yours. Self-discipline allows you to choose to do what is right in every situation regardless of what you feel like doing. It requires focusing feelings and emotions on a future outcome, not an immediate reward. Saints are made in such ways. Pepsi might tell you, "Live for now" because pleasure is about now, but the Church will tell you to live for eternity because you were made for more than what this world has to offer.

There is so much genius in Catholicism. Many people scoff at a Church that requires "disciplines", but that is exactly what the Catholic Church does. She has what we call "Church disciplines", such as fasting and abstinence on certain days of the year. She also has holy days of obligation, certain days of the year when we are required to attend Mass, above and beyond going every Sunday. This means going to Mass even if we do not feel like going. Holy Mother Church is training us in discipline as a good coach trains his athletes in discipline. Mass attendance is not required because it helps God; it is required because it helps us. These disciplines train the will in much the same way an athlete trains the body. The purpose of running a race is to finish with nothing left to give; the purpose of the Christian life is much the same. We must give ourselves away as Christians, sacrificing ourselves for the glory of the kingdom of heaven. The reality is that we cannot give what we do not have. Discipline is self-mastery. Become master over your flesh instead of it becoming master over you. If we do not first possess ourselves, we cannot give ourselves away.

Self-discipline is not about punishing ourselves but about gaining freedom and happiness. Many will say we have to choose between self-discipline and happiness, but I disagree. Not only does self-discipline create more happiness in the long run, but it even creates more pleasure. If you are able to give up something for a period of time, such as certain foods or drinks during Lent or during track season, how much more enjoyable will those products be when the season is over? A treat is a treat precisely because it is infrequent. Hunger is the best spice, and I assure you your favorite "treats" will taste better if you have gone without them for some time. As Matthew Kelly says, your level of happiness is directly proportional to your level of self-discipline. You simply cannot be happy without self-discipline.

It is important to keep in mind when talking of building virtue how quickly the enemy can use our own weapons against us. Remember, Satan is extremely intelligent, and he can turn just about any virtue into pride if we are not careful and lose focus on the mission. So how do we avoid crossing the line from self-discipline to pride? Remember the mission. For years now I have handed out wristbands with the words "Become a Saint—Be Not Afraid" at all my events. The wristband is meant to be a constant reminder of our mission in our everyday lives. The mission is not a list of rules to follow. There is not a black-and-white list of things you should and should not do to become a saint. Which actions are appropriate depend on the situation and the circumstance.

One young man approached me at a conference and told me that he wore the wristband for several months, but eventually he had to take it off because he was becoming too scrupulous, or overly picky about everything he was doing. I assure you, scrupulosity is often more about pride than about self-discipline. If you are scrupulous about sin, that is a good thing. We should never be comfortable with sin. But if we are scrupulous about everyday activities and habits, then we need to step back and ask ourselves again, "What is going to help me become a saint?" Sometimes, self-discipline means setting the "work" aside and having a night out with your friends or eating chocolate ice cream with your children.

So how do we know the difference between being scrupulous and becoming a saint? Scrupulosity is focused on doing and having, while becoming a saint is focused on becoming. Scrupulosity is about pride; becoming a saint is about humility. Scrupulosity sees God as a tyrant and master; saints see God as a loving Father. Scrupulosity is about trying to earn God's love; becoming a saint is about knowing the Father loves you and wanting to love Him in return. Scrupulosity is focusing only on avoiding hell; becoming a saint is about thirsting for heaven.

Perseverance and Passion

Let us not grow weary in well-doing, for in due season we shall reap, if we do not lose heart. (Gal 6:9)

The race of life is not a sprint. It is a marathon. No athlete is inducted into the Hall of Fame because of one game, even if it is the Super Bowl. Our struggle to reach Christian perfection will be reached over many internal battles and will last a lifetime. We cannot claim to have arrived on this side of heaven. Our salvation was won for us in the one perfect sacrifice of Christ, but the journey toward making ourselves completely and permanently available to that sanctifying grace takes patient perseverance.

To persevere means "to continue steadfastly" even in the face of many obstacles. During a marathon, there are times when you feel as if you can fly, and times when you feel as if you cannot take another step. Sometimes the wind is in your face, and sometimes the wind is at your back. Sometimes you are going uphill, and sometimes you are going downhill. That is life with its peaks and valleys. It is when things are not going well that we see what we are made of. When things look bleak and dreary, persevere in doing good. Cling to the hope of brighter days and the kingdom that awaits. We must master the virtues of patience, forgiveness, faith, hope, and love. Love endures all trials.

Many times in my life, my efforts no longer seemed worth it. I often let pride creep into my mind, and I worry about being successful in the things I do. When playing sports, especially when running, there were long stretches of time when I did not feel that I was getting any better, no matter how hard I tried. I became frustrated getting the same result over and over after investing so much time and energy into training. When I started speaking and sharing my Catholic faith, I encountered many of the same moments. There has been a lot of lethargy in the Catholic Church. I wanted so desperately to help people love their faith more, but for five years, I spoke to audiences of ten to twenty people. On more than one occasion, I told myself it was not worth it because I could not possibly make any kind of difference. Thankfully, those ten to twenty people encouraged me, and there has always been someone or something convincing me to keep going.

I have come to discover that our job is to be obedient to God's will. The results of our efforts are often beyond what we can see at this time, and can take many years to bear fruit. There is no way of knowing how and when God will use our efforts to further His kingdom, so we must persevere, even when it seems we are failing. Failure is an important part of success.

It is good to strive for perfection, but we must also remember that we most likely will not reach perfection this side of heaven. We are going to stumble and fall from time to time. However, we must remember that life is not about what we do or have; it is about who we become. A wise man once said that a saint is simply a sinner who keeps trying. The only failure is to quit trying. No matter how many times we sin, no matter how dark and dreary the world seems, no matter how daunting the task seems, we must keep pushing on. We must not quit. We must forgive ourselves and others. We must get back up, dust ourselves off, and keep moving forward. We must never give up. Basketball star Michael Jordan once said, "I've missed more than nine thousand shots in my career, I've lost more than three hundred games, and twenty-six times I've been trusted to take the game-winning shot and missed. Throughout my life and career I've failed, and failed, and failed again. And that's why I succeed."

Perseverance comes from passion. I do not think you can persevere without passion. To have passion means to suffer or to have strong emotion and desire—to pour yourself out. Jesus' passion shows us what it means to empty ourselves of everything we have. Running the race of life, we must run with passion and zeal. Living and teaching our Catholic faith, we must persevere with passion and zeal. All the right words will not inspire anybody if they are not spoken and lived with passion and zeal.

If we live life with passion, then we are able to show others compassion. Compassion—meaning "passion with", or suffering with—is a deep care and concern for what others are going through. Sometimes we can relieve the suffering of others, and we should desire to do so, but that is not always possible. Compassion in the truest sense of the word means going through trials with others and comforting them in their distress, not taking away every trial. Compassion does not mean giving people what they want or avoiding suffering at all cost. "Mercy killing", or euthanasia, is not compassion. Abortion is not compassion. Attempting to remove every consequence to every poor decision is not compassion. We often confuse these things with compassion because we have lost the meaning of the words "passion" and "compassion". Passion and compassion are about perseverance, not about giving up. They are about moving forward (toward heaven) in difficult times, not about staying the same.

Blessed be the God and Father of our Lord Jesus Christ,
the Father of mercies and God of all comfort, who comforts us in all our affliction, so that we may be able to
comfort those who are in any affliction, with the comfort
with which we ourselves are comforted by God. For as we
share abundantly in Christ's sufferings, so through Christ
we share abundantly in comfort too. If we are afflicted,
it is for your comfort and salvation; and if we are comforted, it is for your comfort, which you experience when
you patiently endure the same sufferings that we suffer.
Our hope for you is unshaken; for we know that as you
share in our sufferings, you will also share in our comfort.
(2 Cor 1:3–7)

Obedience

If you love me, you will keep my commandments. (Jn
14:15)

How successful would a basketball team be if the players never listened to their coach? What if all the players
decided to run their own plays instead of running the plays
the coach called? What if they just picked and chose the
drills they thought were necessary and ignored their coach
on the other drills?

How fun would a baseball game be if there were no
umpires? What if there was nobody there to say "Safe" or
"Out", or "Strike" or "Ball"? It would be a bunch of people arguing, and the game would be no fun. The umpires
keep the game moving and provide consistency in how
the game is played.

The role of the coach is not to make his players miserable and crack the whip to see how many hoops they
will jump through. The role of the coach is to help his

team become the best team it can be and reach its fullest potential. The role of the umpire is not to make up rules to make people angry or keep them from having fun. The role of the umpire is not to give one team an unfair advantage or play favorites to control the outcome of the game. The umpire enforces the rules that make the game what it is and creates unity. He guards and protects the rules that were established before the game started.

Typically, "authority" is a bad word in our culture. Many people assume that those in authority have bad intentions of dominating others. However, the role of Christian authority is to serve. Those in power are called to guard and protect those over whom they have authority. A teacher's motivation should be to help students learn. A parent's motivation should be to help his children become saints.

Historically, many people in authority have abused their positions to cause harm instead of good, which is why we have become so suspicious. Sometimes parents lead children in the wrong direction. Sometimes teachers have hidden agendas. Sometimes umpires make bad calls. Sometimes coaches call the wrong plays. And yes, sometimes priests harm those whom they were to protect.

It is for this reason perhaps that we hear so much about the term "cafeteria Catholics", or those who pick and choose what beliefs in the Church they will follow and which teachings they will ignore. After all, they say, everyone can be wrong and make mistakes—why can't the Church?

It is a fact that a very large percentage of priests are good and holy and have laid down their lives in sacrifice for the flocks they serve and love. But it is also true that those in authority in the Catholic Church are human and that some have, by their fallen human nature, caused considerable harm and done terrible things. However, we should not lose our respect for Church authority because of the small number who have fallen. The teachings and doctrines of the Catholic Church are good and true and perfect. We should not toss aside Catholic doctrine based on the actions of certain individuals any more than we should toss aside the rules of baseball because a few umpires made bad calls.

The reality is Jesus established a Church, and He established authority in that Church. Scripture makes this very clear. "And I tell you, you are Peter, and on this rock I will build my Church, and the gates of Hades shall not prevail against it. I will give you the keys of the kingdom of heaven, and whatever you bind on earth shall be bound in heaven, and whatever you loose on earth shall be loosed in heaven" (Mt 16:18–19).

From this Scripture passage, not only can we discern that Jesus established one Church, but we can discern that this Church gives us an unchangeable truth, which hell cannot prevail against. This is not something we made up as Catholics. It is based on Scripture, and in the two-thousand-year history of our Church is an unbroken line of popes, where every bishop was ordained by another bishop whose ordination can be traced back to the original twelve apostles. That lineage is pretty amazing and perhaps some remarkable evidence that Jesus really did establish a Church that cannot be destroyed by any force in hell or on earth.

There is a story I once heard of a bishop who was arrested and put in prison. His captor arrogantly claimed that he would destroy the Catholic Church. The bishop calmly replied, "What makes you think you can destroy what all the priests and bishops of the last thousand years have been unable to destroy?" In other words, despite the failings and human weakness in the members of the Church, the

Church herself will always continue because Christ is the cornerstone and foundation and because the Church is guided by the Holy Spirit, not by men. Although at our best all of us in the Church are saints in the making through whom God works, sometimes God has to accomplish His will despite us. God can draw straight with crooked lines. He builds with "living stones".

Therefore, if the Church is who she says she is, then we should trust her and respect her authority. As with Jesus Himself, we really have only three options of who the Church is. C. S. Lewis points out that Jesus is a liar, a lunatic, or the Lord. Jesus claimed to be God. Because He claimed to be God, He cannot simply just be a nice man with good teachings or just another prophet. If He is not God but claims He is, then He is a liar—and the biggest liar in the history of the world. He changed the whole course of human history, and two billion people continue to follow Him. If He thought He was God and really was not, then He was a lunatic. I find it hard to believe that a lunatic could draw such a following and work deeds such as Jesus did. The evidence is in the fruit. So if Jesus is not a liar and not a lunatic, He has to be God.

In much the same way, the Catholic Church claims to be the one Church founded by Jesus Christ, passing down the faith from generation to generation through an unbroken succession of bishops. She claims to be the Church against which the gates of hell will not prevail, meaning that her teachings and doctrine are given to us by the Holy Spirit, not by the vote of a group of men or by popular opinion. She claims that her dogmatic and moral teachings are infallible even though her people are sinners and do not always live those teachings. So again, we are left with three options:

1. She is an arrogant liar, controlling and manipulating people to follow man-made teaching. This is the position many people hold. Just read any news article about the Catholic Church and then read the comments below the article. So many people view the Church as the "whore of Babylon" and utter all kinds of things against her.

2. She is a lunatic, like an old woman with dementia. I would say even more people hold this position than hold the first position. They respect her and nod their heads and smile (because she is old) but believe she is outdated and off her rocker when it comes to her teachings in relation to the modern world.

3. She is who she says she is. She is the Church founded by Jesus Christ guided by the Holy Spirit, and her doctrine is infallible in the past, the present, and the future.

She cannot just be another pretty face among many. She cannot just have some nice teachings to pick from. Saint Joan of Arc summarized it best. "About Jesus Christ and the Church I simply know they are just one thing, and we should not complicate the matter."

That does not mean we should have blind faith. We should think and use our intellect. I challenge you to research why the Church teaches what she does. If you struggle with a Church teaching, do not just toss it aside and become a "cafeteria Catholic". Oftentimes it is our understanding of Church teaching that is wrong, or maybe we had a bad experience. I remember as a kid I ate a green banana once, and it made me sick. After that, I never wanted to eat bananas and could not stand even to look at them. Because of my experience, I had a bad impression of bananas and told everyone how disgusting they were. If

I were in the "cafeteria", so to speak, I would tell people to avoid the bananas because they are not really good for you. However, if I did that, I would be wrong. If I did the research, I would discover that bananas are in fact good and healthy for you. I am happy to report that I do indeed like bananas now and understand their benefits (and the importance of eating them when they are ripe so they taste better). We can change our opinions and understanding.

Furthermore, if the Church is wrong, you should be able to prove her wrong. Oftentimes we are like five-year-old kids complaining that our parents are wrong about eating healthy food or going to bed at a certain time. Our parents just do not know the truth, right? I propose that if we just look at the facts and be honest with ourselves, we will come to discover that everything the Church teaches makes sense, emotionally, intellectually, and spiritually. Catholicism is not just about the life to come. It is the best way to live ... *now*.

So why should we be obedient to the teachings of the Catholic Church? For one, we can be confident they are true. However, the most important reason we should be obedient is the same reason we should be obedient to a coach, a teacher, and a parent. They love us, and they want what is best for us, even when it seems they are making our lives miserable.

My high school track and cross-country coaches, Russ Stewart and Suzanne Hippley, had a huge impact on my life, not just my athletic career. Many times during the season they made me do things I really did not want to do, and it could be annoying. However, I knew they cared about me as a person, not just as someone who could win a medal. I trusted that they would guide me in the right direction, even when it was a direction I did not want to go. They taught me to find my hidden potential deep inside and to believe in myself. I am glad I was obedient to them.

My greatest "coach" and mentor has been my brother Brian. He is four years older than I, and you can imagine that as the little brother I always wanted to do what my older brothers were doing. When Brian was a senior and I was an eighth grader, I remember a particular practice that the junior high and the high school were doing together under the direction of Coach Stewart: whistle sprints around the football field. When the whistle blew, you had to sprint as fast as you could until the whistle blew again, at which time you could jog. It was a grueling workout because you never knew how long you would have to sprint. Even though Brian was much faster than I at the time and would get ahead of me in the sprints, he kept jogging back to me during the jog, so he could push me during each of the sprints. I remember being so tired, wanting him to leave me alone, but he would not. He pushed me harder than I could have ever pushed myself and was a big reason I became a state champion.

The Church will push you sometimes. Sometimes her teachings are hard and difficult to understand in the heat of battle. Many times we say things like "What is a celibate old man going to teach me about sexual morality?" The reality is, a coach has a unique perspective from the sidelines. He can see the big picture, and he can see the mistakes that all the players he coached previously have made. He is not influenced by temporary emotion that makes you want to take the easy road. He can see all the obstacles surrounding you, like defensive linemen trying to sack a quarterback. The quarterback has to trust the coach to tell him where the hidden obstacles are coming from and how to avoid them, even if that means changing his technique and doing what is uncomfortable to learn better practices.

If you want to be successful in the game of life, be obedient to the authority of the Catholic Church. She loves you, and you can trust her. She wants you to be a champion—a saint.

Repetition and Recreation

One of the greatest basketball players in history is Larry Bird, who was known for his great shooting and passing ability. What is less known is his amazing work ethic. How did Larry Bird become such a clutch shooter? How did he make almost 90 percent of his free throws in his career? How did he become such a great passer, rebounder, and overall player? Repetition. It was said that Larry Bird always showed up hours before a game, when nobody else was around, to practice shooting. In high school, he broke his ankle early in the season, but instead of sitting around doing nothing, he propped himself up on crutches and shot five hundred free throws every morning. During tournament play that year, he made two clutch free throws to win the game, and knew then that repetition would be key to making him the best basketball player he could be.

Shooting five hundred free throws every morning sounds pretty boring, right? Repetition and boredom seem synonymous. Perhaps that is why the rosary seems boring. Perhaps that is why prayer seems boring. Perhaps that is why going to Mass every Sunday seems boring. However, I wonder whether Larry Bird was bored playing in the NBA. I wonder if it was boring to be one of the greatest basketball players ever to play the game. I wonder if he ever had to think about his form when shooting a free throw or a jump shot, or if he had done it so many times before that he could just play. At first, repetition is boring, but the fruit of repetition is recreation.

Do you think Bird would have become a basketball legend with one hour at the gym each week mindlessly going through the mechanics of shooting a basketball? Could a young student ever become a doctor or a lawyer by skimming through textbooks once a week for an hour? Could a man be a good father by just sitting there watching his kids play for an hour a week and then going about his own business the rest of the week?

When young athletes join the basketball team, they know that practice is mandatory every day. They cannot just show up when they feel like it. When they go to school, attendance is required and assignments have to be done, or they will fail and not receive the education needed to be successful.

Why don't we understand that repetition is required in our faith? You cannot be a champion without repetition, and you cannot be a saint without practicing your faith every day. I know that sounds boring, and many people complain because their faith bores them. However, Catholicism is fun when we are trained in the faith. It is fun! But it is not fun like getting drunk on Friday and Saturday night is "fun", leaving pain, misery, regret, and addiction in its aftermath. Catholicism is fun like winning a championship is fun. Winning a championship comes only from self-discipline, perseverance, obedience, repetition, teamwork, and sportsmanship. In the aftermath of this kind of fun, we find peace, joy, and happiness. And it is not just the aftermath that is enjoyable— the process of becoming and developing is fun, even if the end result is not a world championship medal.

Returning to the quote from Moses' farewell speech in Deuteronomy, notice how Moses used the word "drill" when speaking about passing on the faith to children. He said, "Drill [it] into your children" (Deut 6:7). This word really caught my attention. At first I thought this was a little too harsh, like an overbearing parent forcing his children to worship God and follow his rules. My mind tends to wander, and I started picturing Moses pulling out his power drill when he said this. As I pictured Moses holding his drill, I realized that there is a big difference between "drill" and "hammer". I do not think Moses was saying we should beat our kids over the head with this religion stuff. A hammer drives in a nail with a few hard blows. A drill is different. The drill bit spirals round and round and carves out a hole with a kind of design. When a screw is screwed into a hole created by the proper drill bit, the screw fits snugly in those grooves. If you use the claw of a hammer to try to pull out a nail, it comes right out. But take that same hammer and try to pull out a screw—it does not budge. A drill creates a strong foundation with persistent motion and design. How many times does that drill bit spin round and round while creating that hole?

We need to teach the faith to our children by "drilling" it into them. This requires persistent, repetitious motion to form a strong foundation. That way, when the enemy comes to pull out that screw, it will not budge. We do not force religion onto our children with a few hard blows. We do not just send them on a weekend retreat every now and then or drop them off at religion class once a week. We teach them about God by consistently introducing them to God every day of their lives. My wife and I have several prayers we say with our children every night, one of which is "Make us saints, Lord, no matter what the cost." By the time our children leave home, they will have heard or said this prayer more than sixty-five hundred times. That is "drilling" the mission into them.

One "rule" of the Catholic faith to which most people are not obedient is attending Mass every Sunday. Our faith teaches us that it is actually a grave sin to miss Mass on Sunday or a holy day of obligation without a serious reason. Statistics show that less than 25 percent of Catholics attend Mass on any given Sunday,[1] even though the Eucharist is the "source and summit of the Christian life".[2] It is very common for Catholics to scoff at this "rule". One of my religion students anonymously submitted this question: "How is missing Church one or two weekends sending you straight to hell? I understand it is a mortal sin, but if you live an overall good life with minimal sin, how can one sin like missing Church send you straight to hell?"

First of all, you can see from the tone of the question that he sees God and the Church as a tyrant, which is heartbreaking. Twice in that question he mentioned going straight to hell, as if God is just a traffic cop waiting for you to mess up so He can throw you into prison. Second, you can see his complacency with the ordinary. There is no desire for greatness. Our motivation should be more than a fear of hell; it should be a desire for heaven!

The Church is a family. What if my wife came to me and said, "I think we should make it a priority to have dinner together as a family at least once a week", and I replied, "Every week? And holidays? Why do we have to eat together every week?" I think my wife would be greatly hurt just by the fact that I saw it as a burden to be together as a family once a week. God does not send people to hell, but if we choose to be away from Him, he respects our decision. Sadly, many people choose hell,

---

[1] "Frequently Asked Questions", Center for Applied Research in the Apostolate (CARA), accessed October 18, 2017, http://cara.georgetown.edu /frequently-requested-church-statistics/.

[2] Vatican Council II, *Lumen Gentium*, 11, quoted in *CCC* 1324.

for hell is simply the absence of God for all eternity. God respects your freedom, and He will give you what you love the most. If it is not Him, you will not get Him.

Some people say missing Mass is not a sin because the Bible does not say Church attendance is required. Just because the Bible does not specifically state "Missing Mass is a grave sin" does not mean missing Mass is OK. The Bible does not mention the Trinity, but we still believe in the Trinity. We have Scripture and tradition to guide us. The Bible clearly states that Jesus gave authority to the Church He established (see Mt 16:18–19; 1 Tim 3:15). The Bible describes the Mass in many places, including the book of Revelation.[3] The Bible is very clear about keeping the Sabbath day holy, and the New Testament fulfills a great deal of what we read about in the Old Testament, and the Mass is rooted in Old Testament traditions. The Jews worshiped every Sabbath. For a sin to be mortal (meaning it completely separates us from God), the sin must be grave, the person must know it is grave, and he must freely act on it. We can say missing Mass is a grave sin, but to determine whether it is a mortal sin for a particular person is difficult because we do not know the person's knowledge and will.

People often bring up the point that Protestants do not go to Mass. Does that mean they will not go to heaven? Just because a person is not "Catholic" by name does not mean he will not go to heaven. However, he may be missing out on a lot of graces, through no fault of his own. So why is it a mortal sin for an informed and educated Catholic to miss Mass without serious reason? It is not because it is an arbitrary rule to follow. The Church wants us to be saints. Her goal is to get us to heaven. Again, why is attendance

[3] See Scott Hahn, *The Lamb's Supper* (New York: Doubleday, 1999).

required at school? Is it because teachers are mean and want to collect their paychecks, or is it because they want their students to learn and know what they need to know? Why is practice mandatory for someone who joins the basketball team? Is it to make the coaches feel high and mighty, or is it because the coaches want their team to be successful and be the best basketball team it can be?

Going to Mass does not help God. It helps us. When people offered sacrifices in the Old Testament, it was not because God had a thirst for blood and it made Him mightier every time an animal was slaughtered. Sacrifice does not help God; it helps us. You cannot get a proper education by just showing up for class when you feel like it; you cannot become a great athlete by just showing up for practice when you feel like it; and you cannot become the saint God created you to be without worshiping God as part of a community, keeping holy the Sabbath, and soaking in the power of sacramental grace—especially the Eucharist.

It is our human nature to worship God in the way He requests, not just any way we make up. Praying at home is good, but it does not compare to what takes place at Mass. The Mass is literally heaven on earth, a foretaste of the kingdom to come. If you do not have time for Sunday Mass, then you do not have time for heaven. We all worship something. If you do not take time to worship God, you can quickly become too busy worshiping the things of this world.

My former pastor and a good friend of mine, Father Randy Giesige, recently compiled fourteen good reasons why we should want to go to Mass every Sunday. Here is the list:

1. There is no place where we are closer to our loved ones who have died.

2. Mass is the safest and shortest route to heaven.
3. At Mass we experience the fullness of God's love for us.
4. At Mass we receive a foretaste of heaven.
5. Mass gives us strength for life's journey.
6. At Mass we get to be part of the greatest love story of all time.
7. Mass is the most perfect form of prayer that leads us into a deeper relationship with God.
8. Mass provides comfort at our time of death.
9. At Mass we become more like Jesus.
10. Mass gives us the confidence we need to face the Final Judgment.
11. At Mass we experience a closeness and unity with our family and friends still with us.
12. Mass gives us the ability to see those we struggle with as our brothers and sisters.
13. At Mass we give praise to God as we unwrap the many graces and blessings that He has given us as free gifts.
14. Mass is for sinners, and it is there we receive God's mercy.

Who does not want to be a part of something so awesome?

Sometimes I am afraid to tell people that it is considered a grave sin to miss Mass on Sunday. It just seems as if ignorance is bliss, and as long as they do not know it is a serious sin, then they cannot be held accountable. However, that is like refusing to tell a new driver that his car needs gas because you know he is not going to want to fill it up and pay for the gas. Ignorance is not bliss. Without gas, the car eventually will stop running. If you were responsible for telling him but did not out of fear or convenience, then you will be held accountable.

If you are a parent, your children need to know it is a grave sin to miss Mass on Sunday and holy days of obligation. (And they need to know why they must attend—"Because I said so" is not sufficient reason.) They must make their own choices when they go out into the world, and they must be informed choices. Your children should know that Mass is something they spiritually need, like they need air to breathe. A family that prays together stays together. It is not just "me and Jesus". We all are in this together, and we should worship together as a Church family. A coach who wants a championship team would not just want his players to practice at home; he would require them to practice together. We are a team.

Teamwork

My favorite races to run in track were relay races. I discovered that when running individual races, it was much more tempting to slow down when I got tired. It is a lot harder to push through the pain in a race if you are just running it for yourself. When other people are counting on you to give your best, you are much more likely to give everything you have.

This race of life we are in is a relay race. Everybody has a part to play. All the great saints of the past have run their race, and now they have handed the baton off to you and me. We each must run our own race. Nobody else can run it for us.

As we noted in the previous section, Christianity is not just about "me and Jesus". It is true that we need a personal relationship with Jesus, but it cannot just end there. That is only the beginning. Jesus wants much more than a personal relationship with you; he wants a covenant relationship. You can have a personal relationship with your banker or your car mechanic. A covenant is more than just a contract. A contract says, "I'll give you this if you give me that." A covenant says, "I am yours and you are mine." It is a wedding! When we get married, we become part of another family. My wife's brothers and sisters are now my brothers and sisters, and my brothers are now her brothers.

We are in this together, as part of one team, one body in Christ. We cannot claim to love Jesus and not love His Bride. We cannot claim to love God and ignore His children. The Church is the Bride of Christ and the children of God. Our brothers and sisters can be divided into three groups: the Church militant, the Church suffering, and the Church triumphant.

The Church militant, or the pilgrim Church on earth, is all of us here on earth. We are still in the battle of good versus evil. We are still trying to win the internal war and conform our will to the will of the Father as we make our pilgrimage. We are pilgrims because we have a destination. We are going somewhere, and this world is not our home. In fact, the Greek root of the word "parish" means "somebody away from home". Too often we cling to our buildings and our own little community and ignore the fact that we are part of something bigger. We are not just tourists trying to find entertainment. The Church is not a business trying to please customers. She is a family trying to make disciples. Because of the priest shortage, many parishes have had to be twinned or combined. It saddens me to see the fighting over this in many cases. There are many who claim they simply will not go to "that other church". They have severely missed the point and forgotten why they are members of a parish in the first place. Sometimes I wonder, if the second coming of Jesus were to occur at another parish, whether some people would say, "I'm not going to that; it's not my parish."

The second part of the Church family is the Church suffering. These are the souls in purgatory. The Church's teaching on purgatory is beautiful but often misunderstood. Purgatory is a cleansing, a final preparation for eternal joy in heaven. All the souls in purgatory are assured of heaven, and our prayers and sacrifices can help prepare them and help them reach their destination. We are not separated from our brothers and sisters at death.

Finally, there is the Church triumphant. These are the saints in heaven. They are the ones who have run the race before us, and now they are our biggest fans. Their prayers are very powerful, and we ask them for their intercession. In any sporting contest, the fans are a big part of the game. I love the analogy I once heard from Father John Riccardo. The fans who come to a college football game are not there just to enjoy the game. They come with megaphones and painted chests, yelling and screaming the entire game. They are literally trying to change the outcome of the game to help their team win. This is what is called home-field advantage. In football, some teams refer to their fans as the "twelfth man"—there are eleven men playing on the field, and the fans are so loud that they become another obstacle for opposing teams, like an additional player. Similarly, the saints are not just sitting back and enjoying life as we face our challenges and trials. No, they are literally trying to change the outcome of the game—trying to get us to heaven with their prayers and intercession. They are another obstacle for the dragons who are trying to bring us down, and the saints give us "home-field advantage".

While in high school and college, I did almost all of my training for track and cross-country with my teammates and my coaches there to push me. While training for marathons in recent years, I did almost all of my training alone out on country roads. From a prayer aspect, the training in solitude on the country roads was a huge benefit and opportunity for great reflection. Many ideas for writing have come on long runs in solitude.

However, from a training aspect, it is much easier to run with other people. There is a group of long-distance runners in the nearby town, and sometimes early on Saturday mornings I would run with them. First of all, it was so much easier to get out of bed and start my early morning run knowing there was a group of people meeting at a certain time. Accountability makes a huge difference. Second, when I did do the workouts with them, I ran faster and farther with what seemed like less effort. It was a better workout, and the time flew by since I could follow other runners' pace and carry on a conversation.

The Christian journey was never meant to be taken alone. We are not an army of one; we are one army. We certainly need to find silence and solitude to pray and hear our own unique instructions from God, but to conquer dragons and grow in virtue, we need to be part of a team. The enemy is simply too tough to face alone. We need others with us as we face life's failures and successes.

Sportsmanship

With every peak and valley there are trials and temptations. When we fail, we are tempted to give up and become bitter about life. When we succeed, we are easily overcome by pride. In either case, we are tempted to focus on ourselves instead of on God.

Explaining to children how to win and how to lose is one of the greatest challenges when teaching them about sports. Small children often wear their hearts on their sleeves. Many children do not take losing very well. They also cannot help but get overly excited when they win. Everything is a tragedy or a miracle. But learning sportsmanship is about learning how to fail and how to succeed. Both winning and losing are an opportunity to grow in virtue or to grow in vice.

Here is another example of why knowing our mission is so important. I would argue that the goal of sports is not to collect the most medals or trophies, or to have the most bragging rights, or even to experience the most pleasure. The goal is to reach our fullest potential and give everything we have—to finish with nothing left to give. To me, that is success. Failure is not having fewer points on the scoreboard. It is having more left to give.

If we focus too much on the scoreboard, we tend to become lazy when winning and give up when far behind. If we focus too much on having fun, then we will never do what is necessary to reach our fullest potential, because the discipline and training required to do that is not always fun. The scoreboard and fun are both important motivators, but they are not the goal.

So it is with the Christian life. When we keep our goal and mission of becoming saints in mind, then we can avoid putting all our hopes on worldly success or pleasure. We discover that the real opponent is not the "other team"; the real opponent is within. It is you against you. Even the dragons cannot keep you from being a saint. Only you can do that.

In high school, one of my opponents in track, Phil, ran for a nearby school. We seemed to go to all the same track meets, so I was always running against him. Phil would go on to become a state champion in the eight-hundred-meter run our senior year. I knew that Phil was a strong, faithful Catholic, as I could see his scapular always hanging outside his jersey as he ran. I hated running against Phil. He had no off days. He was consistently good and always gave his best, and I knew it would be a huge battle every time I faced him.

Phil was my opponent, but he was another reason I eventually became a champion. He helped me defeat the real opponent within because he pushed me to reach my fullest potential. In this way, Phil was actually helping me become a saint, even though he was on the other team.

In life, we encounter other people who seem to be on the "other team". We get upset when we interact with them, and they often can challenge our faith and our beliefs. It is not just coaches and teammates who push us and challenge us to improve; sometimes it is those who persecute us and utter every kind of evil against us. It is important at those times to remember that people are never the enemy. Becoming a saint is about helping other people become saints. God loves all of His children, and He wants all of us in heaven. When we encounter people who do not believe what we believe, we must remember that sportsmanship is not about winning arguments. It is not about getting more points on the scoreboard to make others look bad or make ourselves look good. Sportsmanship focuses on winning souls for Christ. It is not about being right. It is about helping souls encounter Christ and about sharing the joy of the Gospel.

Nobody's Perfect—but We Are Perfectible

It was June 2, 2010, at Comerica Park in Detroit. Armando Gallaraga of the Detroit Tigers was one out away from

pitching the perfect game. He had faced twenty-six bat-
ters, and retired every one of them. There had been no
Cleveland Indians players on base the entire game, and
Jason Donald was the last Indians player that Gallaraga
needed to retire to complete his masterpiece. Donald hit
a sharp ground ball to the right side of the infield. It was
fielded by the Tigers' first baseman, so Gallaraga sprinted
to cover first base. As the first baseman threw him the ball,
Gallaraga caught it and stepped on first base just ahead of
Donald. All the Tigers players and fans threw their hands
in the air to celebrate, but were shocked when first-base
umpire Jim Joyce declared that Donald was safe.

Armando Gallaraga calmly smiled at the umpire and
then walked back to the pitcher's mound without saying
a word. He went on to get the next batter out and com-
pleted his 3–0 shutout, one out short of the perfect game.

After the game, replays verified that Gallaraga had
indeed caught the ball and stepped on first base ahead
of Donald, and the runner should have been called out.
First-base umpire Jim Joyce, realizing his mistake, immediately told the media that he had blown the call, and
he went to apologize personally to Armando Gallaraga
for taking away his perfect game. Gallaraga hugged Jim
Joyce and forgave him. Gallaraga told the media after the
game, "[Jim Joyce] probably feels more bad than me.
Nobody's perfect. Everybody's human. I understand. I
give the guy a lot of credit for saying, 'I need to talk to
you.' You don't see an umpire tell you that after a game.
I gave him a hug."

Armando Gallaraga is right—nobody's perfect, but he
showed in many ways that we are perfectible. We are not
perfect in the sense that our human weakness causes us
to make mistakes. Our physical capabilities are limited.
However, in a moral sense, we are perfectible because

we can always choose to do what is right. Both Armando Gallaraga and Jim Joyce taught us a great lesson that night of the "near-perfect game". Many people say that Jim Joyce made the biggest mistake of his career, and that may be true. However, his actions were perfect from a moral sense. He said, "I thought [Donald] beat the throw. I was convinced he beat the throw, until I saw the replay." In my eyes, it would have been wrong for Jim Joyce to call Donald out. He saw what he saw, and the umpire's job is to call it how he sees it. We have the advantage of slow-motion replay; he did not. It took a lot of courage to call the runner safe given the circumstances of the situation, but Jim Joyce tried his best to make the right call, not the popular call. After learning of his mistake, he also did the right thing by admitting he was wrong and apologizing. Armando Gallaraga could have thrown a huge tantrum and let his emotions and anger get the best of him, and most people would have understood if he did. After all, Major League Baseball is more than 140 years old, and only twenty-three people have ever pitched a perfect game. But Gallaraga kept his cool. He did not complain or argue or lose his composure. He finished the game and got the final out. Then he forgave the man who took away his perfect game.

Personally, I am glad Jim Joyce botched that call. I could not tell you the name of any of the twenty-three players who actually did pitch a perfect game without looking it up. But I will remember the lesson of sportsmanship we all learned from that near-perfect game. In sports, as in life, the goal is not to be free from mistakes, win the most games, or have the most fun. The goal is to try your best and allow God to do the rest. The goal is to finish with nothing left to give—to leave it all on the field. Life is not about what we have or what we do; it is about who we become. We can choose to strive to become perfectly who God created us to be. Armando Gallaraga and Jim Joyce gave a perfect effort that night. In so many ways, it really was a perfect game.

For all the recommended resources for "Athletics", go to the website: www.saintsinthemaking.com/athletics -resources.html.

Chapter 3

I: INSTRUCTOR'S MANUAL

Color: Red, for God's Love Letter and His Blood Poured Out

Ignorance of Scripture is ignorance of Christ.

—Saint Jerome

The "Instructor's Manual" is the Bible, which is the story of salvation history. Everything in Catholicism assumes we know the story. Unfortunately, many Catholics do not know their story. For the first thirty years of my life, I had no idea there was a story inside the Bible. I knew some characters in the Bible, such as Adam and Eve, Noah, Moses, and King David, but I had absolutely no idea how they fit into the story of salvation history.

I remember being part of an organization called Fellowship of Christian Athletes in college. During one meeting they had Bible races, a game where you see who can find a Scripture verse the quickest. My roommate at the time, Jared, was a devout Christian whose family ran its own church. To this day, I am still learning from Jared. He has a passion, zeal, and love for Scripture and worship that is contagious. During that FCA meeting, I remember Jared rattling off the books of the Bible from beginning to end in order without any hesitation. When they looked at me to participate in the game, I sheepishly declined by saying, "Um, I'm Catholic ... I don't know the Bible." I had little to no interest in the Old Testament, and my only experience reading the New Testament was through "Bible bingo"—opening to a random page and hoping to find an inspiring Scripture verse to help me run a good race or play a good game.

That all changed one day when I went with my brother to a one-day *Great Adventure* Bible study seminar by prominent author and theologian Jeff Cavins, who absolutely changed my whole perspective on the Bible.[1] I discovered an actual story in the Bible that you can read like a novel! Jeff Cavins not only opened my eyes to which books told the narrative but explained where all the supplemental books fit into the narrative's timeline. The Bible is without a doubt the greatest story ever told. You like action and adventure? It is filled with action and adventure. You like mystery? It is filled with mystery. You like humor? You will see God's sense of humor. You like romance? The Bible is the greatest love story ever told. The story has everything.

Storybook Endings

Everybody loves stories. Give me a lecture, and I will forget almost everything you say. Tell me a great story, and I will probably memorize it and remember it for the rest of my life. We all want to be part of a great story. That is why

---

[1] Jeff Cavins, "The Bible Timeline: The Story of Salvation", *The Great Adventure: A Journey through the Bible* (Milwaukee, Wis.: Ascension, 2015).

we love movies and sports so much. In 2011 my favorite Major League Baseball team, the Tampa Bay Rays, had a storybook ending to their season. They won the wild-card spot on the very last day of the season, game 162. It was a long game, ending around midnight in the twelfth inning, so my wife was sound asleep by the time the game was over. When she woke up the next day, I was all excited, and I exclaimed to her, "You're never going to believe this—it's a miracle! The Rays won the wild card!" Of course, her reply was, "What's a wild card?"

I explained to my wife that in baseball there are two leagues, the American League and the National League, and each has three divisions. All division winners go to the playoffs, and then one extra team from each league gets in, and that team is called the wild card.[2] She asked me how many teams there were. I said, "Thirty." She stopped and thought for a minute, did the math, and responded frankly, "So eight out of thirty teams go to the playoffs? That's better than a twenty-five percent chance. That is not a miracle; calm down."

My wife was less than ecstatic, not just because she does not know anything about baseball, but also because she did not know the story. The story changes everything.

She did not know that the Rays started off their season 1–8. She did not know that the Rays' payroll was $40 million, while the two powerhouse teams in their division, the New York Yankees and the Boston Red Sox, had payrolls around $250 million, so they could spend six times as much money finding the best players. That is like a small high school Division 6 team playing against a huge Division 1 team—not fair. My wife did not know that

---

[2] At the time this occurred, there was only one wild-card slot. Now there are two.

the Rays were trailing the Red Sox by nine games in the wild card race in the last month of the season and that no team in the history of baseball has ever come back from a nine-game deficit with one month to play to make the playoffs. She did not know that it came down to the last game and that the Red Sox had to lose to the Baltimore Orioles (the Orioles were woefully bad back then), and the Rays had to win against the New York Yankees. She did not know that the Red Sox were winning their game with two outs in the bottom of the ninth inning and nobody on base. She did not know that the Rays were losing to the Yankees by seven runs with only two innings left to play.

Somehow, the Red Sox blew their lead with two outs in the bottom of the ninth, and the Rays came all the way from seven runs down to beat the Yankees on a home run in the bottom of the twelfth inning. She did not know any of that. All she could see was that the chances were 1 in 4.

As I said, the story changes everything. I saw a newspaper article the next day, and a sports writer did the math. He said the chances of the Rays making the playoffs the way they did was 1 in 278 million! But if you do not know the story, it is 1 in 4.

The Tampa Bay Rays' ending to that season is what many people would describe as miraculous or "magical". A YouTube search of "2011 Tampa Bay Rays miracle ending" shows videos of how people reacted when Evan Longoria hit his home run in the twelfth inning. They were screaming and cheering, dancing, and giving high fives. Grown men who were strangers were hugging and crying. It was pandemonium. In reality, that kind of reaction is not all that uncommon in sports.

However, I am telling you that we as Catholics have a better story. The story of salvation history is way better than any walk-off home run or epic comeback in sports.

Think about this: Jesus fulfilled many prophecies written by more than forty different authors (all of whom were inspired by the Holy Spirit) over a thousand years; the story still applies to the life of every single person to this day; and the narrative climaxes with the God of the universe, who has made Himself man, offering Himself as a living sacrifice on a Cross to save His Bride from the great dragon to get her into the kingdom of heaven. It sounds pretty amazing—and it is true! There is a Divine Author, an uncreated Creator, an all-powerful loving Father who is interested in every detail. Only God could have written a story that fits together so perfectly. It is the greatest story ever told, with the greatest hero who ever lived, the greatest sacrifice ever made, the most epic comeback in the history of the world, and the greatest love ever seen. The Rays may have come back from nine games back and seven runs down, but Jesus Christ came back from the dead! Nothing else even comes close. If you cannot be inspired by this story, there is no story that will ever inspire you. But you have to know the story.

If you are bored by your faith, you probably do not know the story. I certainly did not know the story the first thirty years of my life. Again, everything in Catholicism assumes we know the story. For example, if you come to Mass and you do not know the story, it is like showing up in the middle of a movie you have never seen. You do not know the characters and you do not know the plot, so of course you are going to be bored out of your mind. I am willing to bet, though, that if you were to show up in the middle of your favorite movie, you would probably sit down and watch it, no matter at what point you arrived. You would say, "Oh, I love this part!" because you know the characters and you know the plot. In fact, you may have the movie memorized.

It is my goal that by the end of this chapter, you will have a basic knowledge of our whole story and how it all fits together.

In this chapter, we are going to try to get to know this Instructor's Manual called the Bible. It teaches us who we are, why we are here, and where we are going. We come to discover it is not just a story about a bunch of dead people who lived long ago. The story is alive and is still taking place. We are in the story, and not just minor characters. We each play a significant role. Every character in that Bible acts as a mirror, teaching us something about ourselves and something about our Savior. The entire Bible is Christocentric, meaning it points to Jesus Christ, and by learning about Jesus Christ we learn about ourselves. In fact, the surprise ending to this great romantic story is that after all the sacrifices, forgiving, and searching that the Bridegroom does to save His Bride from evil, you are shocked to turn the final page and discover your own name as the Bride. You are the one He is searching for and trying to save. By reflecting on the characters in the Bible, let us rediscover the story of Jesus Christ and the story of *you*.

The New Adam (Early World)

The story of salvation begins in the book of Genesis with the story of creation. There are two creation accounts, one of which focuses on the objective reality of creation and one of which is a more subjective account on the creation of man and woman. It is important to note that Genesis is not meant to be a science textbook. The author of Genesis uses a style of writing that tells a story to relay a message. One analogy I use on how to read Genesis comes from my vocation as an eye doctor. Every day I look at many human eyes—their corneas, irises, lenses, vitreous, retinas, and whole ocular anatomy. I examine those eyes as a scientist. When I come home from work and I look into my wife's eyes, I see a reflection of eternity. The iris and the pupil are both perfect circles that have no beginning and no end. The strands of the iris never reveal their depth. The pupil is an entranceway for light to enter the body. My wife's eyes are not only a window to her body but a passageway to her very soul. I look at my wife's eyes through the eyes of a lover, not a scientist. When we read Genesis, we should look at the story with the eyes of a lover to gather the spiritual truths of the story.

There are some objective truths we need to accept from the story: God is the Creator of all things; there were an original man and woman who fell from grace by an act of disobedience; there is an enemy that deceived them; and as a result of their fall, we are affected with the stain of their original sin and continue to struggle with concupiscence.

A basic question develops in this "opening scene" that grabs our attention, draws us in, and foreshadows what every character will face through the rest of the story. It is also the question we will all face as we become part of this story: Do you trust God?

In Genesis 2, God gives Adam some specific instructions on his role and duty. He tells Adam "to till ... and keep" the garden, or to translate that from the original Hebrew, to work the land and to guard and protect it (2:15). What he must guard and protect most certainly includes his bride, whom God gives to Adam because "it is not good that the man should be alone" (2:18). We see right from the start that man and woman were made for each other, and it is their differences and complementarities that make them in the image of God. Neither man's nor woman's existence makes sense by itself, but together they reveal the beautiful mystery of God's love for His people.

This opening marriage scene between Adam and Eve foreshadows the end of the story. The narrative begins in Genesis with the story of Adam and Eve and ends in Revelation with the marriage of the Lamb. The story of salvation is the story of a marriage! God's eternal plan is to "marry" us!

In Genesis 3, we see that something goes terribly wrong. This is an important chapter to study and memorize because it is the "game film" of the enemy. The serpent (that former great angel of light, Lucifer, who fell from grace and was cast down to the earth) cunningly convinces the woman to eat the forbidden fruit. The crux of this encounter is how the serpent convinces the man and woman that God does not love them. The real question that emerges from their conversation with the serpent is, Can you really trust God?

Adam and Eve answer that question with a profound no. They mistakenly grasp at the happiness that they suddenly perceive as being held from them by a tyrant master. This is really what sin is. It is our grasping at the things we think we need to be happy because we fear that God does not have our best interests in mind.

In their shame, Adam and Eve cover their nakedness and hide from God. God comes, and by asking, "Where are you?" reveals their situation (Gen 3:9). His question helps them to realize the graveness of their sin. They are now separated from God's grace and surely doomed to death, as God told them they would die if they ate the fruit. God is perfectly just. He cannot take back what He said would happen. He had made a covenant with them, and a covenant is not just a contract or an exchange of goods. God's covenant with them said, in effect, "I am yours and you are mine." When that covenant was broken, and God Himself, the source of life and good, was rejected, the consequence could not be anything other than death—being cut off from Life Himself.

Things look bleak after the fall of man; however, there is hope because God promises them a redeemer. He says to the serpent, "I will put enmity between you and the woman, and between your offspring and hers; They will strike at your head, while you strike at his heel" (Gen 3:15). This is good news! In other words, there will come a new Eve, and she will bear a son, a new Adam, and they will crush the head of the enemy. Eve's response of no to God brought sin into the world, but as the story progresses we will see Mary's yes bring forth a Savior. The Bridegroom Messiah is coming! He will save His Bride (you and me) from the trenches of death by paying the price Himself for the broken covenant.

When I read the story of Adam and Eve, I cannot help but think, "How could they be so stupid?" They had everything they could ever want and need promised to them by God if they would just trust Him. However, I realized this story is not just about Adam and Eve. It is about you and me. I am Adam. His cowardly blood runs through my veins. It is like a cancer that is fatal to my soul, and without a Savior, without a redeemer, without the blood of one who is pure, I am doomed.

Jesus is the new Adam. Just like the first Adam, He found Himself in a garden. Just like the first Adam, He was afraid in His agony in the garden as He cried out, "If this cannot pass unless I drink it, your will be done" (Mt 26:42). Through Jesus' passion and crucifixion, He proclaims to the whole world, "I do not want to suffer, but I am willing to suffer and die for My Bride because I trust the Father! Even if I die, He will raise me up again."

Now we see more of what Jesus accomplished on that Cross and how that Cross is the image of the love of a bridegroom for his bride. When Jesus' side was pierced with a lance, His blood and water flowed out. The water is a sign of baptism, the blood a sign of the Eucharist. Through these sacraments we encounter the very grace that will give us a new birth and eternal life. In essence our life comes from the side of Christ, just as the bride of Adam came from Adam's side. Just as the Lord God "caused a deep sleep to fall upon the man [Adam]" so that He could fashion Adam's bride from his rib (Gen 2:21), the Lord God allowed Jesus to enter the sleep of death so His Bride could have life that flows from His side.

The New Noah

Because of the disobedience of Adam and Eve, sin entered the world, and the heart of every man was corrupted with a tendency to do wrong, and mankind suffered from spiritual death—the absence of the life of God that results from original sin. Humans have disordered desires and must struggle to choose to do what is right. We see the repercussions of original sin in Adam and Eve's first children, Cain and Abel. Abel is a hard worker and makes a good sacrifice to the Lord that pleases God. Cain, on the other hand, goes through the motions with his sacrifice, and God is displeased with his lack of effort. When Cain discovers that God is pleased with Abel and not with him, he goes into a fit of envy and anger, so much so that he kills his brother. We learn an important lesson from this story. God loves us no matter what, but he will be pleased with us only if we do our best in serving others rather than ourselves. Recall Cain's famous question to God when asked where his brother is: "Am I my brother's keeper?" (Gen 4:9). The answer to that question is yes! You are your brother's keeper.

The corruption of mankind does not end with Cain—it spreads throughout the whole world, so much so that God regrets His creation and decides to start over with one righteous man and his family. God comes to Noah with a strange request: Build an ark. This is not just a little ark. It is an ark that would take one hundred years to build. Put yourself in Noah's shoes and ask that question every character must ask: Do I trust God? When God asked Noah to build the ark, it was not raining. He was no doubt laughed at for spending his life building something that seemed useless. Noah had to trust God's plan, even if he did not understand it. Noah does a good job of being obedient to God's will, and he and his family survive the great flood God sends.

Jesus, the new Noah, will also come to build an "ark", a vessel that will carry His people through storms and tribulations into a new life. Jesus built a Church, and that Church is our only hope of salvation. Just as the rains came to cover the land in what seems like total death, the waters of our baptism also symbolize death. Our old self is "drowned" so our new self can live. We die so we can live. Those waters drown the sin of the world, and Jesus makes all things new. We must go through tragedy to get to the triumph.

The New Isaac

After the flood, man repopulates the earth, but so does his sin. At this point in the story, we move out of the early world and into the time of the patriarchs. "Patriarch" means "father, leader"; we read about our forefathers in the faith—namely, Abraham, Isaac, Jacob, and Joseph. God's new covenant with the human race will begin with a righteous man named Abram and his wife, Sarai. God changes their names to Abraham (father of many nations) and Sarah (princess). The three promises he makes to Abraham will be the blueprint for the remainder of the story. God promised Abraham a great land, which later would be described as a land flowing with milk and honey. God promised him that through his line a nation would arise, which later it was revealed would include a royal dynasty. Finally, God promised Abraham that through his descendants all nations of the world would be blessed.

The problem Abraham and Sarah face is that God is promising them a great line of kings, but they have no children in their old age. Abraham is about one hundred years old, and Sarah is ninety. When God promises them a son, it sounds so impossible that Sarah actually laughs at God's plan. Again, they are forced to ask: Do I trust God? At first, their answer to that question is no, and they take matters into their own hands. Sarah gives Abraham her maidservant Hagar to have a son with, and they call him Ishmael. Interestingly, Ishmael would become a forefather of the Muslim religion, which sees God more as a master than a Father. Since Hagar was a slave to Abraham, Ishmael would see him as master. But God's plan was to have a true son through Abraham and Sarah.

And God does get the "last laugh", as they do have a son named Isaac (which means "laughter"—see, God does have a sense of humor). Isaac grows up as the beloved only son of Abraham and Sarah. When Isaac is probably a teenager, God comes to Abraham and gives him an unthinkable order: "Take your son, your only-begotten son Isaac, whom you love, and go to the land of Moriah, and offer him there as a burnt offering upon one of the mountains of which I shall tell you" (Gen 22:2). At this point, I would really struggle with that question: Do I trust God? However, Abraham has learned his lesson. He knows that Isaac is an amazing and miraculous gift from God and that God can do everything He says He will do and can be trusted. Abraham realizes that Isaac belongs to God, and the only adequate response is to give him back, knowing God's promise was that Abraham was to be the father of many nations—if he trusted God.

Notice in this story that God tells Abraham up front what He is asking. He does not say, "Go to Moriah with Isaac, and when you get there I'll tell you what to do next." No, He tells him straightaway why he is going there. The same is true with us. God makes it clear that being Christian is going to be hard—now walk.

When Abraham and Isaac arrive at Moriah, Isaac carries the wood to his own sacrifice, saying to his father, "Behold, the fire and the wood; but where is the lamb for a burnt offering?" Abraham, trusting in God, replies to his son, "God will provide himself the lamb for a burnt offering" (Gen 22:7, 8). Abraham binds Isaac and is about to sacrifice him when the angel of the Lord stops him in the nick of time, proclaiming that he has passed the test. This was not a test to help God discover if Abraham trusted him. This was a test to help Abraham discover that he did indeed trust God and was ready to be the father of many nations. God knows us, but I think He tests us sometimes to help us believe in ourselves.

Have you found Jesus in this story yet? It is the story of a beloved only son of a father carrying the wood to his own sacrifice. As Abraham pointed out, God would provide the lamb. The lamb is not slain in this story of Isaac. Abraham and Isaac end up sacrificing a ram caught in a thicket—which means that at this point in the story we are still looking for a lamb. Later in the story, the Lamb of God will come, the beloved Son of the Father, and He will carry the wood to His own sacrifice to save the world from sin. Interestingly, there is a tradition that this land of Moriah where Isaac was to be offered is the same place as Calvary, where Jesus was offered.

The New Joseph

Isaac grows up and marries a woman named Rebekah, and together they have twin sons named Esau and Jacob. Esau is older, but when the two boys are fighting in their mother's womb, God reveals to Rebekah that the older will serve the younger, so she favors Jacob. Jacob's name means "to trick or supplant", and that is exactly what he does to his father and brother to steal the blessing and the birthright normally given to the oldest son.

Esau is understandably angry at Jacob after having his birthright stolen, so Jacob flees the promised land and meets and falls in love with Rachel. After Jacob serves her father Laban for seven years to win fair Rachel's hand, Laban pulls a trick of his own. After Jacob's wedding night, Jacob realizes that it was Laban's older daughter Leah that he was given in marriage, not Rachel. How Jacob could be tricked in that way is beyond me. You can see that the theme of "what you sow is what you reap" is ever present in the Old Testament.

After this, the story turns into quite the soap opera. Jacob does not love Leah. He loves Rachel. So he agrees to serve Laban for another seven years in return for his daughter Rachel. So now he is married to two sisters. Good luck with that.

In what appears to be a son-making competition between the two wives, God favors Leah because she is unloved, so she is having sons for Jacob, while Rachel remains barren. The two sisters use Sarah's method of making sons by handing over their maidservants to have sons for them. After Jacob has ten sons (and one daughter) with three different women, God finally answers Rachel's prayer begging for a child of her own, and she conceives a son, and they name him Joseph. As you can imagine, Joseph becomes the favored son of Jacob because he is the son of his beloved Rachel. Rachel would later die in childbirth with Jacob's twelfth and final son, Benjamin.

This is how the twelve tribes of Israel came to be. God eventually changes Jacob's name to Israel (God often changes a person's name to mark the essence of his role or character; e.g., Peter is the rock). Jacob's twelve sons would form twelve tribes, from which the Israelite nation would grow.

The story begins to focus on Joseph, the eleventh son, and the favored of Jacob. Joseph is set apart from all of his brothers, and his father treats him differently and gives him gifts, such as the coat of many colors, which most people know from the famous musical *Joseph and the Amazing Technicolor Dreamcoat*.

Joseph is a righteous and upright man with a gift for interpreting dreams. After a dream that he interprets as his brothers all bowing down before him, his brothers naturally become quite indignant and angry. They are so angry that they devise a plan to rid Joseph from their lives. While out working in the fields, they attack him, strip off his coat of many colors, and throw him into a pit. Their first intention is to kill him. However, they see a caravan of Ishmaelites going by and decide to sell him into slavery.

Joseph is taken down to Egypt, where he becomes the slave of a man named Potiphar. Joseph serves Potiphar so well that the Egyptian ruler takes a liking to him and treats him like family. Unfortunately, Potiphar's wife also takes a strong liking to Joseph, and she tries to convince him to sleep with her. Being a righteous man, Joseph refuses, so she tears her own garments and accuses him of attempted rape. Joseph is thrown into prison for a crime he did not commit.

Despite all the bad luck and injustice that comes to Joseph, he remains obedient and faithful to God. In prison, he rightly interprets the dreams of two prisoners, one of whom is released; Joseph tells the released prisoner not to forget about him. Eventually, the Pharaoh has a dream that nobody can interpret. The released prisoner remembers Joseph's gift, so Joseph is brought to Pharaoh and rightly interprets the dream as meaning seven years of plenty followed by seven years of severe famine. The Pharaoh is so impressed with Joseph that he raises him up to be the second most powerful man in the land! He puts Joseph in charge of organizing an effort to store up food during the years of plenty to prepare for the years of famine. The dream comes to fruition as Joseph predicted, and Joseph's plan ends up saving all of Egypt.

Egypt was not the only place experiencing famine. Back home Joseph's family is starving, and so his brothers travel to Egypt looking for food. Joseph recognizes his brothers as they are approaching, and he disguises himself to test the intentions of his brothers' hearts to see if they have changed. He holds one of them prisoner and tells the rest of them to go home and bring back their youngest brother, Benjamin, who had not come on the journey. The brothers obey, against the will of their grieving father, Jacob, who already lost Joseph, his first son born to Rachel. Joseph sabotages Benjamin by placing "stolen goods" in his bag and then accuses him of theft and throws him into prison. The brothers cannot bear the thought of their father enduring more anguish. Judah (the fourth son) especially feels responsible, for it was he who sold Joseph into slavery and promised Jacob, their father, that he would bring Benjamin back to him. Judah refuses to leave his younger brother and offers himself in exchange for Benjamin.

Joseph, overcome with emotion, knowing their hearts have changed, reveals himself, and his brothers all fall down before him, as predicted in Joseph's original dream. They beg for his forgiveness, and Joseph's response is the moral of the story. He explains to his brothers that it was God who sent him to Egypt in order that they would all be saved from the famine. "You meant evil against me; but God meant it for good" (Gen 50:20).

This story of Joseph is one of the best stories in the Bible and makes for an exciting movie script. As you listen to the story, can you find the parallels between Joseph and Jesus? Of all the characters in the Bible, Joseph might be one of the most obvious prefigurements of Jesus.

Now here is the fun part. Let us see all the pieces fall into place. Just like Jesus, Joseph is the beloved son of a father. He is a righteous and obedient man. He is betrayed by those closest to him and sold for twenty pieces of silver. He is stripped of his royal robe and made a slave. He is wrongly accused of a crime he did not commit and is thrown into prison. He uses what seems like a horrible injustice to accomplish the salvation of all the people. And what was his attitude toward those who betrayed him? *Forgiveness.*

The New Moses

As exciting as the story has been so far and as exciting as it will become, the pinnacle of the Old Testament is the story of Moses. After Joseph saves all of Egypt, he brings his entire family down to Egypt to live there. Over the next 450 years, the Israelite nation grows enormously. Unfortunately, after the heroics of Joseph are forgotten and new Pharaohs take over the rule of Egypt, the Israelites become slaves to the Egyptians. They are forced to do hard labor and cry out to God to save them from tyranny.

Despite being slaves, the Israelites grow to such a vast number that the Pharaoh becomes worried they will overthrow his rule. To prevent this, he comes up with the awful plan of throwing all male newborns into the Nile River.

One Israelite mother, from the house of Levi, offers her newborn son a glimmer of hope by placing him in a basket before putting him in the Nile. The baby is found by Pharaoh's daughter, and she calls him Moses, which means "to draw out of the water". (Later in the story, we will see that another tyrant leader, named Herod, will attempt to destroy every male child in and around the city of Bethlehem to protect his throne from a prophesied new King. Herod has his soldiers slaughter the "Holy Innocents" in Bethlehem, but just like Moses, one of them escapes into Egypt—the baby Jesus.)

Moses is raised in Pharaoh's court as a prince of Egypt. However, he knows he is an Israelite. One day Moses witnesses an Egyptian guard treating an Israelite slave harshly, and Moses ends up killing the guard. The penalty for killing an Egyptian guard is death, even for Moses, so with a death sentence on his head, he flees into the desert. He remains in the desert for forty years, until one day God reveals Himself to him in a burning bush.

God tells Moses that He has heard His people's cry in Egypt, and He wants Moses to go back to Pharaoh and ask for the release of the Israelite people. At first, Moses makes excuses: he stutters and cannot speak well; he was raised an enemy of the Israelites, and they will not believe or follow him. He actually begs God, "Oh, my Lord, send, I pray, some other person" (Ex 4:13). Moses has a lot of trouble trusting God and believing he can accomplish what God is asking. Sound familiar? If you are like me, it does. But God reminds Moses (and all of us), "Who has made man's mouth? Who makes him mute, or deaf, or seeing, or blind? Is it not I, the LORD? Now therefore go, and I will be with your mouth and teach you what you shall speak" (Ex 4:11–12).

Moses finally agrees after God offers him the help of his brother Aaron, and the two men approach Pharaoh with the seemingly absurd request. What happens next is the ten plagues of Egypt, which are actually a powerful witness of God showing the whole world that He is the one true God. The Egyptians had many gods and worshiped almost everything, and each one of the ten plagues is a showdown between the real God and the false gods of Egypt.

The Pharaoh remains stubborn, and after he goes back and forth several times on his agreement to let the Israelites go, God finally has enough. The tenth and final plague is the one that will cause Pharaoh to set them free. It is the death of all firstborn sons. This event is referred to as the Passover, because the angel of death will come and "pass over" any house that is marked by the blood of a lamb. The instructions to the Israelites to avoid this angel of death are very interesting and very specific, and the greatest foreshadowing of the coming of Jesus. It is key not to forget the parts of the story we have already read: You will remember that in the story of Isaac, no lamb was sacrificed, and we were told that "God will provide himself the lamb." So, at this point in the story, we are still looking for the "Lamb of God". We will not find *the*

Lamb in the story of the Passover, but we do find another prefigurement of the Lamb to come.

The instructions for the Passover, which the Israelites are to celebrate every year after they leave Egypt, are found in Exodus 12. On the tenth day of the month (roughly March on our calendar), each family was to take a year-old lamb and inspect it for four days to make sure it was an unblemished lamb in prime condition. Then, on the fourteenth day of the month, they were to sacrifice the lamb. They were to take its blood and spread it over the lintel and doorposts of their homes. This bloodstained wood signified their freedom from slavery and saved them from the angel of death. After that, they had to eat the lamb at the Passover meal.

Now we pause in the story to see how this Passover relates to Jesus and how it relates to all of us today. You will recall that during the Transfiguration story in the New Testament, Jesus meets Moses and Elijah on the mountain. This is where we hear God's voice say, "This is my beloved Son, with whom I am well pleased; listen to him" (Mt 17:5). It is a reference to Deuteronomy 18:15, in which Moses says, "The LORD your God will raise up for you a prophet like me from among you, from your brethren—him you shall heed." So what is being communicated at the Transfiguration (among other things)? Jesus is the new Moses, and he is about to perform a new Exodus that will save the people not just from the slavery of a tyrant nation but from the slavery of sin.

It is time to put some pieces of the story together. Jesus, the Lamb of God, comes riding into Jerusalem on Palm Sunday, the tenth day of the month. For four days, he is inspected. He goes before Herod; he goes before Caiaphas, the high priest; and he goes before Pontius Pilate—and what does Pilate say? "I find no crime in him" (Jn 18:38).

In other words, Jesus is a "lamb ... without blemish" (Ex 12:5). Then, on the fourteenth day of the month, at three in the afternoon, the Lamb of God is sacrificed. The blood of that Lamb stains the wood of the Cross. That blood signifies our freedom from the bondage of sin and death. But the connections to Jesus do not end there. What did the Israelites have to do with the sacrificed lamb? They had to eat it! For the Passover ritual to be complete, they had to eat the lamb!

We should get this as Catholics. When do we eat the Lamb? In the Eucharist! When celebrating the Passover meal each year, Jews believe that God not only saved their ancestors but that each individual person is somehow brought back to that very first Passover in which God saved all of them. In the Mass, we believe we are all saved by that one true sacrifice on Calvary two thousand years ago. We eat the Lamb that saves us from death and gives us eternal life. "Unless you eat the flesh of the Son of man and drink his blood, you have no life in you" (Jn 6:53).

Jesus is not just the new Paschal Lamb. He is also the new manna, or bread that came down from heaven. As the story continues, the Israelites leave Egypt after the Passover, only to be chased down by the Egyptian army. This is where the famous parting of the Red Sea occurs, and in a foreshadowing of the sacrament of baptism, the Israelites are brought through water to symbolize the passage through death to life. Pharaoh's army drowns as the sea comes back to its normal level after the Israelites have passed.

Afterward, while out in the desert, the Israelites discover that freedom has a cost, and they must learn to survive without the food and drink they had in Egypt. Many start to complain against Moses and want to go back to slavery in Egypt. God's greatest challenge was not getting the Israelites out of Egypt but getting Egypt out of the Israelites. The same is true with us. God often frees us from sin and addiction, and we often want to go back.

Under the leadership of Moses, God provides for His people in the desert. First He trains them in the law that will keep them free from idolatry. Most people are familiar with the Ten Commandments. Many do not realize that the commandments were given at this point in the story—a time when God sets His people free from slavery. The world often sees the commandments as restrictions on freedom, when in fact God's law is meant to give us freedom and keep us free.

Not only does he give His people the law, but He gives them food in the form of manna. The manna appears on the ground of the desert every morning like a dew frost. The Israelites gather the manna, which tastes like wafers made with honey. This bread from heaven sustains them for forty years while they wander through the desert. The sweetness of the manna is a foretaste of where they are going. They are heading to the land of Canaan, the "promised land" we heard about in the covenant with Abraham. It is a land "flowing with milk and honey" (Ex 3:17). The manna tasting like honey is a great reminder that they are pilgrims on a journey toward a great land.

As already mentioned, Jesus is the new manna. He is the bread that came down from heaven, and Jesus directly tells us this: "I am the bread of life. Your fathers ate the manna in the wilderness, and they died. This is the bread which comes down from heaven, that a man may eat of it and not die. I am the living bread which came down from heaven; if any one eats of this bread, he will live for ever; and the bread which I shall give for the life of the world is my flesh" (Jn 6:48–51). Just as the manna reminded the Israelites that they were on a journey to a promised land, the Eucharist should remind us that we are pilgrims on a journey to the promised kingdom of heaven. The Eucharist is a real foretaste of heaven—an opportunity to experience heaven on earth.

The dew is a beautiful image of how the Holy Spirit works. We wake up to dew in the early morning quiet of the day. It seemingly comes from nowhere, silent and unseen. At Mass we hear how the Holy Spirit comes silently and unseen, changing what is ordinary into what is extraordinary, changing the natural into the supernatural. At the moment of consecration, when the bread and wine are changed into the body and blood of Jesus, we hear, "You are indeed Holy, O Lord, the fount of all holiness. Make holy, therefore, these gifts, we pray, by sending down your Spirit upon them like the dewfall, so that they may become for us the Body and Blood of our Lord Jesus Christ."[3]

This is also one part of the story where we get a foreshadowing of Mary. After the Israelites leave Egypt, God has His people build the "Ark of the Covenant". The ark is where God dwells, and it is kept in the Holy of Holies, the innermost room of the desert tent of meeting. Inside the ark are placed three things: the tablets of the Ten Commandments, a piece of the manna, and the priestly rod of Aaron. Mary is considered the new Ark of the Covenant because inside her womb she carried the One who was to inaugurate the new law of love, who was the new bread come down from heaven, and who was the new High Priest, Jesus Christ.

The New Joshua

The reason the Israelites spent forty years wandering through the desert was not just because Moses was a man,

[3] Eucharistic Prayer II.

and men refuse to stop and ask for directions. The reason they were out there so long was because of their disobedience and lack of trust. Remember the primary question we should ask during this story: Do I trust God? The promised land was not that far from Egypt, and after training the Israelites in the law, God gave them an opportunity to go directly to the land flowing with milk and honey. But first, they had to pass a test.

God commanded Moses to send twelve spies to go up to the land to check it out. The spies discover that it truly is a bountiful land, with great produce and fortified cities. However, the people occupying the land are far more advanced than the Israelites, and the latter believe their chances of overtaking this land to be impossible.

When the twelve spies return after forty days, ten report that there is no way to take the land. Only two of the spies, Joshua and Caleb, trust God and say the Israelites can do it. The overall lack of trust angers God, and he sentences the Israelites to forty years in the desert, during which time every man over twenty years old will die—except Joshua and Caleb.

Moses is a good leader, but even he disobeys God in one instance during the wandering in the desert, and his punishment is that he will not live to lead the Israelites into the promised land. So after forty years of leading them through the desert, Moses dies, and the older generation is gone. Joshua takes over as the new leader. He learned well from Moses how to be a good leader and learned to trust God.

Joshua must have been feeling very nervous after Moses, his mentor and leader for so many years, died and left him in charge of the great task of leading a stiff-necked people into the promised land. At times we all feel like Joshua must have felt, that God asks us to do something we are not ready for or capable of doing. Being a leader takes great courage, and God comes to Joshua from the start to help calm his nerves by letting him know that He will be with him and he has nothing to fear. The book of Joshua, which tells this part of the story, begins with the divine promise of assistance.

God promises Joshua:

> As I was with Moses, so I will be with you; I will not fail you or forsake you. Be strong and of good courage; for you shall cause this people to inherit the land which I swore to their fathers to give them. Only be strong and very courageous, being careful to do according to all the law which Moses my servant commanded you.... Then you shall make your way prosperous, and then you shall have good success. Have I not commanded you? Be strong and of good courage; be not frightened, neither be dismayed; for the LORD your God is with you wherever you go. (Josh 1:5–9)

I refer to this passage often, especially as a father whose task is to lead my family into the promised land of heaven. Often our duties and leadership roles seem too much for our own strength, but this fortifying passage given to Joshua should help us all to realize that we *can* trust God and that He is with us. All we have to do is obey.

Joshua is a good leader and does obey, even when God's instructions seem quite ridiculous. The first city they must conquer to reach the promised land is Jericho, a mighty city surrounded by walls to keep out intruders. God's instructions do not include detailed war strategies. Instead, He simply asks them to walk around the city one time each day for six days, and then on the seventh day they are to walk around the city seven times and blow the trumpets, at which time the walls will fall down (see Josh 6). At this point, I would be saying, "You want us to do what?" However, they have seen God's wonders, and Joshua knows he has every reason to trust God, so he does as commanded, and the walls indeed do collapse on the seventh day.

The Israelites go through the promised land and conquer many of the cities, failing only when their trust in God fails. Although remnants and pockets of enemies remain, the Israelites end up controlling much of the promised land before Joshua's leadership ends. Before Joshua dies, he gives a final challenge to his people. My family has this challenge hanging on our wall at home: "Put away the gods which your fathers served beyond the River, and in Egypt, and serve the LORD. And if you be unwilling to serve the LORD, choose this day whom you will serve, whether the gods your fathers served in the region beyond the River, or the gods of the Amorites in whose land you dwell; but as for me and my house, we will serve the LORD" (Josh 24:14–15).

Joshua and Jesus have the same name in Hebrew, and we see glimpses of Jesus in Joshua. Just like Joshua, Jesus will be obedient to God. He will lead the people out of the desert of this life and into a new promised land of heaven by trusting the Father—even unto death.

The New Gideon

After Joshua dies, the Israelites go through a period without a leader. They are in the promised land but do not heed the warnings that were given to them by Joshua and Moses. As we move forward in the story into the book of Judges, we read in chapter 2 that a generation passed and the Israelites no longer knew the Lord. "They went after other gods, from among the gods of the peoples who were round about them, and bowed down to them; and they provoked the LORD to anger" (2:12). This passage in the introduction to the book of Judges showcases the parallels between these people and our generation today. In one generation, we have lost our story. We failed to teach our children the wonders of the one true God, and they have begun to worship the "gods" of this culture: wealth, power, pleasure, honor, technology, sports—all those things we tend to put before God. In the pews of most Catholic churches, there are few people in their twenties or thirties.

So perhaps this is a part of the story to which we should pay close attention, because we can see what happens to a people who forgets its God and worships false gods. The book of Judges shows us a pattern that recurs seven times, showing both God's patience and mercy and the people's persistence in failing to learn their lesson.

The cycle goes as follows:

1. The people sin.
2. Their enemies overtake them, and they become slaves who must serve.
3. They cry out for help (supplication).
4. God sends them salvation in the form of a judge, or a deliverer from their enemies.
5. There is peace (silence) in the land for a time.

To understand the book of Judges, remember these five words that start with the letter *s*: sin, servitude, supplication, salvation, silence.

For instance, Judges 3:7–11 tells the story of the judge Othni-el:

> And the sons of Israel did what was evil in the sight of the LORD, forgetting the LORD their God, and serving the

Baals and the Asheroth. Therefore the anger of the LORD was kindled against Israel [They sinned!], and he sold them into the hand of Cushan-rishathaim king of Mesopotamia; and the sons of Israel served Cushan-rishathaim eight years [They served!]. But when the sons of Israel cried to the LORD [Supplication!], the LORD raised up a deliverer for the sons of Israel, who delivered them, Othni-el the son of Kenaz, Caleb's younger brother. The Spirit of the LORD came upon him, and he judged Israel; he went out to war, and the LORD gave Cushan-rishathaim king of Mesopotamia into his hand; and his hand prevailed over Cushan-rishathaim [Salvation!]. So the land had rest forty years. Then Othni-el the son of Kenaz died [Silence!].

There are a total of twelve judges we can read about; I would like to focus on one of them. Judges 6–8 tells the story of Gideon. Because of the sin of the Israelites, God has allowed them to be overtaken by the Midianites, and they have become slaves. During their oppression, God speaks to a boy named Gideon and calls him to lead an army against the Midianites. Gideon objects that he is the weakest man from the weakest tribe, and he cannot possibly lead an army into battle.

God explains that Gideon's weakness is precisely why he was chosen. In fact, God orders Gideon to reduce the size of his army twice to make that point: "The LORD said to Gideon, 'The people with you are too many for me to give the Midianites into their hand, lest Israel vaunt themselves against me, saying, "My own hand has delivered me"'" (Judg 7:2). In other words, this victory will be proof to the Israelites that it is not their own power that can save them; it is God's power. Their job is simply to trust God. That is our job also, despite how small and weak we perceive ourselves to be. God can accomplish great victories through us if we just trust Him. Gideon learns this lesson well. He leads the little army to a great victory, and the people cheer him, asking him to rule over them. Gideon, knowing God's desire is to be their King, says to the people, "I will not rule over you, and my son will not rule over you; the LORD will rule over you" (Judg 8:23).

Gideon was the least-expected savior. So was Jesus. Jesus did not come as a mighty king on a lofty throne. He came as a baby, born into poverty in a stable. As C. S. Lewis points out, the Lord came to the world behind enemy lines, in a form his enemies would not recognize. We also are like pararescue jumpers. We are dropped in behind enemy lines, and we are called to save Private Ryan, and Private Rachel, and Private Robert, and every soul we encounter.

The New Ruth

During the time of the judges, a supplemental story takes place that we can learn a great deal from. It is told in the book of Ruth, which is only four chapters long. A Jewish man named Elimelech and his wife, Naomi, leave Israel during a time of famine. They settle in Moab, and their two sons end up meeting and marrying Moabite women. Tragically, Elimelech and his two sons die, leaving Naomi with her two daughters-in-law from a foreign land. Naomi announces that she must return to her native land of Israel and encourages her two daughters-in-law to stay behind. One does, but the other, Ruth, says to her mother-in-law these beautiful words that will be used at weddings for centuries to come: "Entreat me not to leave you or to return from following you; for where you go I will go, and where you lodge I will lodge; your people shall be my people, and your God my God; where you die I will die, and there will I be buried" (Ruth 1:16–17).

What great loyalty Ruth expressed. In the middle of the time of the judges, when the Israelites continually offended God by worshiping false gods, we have the story of a girl from a foreign land leaving her land and rejecting the foreign gods to come to Israel and worship the one true God.

Converts, it is often said, make the best Catholics. Those who were raised Catholic may take their faith for granted, but those who convert to the faith have a firm understanding and appreciation for the faith they chose. It goes to show that all of us must make a conscious choice to follow God, whether we were born Catholic or not.

Jesus has a special place in his heart for the pagans, sinners, and foreigners. Remember God's covenant with Abraham? The third component of the covenant was a worldwide blessing. God would not save just Israel; He would save the whole world! In the Gospels, when the centurion comes to Jesus and requests the healing of his servant, he says, "Lord, I am not worthy to have you come under my roof; but only say the word, and my servant will be healed." Jesus replies, "Truly, I say to you, not even in Israel have I found such faith" (Mt 8:8, 10).

Because of Ruth's loyalty, God makes her a vital and essential part of the story of salvation. Once again, God uses an underdog, just as Jesus himself will come as an underdog. God is not looking for strength and power. He is looking for good-hearted people who will be obedient to Him and trust Him. As Jeff Cavins says, He is looking not for ability but availability.

Ruth comes to Israel and marries Boaz. They have a son named Obed, who will become the father of Jesse, who will become the father of King David, in whose line Jesus will be born. Ruth could not have known how God was going to use her in the story of salvation. If you are obedient and faithful to God, He may have a role in mind for you that you never imagined for yourself.

The New David

At the end of the time of the judges, the Israelites are tired of the vicious cycle in which they keep participating. They seem not to be learning the obvious lesson about faithfulness to God. Rather, they believe their only problem is lack of leadership. In fact, the book of Judges ends with the words, "In those days there was no king in Israel; every man did what was right in his own eyes" (21:25). Sound familiar?

We saw in the story of Gideon that the Israelites wanted Gideon to be their king and rule over them. He refused, knowing that God was supposed to be their King. It is at the end of the time of the judges when the story turns to the book of Samuel, which tells of a woman named Hannah who is barren and desperately wants a child. Hannah does the right thing and puts her trust in God. She makes an offer to Him, promising that if she bears a son, she will give him back to God. She makes a beautiful vow to God: "O LORD of hosts, if you will indeed look on the affliction of your maidservant, and remember me, and not forget your maidservant, but will give to your maidservant a son, then I will give him to the LORD all the days of his life" (1 Sam 1:11).

God hears Hannah's prayer and does indeed grant her a son, whom she names Samuel. As promised, she gives Samuel back to the Lord, and he becomes a great prophet and what many consider the thirteenth and final judge of Israel. The Israelites look to Samuel for guidance and finally ask him to give them a king, like all the other nations. Samuel pleads with the people, telling them God wants to be their King, but they cry out all the more for a human king. Samuel takes his frustration to God, and God tells Samuel to give the people what they want. In the end, God will get what He wants. He will take on human flesh and become their King. Oftentimes this is how God works. He gets what He wants through the things that we want, just as He did for me in my sports.

So Samuel appoints a king over Israel, even though God warned the people that a human king would end up taxing them and taking their land. The first king is Saul, who unites the people but fails to be obedient to God and trust Him. Saul's behavior displeases God so much that He strips Saul of His blessing and goes in search of a man after His own heart who can be king. God sends Samuel to the house of a man named Jesse. Samuel looks over all of Jesse's sons but cannot seem to find the one God has chosen. Jesse then admits he has one more son, little David, who is out tending the flocks. He brings David to Samuel, and immediately Samuel anoints David, and he is destined to rule over the people.

David first shows his heart of courage in the famous story of David and Goliath, perhaps the most famous underdog story of the Old Testament. The giant Goliath challenges the Israelites to a duel, him against their best man, winner take all. All the Israelites are afraid to fight the giant man, but little David, who comes to the battlefield simply to bring food to his older brothers, volunteers to fight him. Goliath laughs at such a young, small kid and does not realize that David's heart and courage come from his pure trust in God—so David is able to slay the giant with a sling and a stone.

After Saul's death, David does indeed become the new king of Israel, and he is a mighty warrior. He brings the Ark of the Covenant to the holy city of Jerusalem and vows to build a temple to God. However, David is a warrior, not a builder, and God reveals that it will be his son who will later build the temple.

David is not without his own faults. In fact, he commits one of the most heinous crimes. When he is supposed to be out on the battlefield with his army, he decides to stay home and glimpses the beautiful Bathsheba, the wife of one of his generals, Uriah. David commits adultery with her. Later, she discovers she is with child. In an attempt to cover his sin, David tries to convince Uriah to go home and sleep with his wife so the child will appear to be his. Uriah refuses, so David sets up a plan to have Uriah killed in battle. The plan is successful.

It is a horrible sin, and God sends the prophet Nathan to David to tell him a parable of a rich man and a poor man. The rich man, who has many lambs, steals the only lamb of a poor man. The story infuriates David, who says the rich man deserves to die—at which point Nathan tells him that he, David, is the rich man. David's reaction is key. Unlike Saul, who was never sorry for his mistakes—he was worried only about his reputation among the people—David is filled with sorrow. He begs the Lord for forgiveness. You can read David's response in Psalm 51, a beautiful psalm to reflect on before going to confession.

The story of David should give us all hope. David was a sinner, just as all of us are, but he had a heart after the Lord. He wanted to please the Lord, and when he fell on his face with the most horrible sin, he pleaded for mercy and forgiveness. We see the mercy and compassion our God has when God not only forgives David but promises him that the King of Kings will stem from his line. A Savior, a Messiah, will come from the line of David. Jesus will be the new David. He will be the Israelites' King in the everlasting covenant that will never be broken.

The New Prophet and King

After David dies, his son Solomon takes over as king and does indeed build a temple to the Lord. Solomon asks God for wisdom, which pleases the Lord, and God makes him the wisest man ever to live. Solomon's wisdom helps him to build a mighty kingdom in Jerusalem. However, in doing so, he begins making many covenants with other nations. As the prophet Samuel predicted, Solomon becomes a king who taxes the people and steals their land. When Solomon makes a covenant with a nation, a woman from that nation is often given to him in marriage, and Solomon ends up with seven hundred wives! Scripture tells us that his wives changed his heart and that he began treating the people harshly and worshiping pagan gods.

As you can imagine, Solomon's downfalls at the end of his reign cause a rebellion among the people. When his son takes over as king and vows to treat the people even more harshly, the kingdom splits in two. Ten of the tribes break off into the northern kingdom, called Israel. Two of the tribes stay in Jerusalem and form the southern kingdom, named Judah, where we get the term "Jews". The stories of these kingdoms are found in the books of Kings and Chronicles.

Neither kingdom has very good leaders. The northern kingdom has no good kings, and its people quickly begin worshiping pagan gods, since they do not have the temple in which to worship. The southern kingdom is not much better, although it does have a few good kings, including Josiah. I love the story of Josiah, a young kid whose father's murder makes him king at the age of eight. Josiah's story is in 2 Kings 22, where we learn that Josiah's father and grandfather were two of the worst kings in Judah's history, building many altars to pagan gods and desecrating the temple. When Josiah becomes king, he has a heart for the Lord, unlike his father and grandfather. He cleans the temple of its pagan altars and vows to worship the one true God again. He turns the kingdom around. We need that kind of leadership today. We need a Josiah to lead the people back to the Lord and "clean house" of foreign gods. Josiah is a good reminder to all of us that no matter who our parents are or what our lot in life is, we can always choose to do what is right.

However, Josiah's heroics are too little too late. The people are simply too hard-hearted. The prophets of God come mostly during this time of the kings; some of the prophets speak to the northern kingdom, and some of them speak to the southern kingdom. Their work is to speak for the Lord. They warn the people that God's patience is running thin, and soon they will be exiled from the land if they do not repent and turn from their ways. The prophets not only give warning but also give hope, many describing and predicting the coming Messiah in great detail. My favorite prediction and description of the coming of Jesus is in Isaiah 53. Describing the suffering servant, this passage in Scripture has inspired me so much that I named my son after this prophet: "Surely he has borne our griefs and carried our sorrows; yet we esteemed him stricken, struck down by God, and afflicted. But he was wounded for our transgressions, he was bruised for our iniquities; upon him was the chastisement that made us whole, and with his stripes we are healed" (53:4–5). These words were written seven hundred years before Jesus Christ was born.

Being a prophet was no easy task. Most were brutally executed. Nobody likes to hear he is doing something wrong, and nobody likes to be challenged to change. We must have the courage to be prophets in this land and to speak for the Lord even when it is hard, and even when we are persecuted for it.

Unlike the prophets and the kings of the Old Testament, we know how the story ends. We know there is one true King and one true Prophet who makes up for what is lacking in all the kings and all the prophets, past, present, and future. We simply have to trust in Jesus Christ, who will lead us and protect us from our enemies. He will teach us what to say. He will change hearts and minds, and He will help us spread the good news of salvation to the ends of the earth. He introduces us to the one true God, a Father filled with mercy, compassion, and forgiveness for His children who have gone astray. By His wounds, we truly are healed and given new life. That is good news.

The New Esther

As the prophets predict, the Israelites end up in exile because of their disobedience. The Assyrians come first to conquer and scatter the northern kingdom. Later, the Babylonians take over, and they bring the southern kingdom under their rule, sending its inhabitants into exile. The exile is a sad story that includes the destruction of the temple and the king being forced to watch his sons being killed. Then he is immediately blinded and put in chains. The last thing he sees is the death of his sons. As he walks to Babylon in chains, you can imagine how hopeless things must seem.

The exile does not last forever, though. Eventually the Persians take over and allow the Jews to return to the land, after 70 years of exile. The prophet Daniel predicts that even though they get to return to the land after 70 years, their hearts will remain in exile for 70 times 7 years—or 490 years, which brings them to the time of the coming of the Messiah, Jesus Christ. At that time, Jesus will come and quote the prophet Isaiah, announcing "release to the captives and recovering of sight to the blind" (Lk 4:18; cf. Is 61:1). Jesus will undo what happened to that last king who was blinded and put in chains: this king symbolizes all of us who are blinded by our sins, which make us prisoners.

At the time when the Jews are returning to their land comes the great story of Esther. The book of Esther tells of a young Jewish woman in Babylon. The Persian king banishes his own wife and goes in search of a new wife. Esther, against her will, is chosen as his new queen. Not long after, the king's right-hand man, a great enemy of the Jews, tricks the king into believing that the Jews are a threat to his kingdom and has him sign a decree to massacre all the Jews, a story eerily similar to that of the Holocaust. Esther's uncle informs Esther that she is their only hope. She must appear before the king uninvited and ask for mercy for her people. Appearing before the king uninvited is punishable by death, even for the queen. Esther struggles with what to do. After all, she is queen, and the king does not even know she is a Jew. She has it made in a life of luxury if she keeps quiet, but her people will be destroyed.

The message coming to Esther is clear, though. As she tries to understand why she was chosen as queen, she hears the words, "And who knows whether you have not come to the kingdom for such a time as this?" (Esther 4:14). Esther's time is not so different from ours. Christianity is slowly being stamped out of our culture and in many cultures around the world. It is unpopular and increasingly more unaccepted. Perhaps you were born for a time such as this. It would be easier just to "fit in" with the culture around you, but you are called to live and speak the truth, even if you lose your job, or your family members, or in the not-too-distant future, possibly even your life. God comes before all those things. Esther does the right thing. She risks her life, and she saves her people from annihilation.

Jesus also does and says what is right, even though it is unpopular. He proclaims the truth, even at the cost of His own life—because He trusts the Father.

The New Zerubbabel, Ezra, and Nehemiah

After the king of Persia gives the Jews freedom to return to the promised land, many stay in Babylon. They have become comfortable in the foreign land and simply do not want to go back. This is a danger we all face. Many people fall into a sinful lifestyle and become comfortable in "exile". We can become comfortable being separated from God in this life, and that is a huge danger. The Jews who do return come back in three waves.

This return to the land happens about five hundred years before the coming of Jesus Christ. In the first wave, the Jews rebuild the temple under the leadership of their new king, Zerubbabel. Rebuilding the temple is no easy task—they encounter resistance both externally and internally. People from foreign lands want to help them build the temple, but the Jews simply have to turn them down. The reason they do so is that the foreigners worship other gods, and the God of Israel is just one God among many to them. This lack of belief in one true God is an obstacle to unity. It seems harsh to turn people away who are trying to help, but you cannot build something you do not believe in. Many people wonder why the Catholic Church does not allow people of other faiths to receive the Eucharist. The reasons are similar. It is not to be mean; the Eucharist is a sign of unity. We cannot pretend there is unity when there is not. When we receive the Eucharist, we say "Amen", which means "I believe" or "It is true." We should never receive the Eucharist if we do not truly believe it is the body, blood, soul, and divinity of Jesus Christ. That would be dishonest, and there is no way we would have the proper reverence for what we are receiving.

The Jews also face internal obstacles to rebuilding the temple. They grow busy building their own houses. It takes them much longer to build the temple the second time because they have so many distractions. Again, we can see parallels to Catholics and the Eucharist today. Oftentimes we get busy with the things of this world and with our own interests, and we simply get "too busy" to receive the Eucharist or to show the proper reverence toward it.

After rebuilding the temple, the Jews need to rediscover their faith again, much the same way Moses had to teach the Israelites the law after they were freed from Egypt. The book of Ezra tells the story of the second wave of the return from Babylon. Ezra is a teacher who helps the people rediscover their roots and the laws of their faith. It is not enough for them just to be in the land. They must live their faith.

In the third and final wave, Nehemiah comes and helps to rebuild the city walls. Once again, we see the internal and external obstacles to living the faith. Nehemiah 4 says the people built the city with a shovel in one hand and a weapon in the other hand. It is a good reminder to us that we do have an enemy that is going to try to prevent us from living the faith. We must always be awake and ready for that enemy with our "spiritual weapons" (explained in chapter 1), but we cannot allow the enemy to fill us with so much fear that we stop building the city of God. We must continue to build. We cannot just be on the defense—we must be on the offense.

This rebuilding of Jerusalem in the return from Babylon is a great foreshadowing of what Jesus will do when He comes. As we know, He is the new temple; He will teach the new law of love in the new covenant; and He will announce the new heavenly Jerusalem, or the City of God, that we read about in the book of Revelation. Jesus gives us the model for building the new Church, and the model mirrors the model we read about in the return from exile. We must build the Church, teach and share the faith, and protect the Church from outside forces.

The New Maccabees

The books of Maccabees are not found in Protestant Bibles. They are part of the deuterocanonical books, seven books contained in the Catholic Bible that are not in Protestant Bibles. (Protestant Bibles have sixty-six books, and Catholic Bibles have seventy-three books.) We will not explore the reason for the differences here, but I invite you to research where the books of the Bible came from.[4] The books of Maccabees provide an important bridge from the time of the return from exile to the time of the coming of the Messiah. It is indeed an important and exciting part of the story of salvation.

---

[4] This is discussed in Jeff Cavins' *Great Adventure* Bible study.

Under the leadership of Alexander the Great, the Greeks begin to conquer the world. At first, the Greeks allow the Jews (the word "Jew" comes from the name Judah, the son to whom Jacob [Israel] passed on the blessing and the birthright) to stay in the promised land and continue with their religious traditions of the past. However, Antiochus Epiphanes becomes king, and he has other ideas. He is determined that the whole world will eat Greek food, speak the Greek language, and worship Greek gods. He takes control of the holy temple in Jerusalem and desecrates it, sacrificing pigs inside—which is abominable to the Jews—just to prove a point and make a statement.

Unfortunately, many of the Jews are not strong at all in their faith. They are "low-hanging fruit", simply going through some motions, and at the first sign of persecution, they cave. Many Jews begin to worship Greek gods and actually enjoy the newfound rule and religion. Some Jewish men are so afraid of being rejected by the culture surrounding them that they actually have reversal operations for their circumcisions, the sign of the covenant God made with Abraham. These people want to fit in and be successful, so they conform to the culture around them.

Sound familiar? There are about fifty million Catholic adults in America. The research of Dynamic Catholic shows that only about 7 percent of Catholics are highly engaged in their faith.[5] I wonder, at the first sign of inconvenience or persecution, how many of the fifty million Catholics in America would cease to call themselves Catholic so they could be successful and fit in with the culture around them. We are clearly seeing this, a heartbreaking

[5] Matthew Kelly, *The Four Signs of a Dynamic Catholic* (Cincinnati, Ohio: Beacon Publishing, 2012), 12.

betrayal of the faith to fit in with new cultural norms. If you had to choose between your faith and your job, what would you choose? If you had to choose between your faith and your sports, what would you choose? If you had to choose between your faith and the woman or man you want to marry, what would you choose? (That sounds like a harsh question, but God should always come first, and many people are willing to put earthly marriage before the heavenly marriage. Many people do leave the faith for the sake of a spouse. That does not make sense when the goal of marriage is to bring each other closer to God.) If you had to choose between your faith and your family, what would you choose? As hard as these questions seem, the day may be coming in America, and has already come in many countries, when you have to ask the ultimate question: If you had to choose between your faith and your very life, what would you choose?

Fortunately for the Jews, an honorable family, the Maccabees, stand for the truth in their time of persecution. Antiochus comes to the father of the household, Mattathias, in the city of Modein, to make an example of them. He knows they are well-respected Jews, and he wants them to make a sacrifice to the pagan gods so the rest of the Jewish population will follow. Mattathias not only refuses but starts what is called the "Maccabean revolt", and they fight for their religious freedom and eventually win. Not long after the revolt starts, the Jews recapture the temple and dedicate it to the Lord. They have enough oil to light the lamps only for one day, but miraculously the oil does not run out, and the fire stays burning for eight days. The Jews would forever commemorate this feast in a celebration we now know as Hanukkah.

Before Mattathias dies, he passes on the leadership to his sons. He reminds his sons of their story and who they are as a people. In 1 Maccabees 2:49–64, Mattathias goes through a litany of the great heroes of Israel's past, people like Abraham, Joseph, Joshua, David, and Daniel. He helps his sons prepare for battle by answering the biggest question in this story: Can you trust God? Yes! Mattathias' message is clear. God has never forsaken His people. Just believe and trust in the one true God, and He will take care of you. You may suffer, be persecuted, or even die, but you will win in the end because God loves you, and you will spend eternity with Him in the kingdom to come. "My children, be courageous and grow strong in the law, for by it you will gain honor" (1 Mac 2:64).

Throughout 1 and 2 Maccabees, we read many stories of how the Jews gain strength in their persecution. Through their suffering, they return to the Lord and trust Him unconditionally. Sometimes when the skies are blue we forget about God, but when the storms come, we cannot help but return to His love and mercy, knowing that without Him we have nothing. All the things of this earthly life that we find contentment in will pass away. God alone is worth living for and dying for, because God is our beginning and our end. He created us for communion with Him.

In 2 Maccabees 7, we read perhaps the greatest story of courage under persecution. A mother and her seven sons are arrested by the Greek king Antiochus and tortured in an attempt simply to get them to eat pork, a violation of God's law that was given in the old covenant to prevent idolatry. One by one, each of the sons is brutally tortured and put to death in front of his mother. All die proclaiming they will never violate the law of the one true God and their belief in eternal life with Him. The executioners demand that the mother convince her last remaining son to eat the pork. In return, Antiochus offers to make the boy "rich and enviable" and to "take him for his friend and entrust him with public affairs" (2 Mac 7:24). After six of the sons have been executed, you would think the mother's will would be completely broken. The mother's response is beyond inspiring:

> After much urging on his part, she undertook to persuade her son. But, leaning close to him, she spoke in their native tongue as follows, deriding the cruel tyrant: "My son, have pity on me. I carried you nine months in my womb, and nursed you for three years, and have reared you and brought you up to this point in your life, and have taken care of you. I beg you, my child, to look at the heaven and the earth and see everything that is in them, and recognize that God did not make them out of things that existed. Thus also mankind comes into being. Do not fear this butcher, but prove worthy of your brothers. Accept death, so that in God's mercy I may get you back again with your brothers."
>
> While she was still speaking, the young man said, "What are you waiting for? I will not obey the king's command, but I obey the command of the law that was given to our fathers through Moses. But you, who have contrived all sorts of evil against the Hebrews, will certainly not escape the hands of God.... I, like my brothers, give up body and life for the laws of our fathers, appealing to God to show mercy soon to our nation." (2 Mac 7:26–31, 37)

The Maccabean revolt was a time of great testing for the Jews. In the end, they were victorious and through their trials would prepare themselves for the coming of the one true King, the Messiah. Jesus would come and relive their persecution, and He would trust and obey His Father, even unto death, even death on a Cross. He would usher in God's mercy and show compassion for His people. While many of the Jews during the Maccabean revolt died coura-geously, they also died warning their persecutors that God would not grant them mercy for their actions. In contrast, Jesus not only allowed himself to be crucified, but He died praying for those who persecuted Him: "Father, forgive them; for they know not what they do" (Lk 23:34).

The New You

As we move into the New Testament, we see Jesus Christ, the Savior of the whole world, come onto the scene in the fullness of time. He relives the life of Israel, showing the Israelites and the whole world who God really is and how to trust Him with everything they have. While Jesus relives the life of Israel to usher in a new and everlasting covenant, He calls all His apostles, all His disciples, and everyone who comes after Him to relive the life of Christ. We see in the book of Acts how the early Church starts in Jerusalem and begins to spread like a wildfire to the ends of the earth. Before Jesus ascends to the Father, He tells the apostles, "You shall receive power when the Holy Spirit has come upon you; and you shall be my witnesses in Jerusalem and in all Judea and Samaria and to the end of the earth" (Acts 1:8).

This is where the era of the Church comes in and where you and I enter the story of salvation history. While we catch a glimpse of the end of the story in the book of Revelation, there is still much to be written in this time between Jesus' Ascension to the Father and His second coming. This is our time, a time in which we know that the war has been won and that good will be victorious, but a time in which many battles remain and many souls are still at stake. It is a time of great evil, when the dragon and his demons will unleash all of their anger and fury in one last temper tantrum to destroy whatever they can in defeat. But it is also a time of great saints. As Saint Paul noted, where sin abounds, grace abounds all the more (see Rom 5:20).

There is a question we must all ask ourselves as we put ourselves in the story, the same question every character had to ask himself in this story: Do I trust God? Will I be like the first Adam, a coward afraid to stand up for his bride, or will I be like the second Adam? Will I be like the first Eve, whose no to trusting God brought sin into the world, or will I be like the second Eve, Mary, whose yes brought forth a Savior? Will I be like Cain and go through motions halfheartedly, jealous of others when God shows displeasure in my apathy? Will I be like Noah and trust God enough to build something that will sustain life through the storm—even when the sun is still shining and the whole world ridicules me for it? Will I be like Abraham, a father in faith, and bring everything I have to Mount Moriah and place it on the altar—even my dreams, talents, and hopes, my own children and family? Will I be like Isaac and be obedient to the Father, even if I find myself carrying the wood to my own sacrifice? Will I be like Jacob and go from being a "deceiver" to being "Israel", one who is "victorious with God", and wrestle with God enough to become intimate with His plan for me to be victorious in building a great nation?

Will I be like Joseph and persevere through trials and persecution, knowing that in the end God will take what was meant for harm and turn it into salvation for others? Will I be like Moses and help lead the people of God to freedom from bondage by helping them rediscover their faith? Will I be like Joshua and be strong and courageous in my obedience to God's plan? Will I be like Gideon and testify to the power of God by allowing Him to use my weaknesses to accomplish great things? Will I be like Ruth and be loyal enough to go wherever God leads me? Will I be like Hannah and offer my children back to the Lord in service? Will I be like King David and lead with courage and valor and be willing to seek God's mercy and compassion when I fall to the temptations of sin? Will I be like Samuel, Isaiah, Jeremiah, and all the great prophets of the past and speak for the Lord in convincing His people to turn back to Him, even if they persecute me for it?

Will I be like King Josiah and throw out all the pagan gods that threaten the salvation of my family, or will I be like so many of the other kings of Israel and sell my allegiance to foreign gods? Will I be like Esther and be willing to risk my everyday comforts in an effort to save God's people from annihilation, knowing I was born for a time such as this? Will I be like Zerubbabel, Ezra, and Nehemiah and build God's Church, teach the faith, and protect her from the enemy? Will I be like the Maccabees and stand up for the truth of the faith and the one true God in the middle of a culture that has abandoned His ways to fit in with the new order of the day?

Will I be like John the Baptist and testify to the truth, allowing myself to decrease so Jesus can increase? Will I be like Peter and be a fisher of men and repent of my failures, or will I be like Judas and betray my master and allow that failure to lead me into despair? Will I be like Andrew and lead everyone I meet to Jesus? Will I be like John and be loyal to Jesus and stick with Him, even when things get hard, or will I run away like everybody else?

Will I trust God, knowing that His ways are better than my ways and that He loves me more than I love myself? Will I allow Jesus Christ and the power of the Holy Spirit to flood my whole being, so it is no longer I who live but Christ who lives in me? Will I die to myself so that Jesus Christ can be alive in me?

The Story in Three Minutes

Billy Joel has an amazing gift for music. What if we used Billy Joel's talent to attract people to the truth of the faith? Perhaps you are familiar with his song "We Didn't Start the Fire". It gives a review of history between the years 1949 and 1989 in a rapid-fire list of people and events.

I decided to use the basic tune of this song to tell the entire story of salvation history in three minutes. I have started singing this song at some of my events. Even though I cannot sing worth a darn, people really like it. Because of the attractive tune, the song gets stuck in your head, and having the story of salvation history stuck in your head is a wonderful thing. If you have never heard "We Didn't Start the Fire", look it up on YouTube to catch the tune; then try singing the following words to the same melody.

Song of Salvation History:
We're Going to Start a Fire

To the melody of "We Didn't Start the Fire" by Billy Joel
Lyrics by John R. Wood

Verse 1: Early World (Gen 1–11)

Formless void, Word of the Lord,
Dark as night, let there be light,
Breathe life, man and wife,
Living in a paradise.

Serpent came, played his game,
Wrong and right, lost the fight,

The Father's love within them dies,
Falling for the dragon's lies.

Exile, death came near,
Sin and suffering, filled with fear,
Hope came in a prophecy,
The woman's seed will set them free.

Abel, Cain, a brother's slain,
Evil spreads, God regrets,
Only hope is Noah's good,
Ark is built with gopher wood.

Waters came, start again,
Baptized with torrential rain,
Shem's the name, tower's built,
Man shows he's still filled with guilt!

Refrain

We're going to start a fire! Set the world ablaze;
    God's saints will love and praise Him.
We're going to start a fire! Set the world ablaze;
    God's saints will love and praise Him.

Verse 2: The Rest of the Old Testament

Righteous man, Abraham,
Journey to a promised land;
Isaac, Jacob, and his sons,
Joseph is a righteous one.

Egypt, Pharaoh, now their slaves,
Burning bush, ten plagues,
God tells Moses, set them free,
Parting of the Red Sea.

Ten Commandments, broken laws,
Joshua, Judges, Samuel,
Prophets, Kings, and promised land,
David slayed a giant man.

Exile, Babylon,
Esther saves, hope is strong,
Return to peace, gods of Greece,
Courage of the Maccabees!

Refrain
We're going to start a fire! Set the world ablaze;
    God's saints will love and praise Him.
We're going to start a fire! Set the world ablaze;
    God's saints will love and praise Him.

Verse 3: Life of Christ

Gabriel, Mary,
Let it be done to me,
World has a new Queen,
This one's everlasting.

Prophet says prepare the way,
Word made flesh has come to save,
Holy Spirit, like a dove,
A faithful Son, a Father's love.

Miracles, the blind will see,
Freedom from captivity,
They betrayed, ran away,
He was scourged in agony.

Crucifixion, price is paid,
Sin and death, destroyed that day,
Jesus rises from the grave,
What else do I have to say!

Refrain
We're going to start a fire! Set the world ablaze;
   God's saints will love and praise Him.
We're going to start a fire! Set the world ablaze;
   God's saints will love and praise Him.

Verse 4: Life of the Church

Resurrection, Pentecost,
Grace abounds where hope is lost,
Church is born, Peter's pope,
Missionary zeal provoked.

Lamb's blood set them free,
Martyrs' blood is the seed,
Saints begin to make their mark,
Saint Augustine, Polycarp.

Virgins Agnes, Philomena,
And Saint Catherine of Siena,
Crown of thorns of Rose of Lima,
Joseph is the terror of demons.

Holy Mary, she's our Mother,
Holy Francis, he's our brother,
Little Flower, JPII,
Passing the baton to you!

Refrain
We're going to start a fire! Set the world ablaze;
   God's saints will love and praise Him.
We're going to start a fire! Set the world ablaze;
   God's saints will love and praise Him.
We're going to start a fire! And it will keep
   burning on and on and on and on and on ...

For all the recommended resources for "Instructor's Manual", go to the website: www.saintsinthemaking.com /instructors-manual-resources.html.

Chapter 4

N: NEED TO KNOW HIM

Color: Purple, for Royalty

You have made us for yourself, O Lord, and our heart is restless until it rests in you.

—Saint Augustine

What motivates you: heaven or hell? Let me ask the question again with this analogy. Are you like a rebellious teenager who comes home by curfew only because he is afraid his parents might take away his cell phone, or car keys, or freedom? Or are you like the teenager who comes home by curfew because he loves his parents and wants to make them proud of him, and he trusts that his parents love him and know what is best for him? Too often we view God the Father through the eyes of a rebellious teenager. We expect Him to give us everything we need (and want), we see Him as an obstacle to being free, and we do not trust that He has our best interests in mind. The rebellious teenager does not want to be seen with his parents in public and believes that his parents give him rules and regulations to follow only to control and manipulate him. Consciously or subconsciously, is that how you see

God? Why do you go to Mass on Sunday? Is it because you long to be one with Christ, or is it because attendance is required according to the Catholic rules, and just in case what the Church teaches is true, you do not want to go to hell?

We should strive to be saints not merely because we are afraid of what God might do to us if we do not try to be saints but because God is our Father and we love Him. It should break our hearts to be anything less than the saints God created us to be. If we are just going through the motions and see our faith as a lifeless set of rules and regulations, it is because we see God not as a loving Father but as a master, forcing us to do things we do not want to do. We love what we know, and the only way we are going to love our faith is if we come to know the Father in heaven.

This class is about getting to know the family of God. We cannot perfectly define God, because He is a mystery beyond full comprehension, but we can get a glimpse of His love for us as He reveals Himself in the structure of a family. The last chapter told the story of salvation history in a nutshell. If you dig further into the story, looking at the language and background, you will quickly discover that above everything else, it is a love story about a family. God is our Father. Mary is our Mother. Jesus is the Bridegroom Son. We are the Church, His Bride, all brothers and sisters. The Holy Spirit is the power binding all those relationships together in love.

Catholicism is not primarily about rules and regulations but is about relationships. Rules and regulations and rituals are necessary to make families strong and keep them together, but they are not the purpose of families. It is no coincidence that as we see a decline in the value of the family in our culture, we see an increase in the number of people who describe themselves as "unaffiliated" when it comes to religious beliefs. God lives inside a family, and He reveals Himself to us in many ways: through the beauty of creation, through other people, through our own families, and through His holy Church. In this chapter, I would like to share with you my experience of coming to know God.

Revealing God

I believe the greatest compliment a child can give his parents is "You introduced me to God and His Church." Ask yourself how you came to know all the people in your life. Occasionally you randomly meet a stranger and become good friends, but most of the time we come to know others through a mutual acquaintance. Somebody introduces us. God is no different. Some people randomly stumble upon the reality of God, but most come to know God because somebody introduced them to Him—and that somebody is ideally their parents.

Have you ever been at a party talking to somebody and you cannot remember his name? You have met the person several times before, and at this point it is too late to ask because you really should know it by now, and you are embarrassed to ask again. To complicate matters, somebody else walks up and joins the conversation. Now you are talking to two people who do not know each other, and they are expecting you to introduce them. It is pretty awkward, isn't it? How can you introduce the person you are talking with to somebody else if you do not even know his name? I think that is how we Catholics are sometimes. We are supposed to evangelize by introducing our friends and family to God, especially our own children, but we do not even know God ourselves. We cannot give what we do not have, and that is why it is so important to know God personally and have a real relationship with Him. He should be our best friend whom we cannot wait to introduce people to, not somebody we accidently bump in to and with whom we are forced to have an awkward conversation.

I would like to honor my parents by saying they did a good job of introducing me to God. My mother was heroic in her humble witness of introducing her husband and four sons to Christ and His Church. Her Catholic faith emanates from her. She taught us the faith with some words but mostly with the way she lived. She faced endless resistance, complaining, and ridicule from us boys on matters of religion, going to Mass, and prayers, but she never wavered. It would be impossible for me not to have been profoundly influenced by her persistent witness and humility. I have never seen her put herself before others or feel sorry for herself, even as a widow. She is in constant joyful service. She remains persistent in her faith and her motherly prayers that have no doubt showered my life with graces. I cannot help but want the peace and joy that she has. Perhaps that is one of the biggest reasons that in my adult years I have vigorously sought that relationship with God and His Church myself.

My father, on the other hand, was not a deeply religious man. He converted to Catholicism after he married my mother, and I always saw him as being more obedient to my mother than to the Church. He went to Mass every Sunday, but I figured it was just because Mom wanted him to go. I remember saying family rosaries during Advent and Lent that my mother would insist upon. My father, my brothers, and I would often complain, but secretly I liked saying those rosaries, especially around a lighted Advent wreath and Christmas lights. The rosaries were always led by my mother. When she finished her part of the Hail Mary, the race was on. We boys would then recite the rest of the prayer as fast as we could to see who could finish the quickest. My father would always win. He won at everything.

I lost my father to cancer in August 2008. Even though he was not a deeply religious man, I cannot think of another person on this planet who introduced me to God the Father more than he did. I did not recognize the connection until after he was gone, but now I can plainly see how the qualities he had as a father and the way he treated his sons greatly mirrored God the Father.

God the Father

I would not say my father was always an extremely patient person, but his patience with me was impressive. I do not ever remember him losing his temper with me. For the most part he was calm and cool, whether coaching me in a sport or encouraging me to share my thoughts. Looking back, I realize I was a closed book as a teenager. My father desperately wanted to know everything about my life, but he tried his best not to pry. He was curious how practices went or how things were in school, and the only answer I ever gave was "Fine." My father was so patient and laid back with me that I often wondered if there was anything I could have done to make him lose his temper. One day I decided to test him. On the way back from a college hockey road trip, I got a speeding ticket. I was complaining to my friend that I would have to call my dad and tell him, and my friend came up with a brilliant idea—tell him I got a DUI. Then when he "freaked out", I could say I was kidding and that it was only a speeding ticket, which would not sound nearly as bad. I was curious what his reaction would be, so I tried it.

Anytime I had a problem or a question about anything, I called my dad at work. So I called and told him I got a DUI. He said, "You did?" I replied, "Yes", and then there was awkward silence. Finally he said, "OK", as if he was not sure what else to say. It was not an angry "OK". It was an "OK" filled with the most disappointment I have ever heard, and it absolutely ripped my heart out. I could not take it. I immediately blurted out, "I'm kidding! It was just a speeding ticket." I knew at that moment that I never wanted to disappoint my father.

I do not ever remember being bored around my dad. Being with him was either really exciting or really annoying. It was exciting because he was always there. The one quality my father had that most mirrors God the Father is always wanting to be with his children. My father would go to great lengths to be with us. He attended all my games and track meets, and even when I moved away to college, he looked for any excuse to visit. I knew I could call my dad at any time and he would be happy to hear from me; and I could ask him for almost anything and he would do whatever he could to get it. Again, he would try not to pry into my life and allowed me to do things on my own, but if he could come up with an excuse to help me out financially or drop by the neighborhood to take me out to eat, he would use it.

There were times in college when my track season overlapped with my hockey season. My dad knew I loved playing hockey, but he knew how successful I was in running, so he wanted me to be able to do both. His best friend had a pilot's license for small planes, so he occasionally talked his friend into flying me from track meets to hockey games so I could do both on the same weekend. One year my national championship track meet was on the same weekend as my league championship in hockey. My dad quickly offered to fly from Ohio with his friend to pick me up at my track meet in Nebraska and transport me to my hockey game in Pennsylvania. I told him it would be too much of a hassle, but he insisted. Tornado warnings prevented him from making the trip to Nebraska in the small plane, so the next thing I knew he was calling me to say he had booked me a commercial flight and would meet me in Pennsylvania.

I ended up making it to my hockey game, and I played the worst game of my life. I played so bad I actually felt guilty about how much my parents went through to get me to that game. I wrote an e-mail to my mom telling her I was sorry, and in her reply she simply stated, "You know your dad—he just wants to see you play."

It was exciting knowing that my dad would always be there, but it was annoying for the same reason. Sometimes I did not want him to be there because I did not always feel like trying my best. He would be at all my track meets with his stopwatch. I think he timed every lap I ever ran around the track. Even in college, when running somewhere across the nation, I knew that if my dad could not be there physically, I was going to get a phone call from him later, asking my times. I hated my father's stopwatch because that stopwatch knew my potential. It knew what I had accomplished in the past and held me accountable. I was nervous and afraid before every race because in every race I knew that my opponent was myself. The purpose of running a race is to finish with nothing left to give, and I knew that if I crossed that finish line with something more to give, my father would know. I did not want to let him down.

Now, before the psychoanalyzing begins, please know that never once have I doubted that my father loved me or was proud of me. He did not come to those track meets and ball games because I was successful. He still would have been there if I had been the worst athlete on the team. I was not trying to earn his love, and I am not trying to earn it now. I was not trying to be successful to make him love me. I was trying to be successful because I loved him. I was not afraid of what he would do to me if I ran poorly. He never complained about my performance. He never said anything. He was just there, timing me, and he loved seeing my name in the newspaper. By the time I graduated from high school, he had four scrapbooks full of articles and times I had run. He was so proud of my accomplishments, and he loved to see me run.

God the Father is exactly the same way. He is extremely patient with us. He does not disown us when we make mistakes. He is always looking for an invitation from us to be together. He is always excited to hear from us. He does not pry or force us to love Him, but He patiently waits for us. He looks for every opportunity to be part of our lives, and yes, He can be annoying. God is always watching us, and we do not always want Him to be watching. But He is there, timing us in the race of life. He is concerned that you learn to give your all, and He loves to see you use your talents and abilities to glorify His kingdom. You cannot earn your way into heaven, and we should not try to make God love us. He loves us no matter what. We should strive for perfection because we love Him.

A Letter to the Father

In this reflection on what a father is, I am not trying to introduce you to my earthly father; I am trying to introduce you to God the Father, and explaining my relationship with my own dad is the best way I know how to do that. On May 1, 2008, I sat in a hospital lobby and listened to some doctor explain how there was nothing that could be done for my dad, who was going to die. Ask yourself, what would you do in that situation?

I started thinking of my relationship with my father. I loved him, and I knew he loved me, but we were not the type of people who say those kinds of things. Neither of us was very good at revealing himself. I always admired and respected my father. I always wanted him to be proud of me, and I know he was. Much of my success was because I never wanted to do anything to let down my father. However, I could not help but think about how I treated him. I never gave him the satisfaction of knowing my feelings and joys in life. I was a closed book around him. I was a teenager who was always "the victim", stuck doing things I never liked to do. Even if I was happy, I would have never led him to believe it.

I do not know why I did this. It was a habit I developed as a teenager, and I never got rid of it. We are creatures of habit, I guess. Even when my life and career began going well and I was genuinely happy, whenever I would talk to my parents I would use the same disappointed voice I always had, never excited about anything. My father was my safety net, and I would go to him with all my problems, questions, or frustrations in life, but rarely would I go to him when things were going well. Hearing that my father was going to die, I was afraid of losing him; but more than that, I was afraid of losing my father without revealing myself to him.

When I returned home after learning my father's fate that weekend, I decided to write him a letter. I wanted to give him what he had deserved for a long time. I was going to keep this letter just between him and me. I had planned on putting it in his casket the day of his funeral. However, I forgot it that day, perhaps for a reason. The months following his death, I had a lot more conversations with God. I guess it took losing my father on earth before I realized I had a Father in heaven. It struck me that I treated them both the same. I loved them and deeply appreciated them both, and I told them both all my frustrations and bitterness about life. I asked them for a lot of things. However, I never thanked them. I never shared the glory of life with them. I never gave them the satisfaction of knowing I was truly happy. I wrote the letter to my dad but realized I needed to write it to my God as well. If I needed to write it to my God, maybe other people do too. So I am sharing it with you.

Dear Dad,

Whatever happens in the next weeks, months, or years, there are things I need you to know. I have been a father for only three years, but I have quickly discovered that all I really want is for my children to be happy. When they are this little, it is easy to see their excitement (and disappointments) about life, and I am sure that when we were very young it was easy for you to see when we were happy and when we were upset. As I grew older and went to high school and college, I know my outlook on life changed, and I lost some of the passion I had had as a child. As I look back at how I acted now, it seems my goal must have been to convince you and Mom that life was not fair. No matter how successful I was, I wanted you to think I was always the victim of some injustice. I was successful at running and in school, but I always led you to believe I was miserable doing those things.

In the last few years I have been able to regain some of the passion for life that I had as a child. I have been able to look back at the things I have accomplished and be proud of them. I have been able to see the struggles I went through not as an injustice but as an integral part of forming me into who I am now. I am excited about my present and my future, and I have been able to open my shell and share my enthusiasm for life with the patients I take care of, the friends I have, and the community I live in. Never did I ever wish or think I could stand up in front of people and talk, but for some reason, over the last year I kept getting put in situations to do it, and I have been able to inspire people to renew their passion for life. I have shared with them the things that have made me happy and the lessons I have learned along the way. But, for some reason, I have never shared those things with you. I have never shaken off my attitude as a teenager around you. I talk to you not about happiness and passion for life but about my problems, injustices I suffer, and the things in life that are not fair. I need you to know that I am happy. I love my life, I love my wife and my children, I love my home and my job, I love my family, I love the friends I have made and the opportunities I have been given because of you. I love God, and I am now able to look back at the kaleidoscope of my life and see how all the pieces were placed together perfectly, not by chance. I do not regret any of the races I ran or any of the tests I took. I do not regret any of the crosses you encouraged me to carry.

When I was going through all those struggles, I learned to have faith in something I cannot see. I learned to rely on God to get me through all the things I was afraid to do or did not want to do. I used to stop at church before every track meet and every basketball game—and sometimes, late at night, when the church was empty and dark—and just sit in front of the tabernacle, hoping, believing, that God was truly in there listening to my requests. When I had to face the reality that I may have to spend the rest of my life without my father, I felt that cold brush of fear and self-doubt that I had experienced so many times before— except this time it was much worse. So I returned to that same dark and empty church late at night and sat in front of that tabernacle looking for answers. I got those answers not in a voice but in the depths of my heart. I told God that I was afraid, and He replied, "I've been there, in the agony in the garden." I told God that the pain was more than I could bear, and He replied, "I've been there. I felt the scourge of the whip and the thorns pierce my skull." I told God that the suffering was too much, and He replied, "I've been there. I carried the weight of the Cross and the weight of the sin of the entire world on my shoulders." I told God that it was not fair, and He replied, "I've been there. I made Myself man to save the world from sin, and they crucified Me on a tree." I asked God, "Why?" He replied, "To you who have lost the meaning of birth, life, suffering, and death, turn to the One who was born, lived, suffered, died . . . and rose again."

I have not given up hope that God will grant us a miracle. I have prayed for a miracle, but only if it is God's will. I know you are suffering now, and I will pray for your continued courage to fight this to the end. Please know that your suffering is not in vain. We suffer with you, but we will win this fight, no matter what. I am proud to be your son. I appreciate how you have given us all you have— you have always put us first, and you have always been there for everything I have done. Without you, I would have never become who I am. If it is God's will for you to join Him soon, it will leave a huge void in my life and the life of my family. We will miss you every single day, but we will face the emptiness with courage. We will be OK. We will take care of each other, and we will take care of Mom, as you have taken care of us. Pray for us. I am looking forward to seeing you in the eyes of my unborn child—a third child, like you and me, who will have the honor of carrying the name of his grandfather, just as I did. I hope I have made you proud. Please let me know if there is anything you need from me, anything you want me to do with the life you have given me. I will spend the rest of my life trying to fulfill my purpose of becoming the saint I was created to be and inspiring others to do the same. I will try to become as good a father to my children as you were to me. I love you with all my heart and soul, and I will pray for you every day of my life.

Love,
Your son, John

I wanted my father to know that he did not need to bribe me with financial help or taking me out to eat so we could be together. If he wanted me to clean the garage with him, I would be there. I want God the Father to know that He does not have to get me into the NHL for me to love Him. He does not have to answer my prayers the way I want them answered. He does not have to follow my plan for my life. If He wants me to speak, I will speak. If He wants me to write, I will write. If He wants me to run, I will run. Everything I have is a gift from the Father, and even though I can offer so little compared with what He gave me, I give it all back—my life, my heart, my hopes, my dreams, my time, my talent, my treasure, my wife, my children, my soul. I give it all back to the Father to do with as He pleases.

Lord, let it be done to me according to Your will. My will is to do Your will, no matter what the cost. I ask for Your love and Your mercy, and nothing more.

Prayer of Abandonment

Father,
I abandon myself into Your hands;
do with me what You will.
Whatever You may do, I thank You:
I am ready for all, I accept all.
Let only Your will be done in me,
and in all Your creatures—
I wish no more than this, O Lord.
Into Your hands I commend my soul:
I offer it to You with all the love of my heart,
for I love You, Lord, and so need to give myself,
to surrender myself into Your hands without reserve,
and with boundless confidence,
for You are my Father.

—Blessed Charles de Foucauld

*And in the end . . . everything else will turn out to be
unimportant and inessential, except for this: father, child,
and love.*

—Saint John Paul II

Through the Eyes of a Child

Being my father's son taught me a lot about God, and being
my children's father taught me just as much. I currently
have four children, ranging from five to twelve years old.
I cannot tell you the joy my children have brought to my
life. Little children are so full of life and curiosity, and they
love being around their parents. My children are excited
when I come home. They love spending time with me,
they are always trying to get my attention, they want me

to be proud of them, and they believe what I tell them. They may not always agree with me and may throw a temper tantrum when I do not give them what they want, but five minutes later they love me again. They are never bored when we are doing something together, and they feel safe with me. My children trust me, and they love me unconditionally.

I have often wondered, if my children can have that kind of faith in me, a sinful and weak man, how much more should we have faith in God, who is a perfect Father? Being a father myself has given me a new perspective. I want to be with my children. I want my children to be happy and safe. I want to see my children reach their fullest potential in life. God the Father is no different. If we could just look at Him through the eyes of a little child, we would see that He loves us more than we love ourselves. He wants us to be happy more than we want it for ourselves. He desires to be with all of His children around the dinner table of a heavenly banquet. He longs to see his children become the saints He created them to be. He is a loving Father, not a master who wants to whip our backs. Catholic author Christopher West points out that God loves us so much that He took on human flesh and allowed us to whip His back to prove to us that He has no desire to whip ours.

Daddy Days

There are a lot of books I will be recommending for you in this class of getting to know God. They are books that have helped me learn about God and His Church. However, the primary purpose of the class is not to know *about* God. The purpose is actually to know Him. You cannot really come to know somebody by reading a book. You have to experience a relationship with the person. So this class is less about what you read and more about what you do. The primary activity I am going to recommend is Daddy Days (or Mommy Days, if you are a mom). A Daddy Day is a day when I take one of my children out so we can spend some time together. I might take him to a ball game, or a movie, or bowling, or fishing, or we might go on a nature hike or out to lunch. I let my child pick what he wants to do, and we do it together. It is an opportunity for my children to have my undivided attention. Each child gets two or three Daddy Days apiece throughout the year, and they really look forward to these days. These days do not have to be just for parents and children. They can build any relationship—with nieces, nephews, grandchildren, friends, siblings.

By having these one-on-one days with my children, I hope to introduce them to God the Father. I want them to understand that God is not limited by time or space; therefore, although I cannot always be with them, God can. They have an opportunity for a Daddy Day with God every day of their life. I want them to long for Daddy Days with God, but the only way that is going to happen is if they know God. During one of our Need to Know Him classes, I asked my children if they liked Daddy Days. They emphatically cried out, "Yes!" I asked them why. They said, "Because we get to go to fun places and do fun things." Then I asked, "What if you had the opportunity to go out and do those same fun things and go to those same fun places with some other guy? Would you still want to go?" They all shook their heads. I asked why not. They replied, "Because we don't know the other guy. We know you. We want to go with you." As obvious as that sounds, that is precisely the point. We love what we know. The class is not about the fun things and fun places; it is about spending time with somebody you love. Catholic youth would do well to remember this when they go to Mass and complain because it is "boring". I would rather clean the garage with my dad than go anywhere in the world with a stranger.

God the Son

As Christians, we seem much more comfortable talking about Jesus than about God the Father. We picture the God of the Old Testament with an iron fist, striking people dead for breaking the tiniest letter of the law, and we often picture Jesus with "lambs around his neck and a marijuana glaze in his eye",[1] as Jeff Cavins puts it. However, the differences we claim exist between the God of the Old Testament and the God of the New Testament are heretical. The two deities are one and the same God, and if anybody's law is harder, it is the New Testament God's. In the Old Testament, there were a lot of laws, more than six hundred, because the more sin, the more laws. The people were slaves to sin, so they were given many laws to help them do God's will. However, in the New Testament, Jesus makes it very clear that God is not just after your mind—He is after your heart. The law is written not on stone but on the heart of every man. In the Beatitudes, Jesus ups the ante on the laws of the Old Testament. The previous mentality of an eye for an eye is changed to "To him who strikes you on the cheek, offer the other also; and from him who takes away your cloak do not withhold your coat as well" (Lk 6:29).

[1] Jeff Cavins, *The Great Adventure: A Journey through the Bible* (Milwaukee, Wis.: Ascension, 2015).

Jesus shows us that faith and love are not only about following rules and regulations. They are about doing the will of the Father. If you read the Gospels, you will discover that the Father is always on Jesus' mind. Jesus told us, "I do as the Father has commanded me, so that the world may know that I love the Father" (Jn 14:31). Jesus came to reveal the Father to us.

Saint John Paul II once said, "It is Jesus in fact you seek when you dream of happiness."[2] Jesus does not want to replace the things in this world that make you happy. He wants you to realize He is the source of your happiness, and you cannot really find fulfillment in creation when you forget the Creator. Jesus finds His happiness and freedom not in doing His own will but in doing the will of His Father. Jesus and the Father are one, so in seeking Jesus, we seek the Father, and in seeking the Father, we discover our own happiness.

Brant Pitre's book *Jesus the Bridegroom* beautifully illustrates that the story we told in the last chapter is all about a marriage;[3] and if we understand the roots of a Jewish wedding, we will see that Jesus is constantly referring to Himself as the Bridegroom, and the consummation of the wedding takes place on the Cross.

Most of us have been asked a question very common in the Protestant world: Do you have a personal relationship with Jesus Christ? Pitre reminds us that the answer to this question as Catholics should certainly be yes. It is a good question and a key starting point in our journey—but only a starting point. Jesus wants so much more than a personal relationship. We can have a personal relationship

---

[2] Address, Vigil of Prayer, Fifteenth World Youth Day, Tor Vergata, August 19, 2000.

[3] *Jesus the Bridegroom* (New York: Image, 2014).

with our banker, our accountant, and our car mechanic, and those are great. If I run into these people on the street, I will probably ask about their families and lives. However, my relationship with these people is nothing compared with my relationship with my wife. I spend time with my wife every day, check in throughout the day to see how things are going, share my problems and concerns, and share my very self in much more intimate ways than I would ever share with anyone else. Intimacy can be thought of as "In to me, see." It is self-revelation.

Our relationship with Jesus should be the same. He wants so much more than a personal relationship. He does not just want to be our friend—He wants to be our Bridegroom. He wants a covenant that transcends any earthly wedding. He wants an everlasting covenant: "I am yours and you are Mine for all eternity." Our relationship with Jesus has to be more than just an acquaintance. You cannot just bump into Him once a week and engage in small talk.

Sooner or later we have to ask ourselves whether we really believe what Saint John Paul II said. We all want to be happy, but is Jesus what we are really seeking in that search? Most of us unfortunately do not live as if that is true. Saint Thomas Aquinas said that most people seek four things in their search for happiness: wealth, power, honor, and pleasure. There is nothing wrong with these things in and of themselves, but if we try to make them our source of happiness, we create huge problems.

Let us use the analogy of somebody completely dehydrated, dying of thirst. Instead of drinking water, what if he were to try to quench his thirst with alcohol? The alcohol might actually take away the pain for a short time, but the problem will come back even worse because alcohol dehydrates you even more. This may give the person the illusion that he needs more alcohol to douse the pain again. This is the mark of addiction—an increasing desire for something that gives less and less satisfaction. On the other hand, what if the person first quenched that thirst with water, which is what is really needed? The water would satisfy the thirst and fix the problem. No longer in survival mode, the person now could actually enjoy an alcoholic beverage in moderation.

As the living water, Jesus is the only one who can quench your "thirst". He said, "Seek first his [God's] kingdom and his righteousness, and all these things shall be yours as well" (Mt 6:33). In other words, if you make pleasure a god, it will consume you and make you a prisoner. If you make Jesus your God, you will experience pleasure in a healthy way. If you make wealth a god, it will destroy you. If you understand that your wealth was meant to serve God and others, you will avoid much unnecessary suffering. If you seek honor as a god, you will be consumed with selfish ambition. If you put Jesus first and yourself last, you will receive great honor and respect—if not in this life, then in the next. The first will be last, and the last will be first. If you seek power as your god, you will be crippled in weakness. If you become weak so that Jesus can be your strength, then you will receive great power—not to rule and conquer but to love and serve.

The fact is, the most profound case of being unequally yoked is the marriage between Christ and His Church. We get to marry "way up". I actually married way up in my earthly marriage. My wife is the most beautiful and amazing person I have ever met, and I still cannot believe she agreed to be my wife. Think about how foolish it would be for me to cheat on my wife for a moment of pleasure. I would be trading something of immense value for something of far less value. This is exactly what we do when we sin. In fact, throughout the Old Testament, whenever the people of Israel sin against God and worship false gods, the prophets refer to them as harlots and adulterers. When we worship "false gods", we cheat on the Bridegroom, an incredibly foolish thing to do that hurts us and breaks God's heart.

You have a huge dowry, and you were purchased for an unbelievable price. You are expensive. If you were a million-dollar bill, sin would be like taking that million-dollar bill and crumpling it, stepping on it, and throwing it in the mud. The bill would be ugly, as sin makes us ugly and broken. But its value would not change. In God's eyes, it is still worth every drop of His blood for the chance to spend eternity with His Bride. He makes all things new. You cannot earn the gift you have been given, but you can glorify God by making the most of it. Do not waste the gift. The million-dollar bill is worth nothing unless you use it for something valuable. Give the gift back to the One who gave it to you, and see how it multiplies. In this way, you will prepare yourself for the wedding feast of the Lamb, which is our goal in this life. As we read in Revelation, a time is coming when the Bride will be made ready. "I also saw the holy city, a new Jerusalem, coming down out of heaven from God, prepared as a bride adorned for her husband. I heard a loud voice from the throne saying, "Behold, God's dwelling is with the human race" (Rev 21:2–3).

Before ending this reflection on God the Son, I think it is important to return to the crucifix and perceive what it teaches us. Oftentimes, Protestants will wonder why Catholics are so transfixed by the crucifix. We do not just have crosses in our churches and homes; we have crucifixes, which display the corpus of Jesus on the cross. Why do we do this? Isn't it a denial of the Resurrection of Jesus when we leave Him on the cross? Absolutely not. In fact, the crucifix is key to understanding all of life's questions and problems. The crucifix is a wedding picture. You would not ask someone, "Why do you keep your wedding picture up in your home? You are already married!" I keep crucifixes up all over our home because I do not ever want to forget what my Savior did for me and what He said on that Cross, where He wed Himself to humanity.

What were Jesus' final words on that Cross? "Father, forgive them" (Lk 23:34); "Why have you forsaken me?" (Mt 27:46); "Behold, your mother" (Jn 19:27); "I thirst" (Jn 19:28); "It is finished" (Jn 19:30). All of these utterances can have marital implications. Everyone who is married knows the importance of forgiveness. We have "cheated" on the Bridegroom over and over, but Jesus took our shame upon Himself to make us new again. He does not abandon His Bride, and His message is forgiveness.

"Why have you forsaken me?" is a question directly from Psalm 22 (v. 1). It is important to note that Jesus is God, and whenever God asks a question, it is not for His sake but for ours, since He already knows the answer. You better take notice because He is trying to teach you something. In this case, He is showing you that marriage is hard, and you have to pass through Good Friday to reach Easter Sunday. We are allowed to die so we can live. Even though God seems far away sometimes, He is really near. If we read further in Psalm 22, it states, "From you comes my praise in the great congregation; my vows I will pay before those who fear him" (v. 25). Jesus will not violate His wedding vows even when things get hard. He will be faithful even when we are unfaithful. Of course, we know that Psalm 22 is followed by Psalm 23, which is one of the most important psalms to help us know God. "Even though I walk through the valley of the shadow of death, I fear no evil.... I shall dwell in the house of the LORD for ever" (vv. 4, 6).

"It is finished" comes from a Greek phrase that literally means "It is consummated." It is not simply over; it is brought to completion. What else do you consummate? A wedding! That is why some theologians refer to the Cross as the "marriage bed". It refers to the mystical marriage of Christ and His Church. The wedding is brought to completion when the covenant is sealed.

When Jesus said, "Behold, your mother", He was giving us Mary as our Mother. Of course, when we get married, our spouse's mother becomes ours as well, but Mary is more than your typical mother-in-law, and we will see her importance in our reflection on the mother later in this chapter.

The words I would really like to focus on are "I thirst." Nobody understood these words as well as Saint Teresa of Calcutta, the nun who caught the world's attention by serving the poorest of the poor in Calcutta, India. This phrase "I thirst" could be considered the central theme of all the work Mother Teresa did. She came to understand Jesus' thirst for human souls and in doing so was able to treat every human soul she encountered with awe and wonder. She treated souls as if they were Jesus Himself. I would like to share with you a portion of a popular reflection that Mother Teresa wrote called "I Thirst for You". These are the very words Jesus is speaking to every single one of us. If you want to know how He feels about you, then read these words.

> It is true. I stand at the door of your heart, day and night. Even when you are not listening, even when you doubt it could be Me, I am there. I await even the smallest sign of your response, even the least whispered invitation that will allow Me to enter....
>
> No matter how far you may wander, no matter how often you forget Me, no matter how many crosses you may bear in this life; there is one thing I want you to

always remember, one thing that will never change. I THIRST FOR YOU—just as you are. You don't need to change to believe in My love, for it will be your belief in My love that will change you. You forget Me, and yet I am seeking you every moment of the day—standing at the door of your heart and knocking. Do you find this hard to believe? Then look at the cross, look at My Heart that was pierced for you. Have you not understood My cross? Then listen again to the words that I spoke there—for they tell you clearly why I endured all this for you: "I THIRST ..." (Jn 19:28). Yes, I thirst for you—as the rest of the psalm verse I was praying says of Me: "I looked for love, and found none ..." (Ps 69:20). All your life I have been looking for your love—I have never stopped seeking to love you and be loved by you. You have tried many other things in your search for happiness; why not try opening your heart to Me, right now, more than you ever have before. Whenever you do open the door of your heart, whenever you come close enough, you will hear Me say to you again and again, not in mere human words but in spirit, "No matter what you have done, I love you for your own sake. Come to Me with your misery and your sins, with your troubles and needs, and with all the longing to be loved. I stand at the door of your heart and knock. Open to Me, for I THIRST FOR YOU."[4]

The Bridegroom longs for His Bride. He longs for you. He thirsts for you. We should thirst for Him. He is the living water. He is the only one who will satisfy the unquenchable thirst in your heart. The mystery of the Cross and the mystery of the Eucharist are the same mystery. They are a wedding banquet. At the Eucharist, we as the Bride walk down the aisle. We receive the Bridegroom, become one with the Bridegroom, and conceive

[4] Mother Teresa, "I Thirst for You", Mother Teresa Center, accessed October 23, 2017, http://www.motherteresa.org/11_encounter/I_T_7.html.

"new life" within us. When the priest or deacon says, "Go forth", we should bear forth that life to the whole world—become whom we eat. We should be Jesus to everyone we encounter. We should thirst for souls. We should love and serve others as Mother Teresa and all the saints of God have done.

God the Holy Spirit

We have already discovered that the story of salvation history is the story of a marriage. If Jesus is the Bridegroom and we are the Bride, then the way I see it is that our life on earth is like the engagement period. We should be spending this life preparing to spend eternity in heaven with the Bridegroom. We are supposed to spend this time getting to know the Bridegroom. I do not think anybody would like an arranged wedding, in which your parents choose your spouse when you are very young and then you meet your spouse for the first time on the day of your wedding. Talk about a serious case of cold feet. Perhaps that is another reason that we fear the horizon of death. We do not know to whom we are betrothed.

God knows we are bodily creatures, and we experience God in and through our senses. I did not prepare to marry my bride by simply reading a book about her or asking other people what they thought of her. I spent time with her and actually experienced her presence. I can see her beauty. I can feel her touch, hear her voice, and smell her perfume. Our love for each other is not sterile—it is life-giving, and we literally experience the fruit of that love in the lives of our children. In a similar way, God allows us to experience Him in this life, and the love we share with Him actually bears much fruit through the power of the Holy Spirit and sacramental grace.

We taste and see the body and blood of our Lord and Savior in the most humble form of bread and wine. We see the liturgical colors at Mass—red for martyrs, green for Ordinary Time, purple for preparation and anticipation or penance, and white for celebration. We sing some of the same choruses as the choirs of angels and saints. We hear the most beautiful sound in the world: "I absolve you from your sins, in the name of the Father, and of the Son, and of the Holy Spirit." We feel the touch of the marital embrace, which is a sacramental sign of the covenant of marriage. We feel the waters of baptism. We feel the oils of baptism, confirmation, holy orders, and the anointing of the sick. We see and smell the incense as it rises up to the heavens, representing the prayers of the faithful rising to God. As one small child said when he walked into church, "Mommy, I can smell the saints praying."

The smell of incense is perhaps my second-favorite smell in the world. My favorite smell is sacred chrism. It represents Christian purity. When each of my children was baptized, I negotiated with the priest for an extra-thick application of oil on the baby's forehead, and I did not let my wife wash his little head for a week because I did not want her to wash it off. My favorite part of a newborn baby is his soft little head, and when you put that chrism on there, I end up calling into work saying, "I can't come in today. My baby's head smells good." Interestingly, smell is the sense most tied to memory because the olfactory nerve runs right past the part of the brain tied to memory. Whenever I smell those holy oils and incense, it is like déjà vu. The smells of the Church seem to have a thread through my entire life and bring me back to a faraway time and place that I cannot quite remember with my conscious mind. It is almost as if I am suddenly present at my own baptism. And it is at baptism when we become children of God, summoned to battle against sin and evil. Those holy oils are similar to the oils an athlete may use before a competition. They limber our spiritual muscles and make us slippery to escape the grasp of the enemy.

In all of these sacramental situations, we experience God's love here on earth, and that love is not sterile. The sacraments give us the power to do things that we do not have the power to do. They are not just empty rituals. The symbolism, the form, the matter, and the words of each sacrament are absolutely beautiful and profound.

The transformation that takes place at baptism and confirmation especially is unchangeable. These sacraments literally transform who we are, changing our very identity. That is why those sacraments can be received only once. I call it the "pickle effect". In college, I came home one day and I was starving. I went to the fridge to find something to eat and found it was pretty much empty. Inside were some pickles, some mustard, and a few other random items that a typical broke college guy has. So I found myself sitting at the kitchen table eating pickles for lunch, reading the food label on the jar. Can you guess the first ingredient in a jar of pickles? That's right—cucumbers. I was twenty-one years old at the time, and I sat there thinking to myself, "Why would they put cucumbers in the pickles?"

It had never dawned on me up to that point that a pickle was a cucumber. Even though pickles and cucumbers are the same size, the same shape, and the same color, it just never clicked. Why do you think that is? Well, I probably just never stopped to think about it, but I also think that the vinegar that transformed those cucumbers into pickles was so powerful that I could not even recognize the cucumbers anymore. That vinegar is like the power of the Holy Spirit. It transforms you into something new. Once you go from being a cucumber to being a pickle, you simply cannot go back to being a cucumber again. You are changed forever! Once you become a child of God, you cannot lose that honor and vocation. It is who you are. Once you are sent to be a disciple of Jesus Christ, you cannot be unsent. You may rebel against your Father and run away from your mission, but that does not change who you are or the power you have been given.

The power of the Holy Spirit that we receive in all the sacraments is the same grace given to all the great saints of the past. It is the same Spirit who transformed people like Saint Paul, who was a murderer of the early Christians; Saint Peter, who denied Jesus three times; Saint Augustine, whose mother was drawn to tears at his early wanderings from the Church and his wretched sins; and Saint Francis, who spent his youth as an arrogant, rich ladies' man. Some of the worst sinners in the history of the world became some of the greatest saints because of the power of the Holy Spirit and sacramental grace. After the Holy Spirit flooded the lives of these men, they probably looked the same, probably had the same haircut, but they were different men. They were so different that you would not be able to recognize them.

We need to rediscover the power and the love of the Holy Spirit, and the privilege we have in receiving His grace, and take responsibility for that power to make love visible to the world. The love given can and should bear much fruit. It is not sterile, and we should seek to set the world ablaze with the fire of the Holy Spirit. When I speak to people or when I write, I do not dare start without saying the words, "Come, Holy Spirit; let my words be Your words." I want to get out of the way so the Holy Spirit can work through me.

A couple of the books I read to my children about the lives of the saints were written by Father Daniel Lord, a popular priest of the twentieth century. After receiving a diagnosis of lung cancer, he wrote an article in a newspaper titled "Cancer Is My Friend". This sounds like a very strange thing for somebody to say, but the reason he gives is striking. In regard to his diagnosis, he says, "I was relieved. I expected to die someday of heart trouble, or a stroke, and I dreaded that sudden and perhaps sacramental-less death." In other words, Father Lord was so confident in the power of sacramental grace and felt so much comfort in its healing power that his fear was not of dying, but of dying without the opportunity to prepare with sacraments. The sacraments were his ladder to heaven, and whenever he prayed a litany to the saints he added, "From a sudden and unprovided death, O Lord, deliver me." That is why cancer was his friend, because it afforded him the time to prepare for his journey. Before my death, I hope to be showered with the presence of the Holy Spirit that we find in the Eucharist, reconciliation, and the anointing of the sick. As we end our reflection on the Holy Spirit, the fruit of God's love, let us marvel at the beauty of the words prayed over a dying person, a prayer that I hope to hear one day as I prepare for my journey.

> Go forth, Christian soul, from this world
> in the name of God the almighty Father,
> who created you,
> in the name of Jesus Christ, the Son of the
>   living God,
> who suffered for you,
> in the name of the Holy Spirit,
> who was poured out upon you.
> Go forth, faithful Christian!
> May you live in peace this day,
> may your home be with God in Zion,
> with Mary, the virgin Mother of God,
> with Joseph, and all the angels and saints.

Our Mother

"When Jesus saw his mother, and the disciple whom he loved standing near, he said to his mother, 'Woman, behold, your son!' Then he said to the disciple, 'Behold, your mother!' And from that hour the disciple took her to his own home" (Jn 19:26–27).

We should all behold the Mother that Jesus gave to us. We know the importance of mothers in families, and Mary plays an important role in our lives as part of the family of God. Christians have always given Mary great respect and honor. As the Mother of God, she has a unique role. In recent centuries, many Christians have lost touch with Mary, including many Catholics. It is important to note that Catholics do not worship Mary, but we can and should be greatly devoted to her and show her tremendous honor. Jesus certainly honored His own Mother.

We saw in chapter 1 how Mary's humility is a great weapon in destroying dragons. So what is the significance of Jesus giving us Mary as our Mother? One of my favorite talks about Mary that I have ever heard is from five-time Major League Baseball All-Star Mike Sweeney. It is entitled "The Four Pillars of Marian Spirituality". He uses the acronym MARY to help us remember Mary's role in our life. The *M* stands for "Mother". First and foremost, she is our Mother. She does everything that mothers do, and we should honor her as our Mother. The *A* is for "advocate". We know that Mary's prayers are powerful and that she intercedes for us just as she did for the married couple in Cana. The *R* stands for "rosary". The rosary is Mary's scrapbook of her Son. She invites us into the mysteries in the life of her Son so we can walk with Jesus. The *Y* stands for "yes". It was Mary's yes that brought forth a Savior. She teaches us to say yes and trust God.

A recent popular book, *33 Days to Morning Glory* by Father Michael Gaitley,[5] offers a thirty-three-day do-it-yourself retreat to prepare for consecration to Jesus through Mary, based in part on Saint Louis de Montfort's *True Devotion to Mary*. Saint John Paul II said that reading *True Devotion to Mary* as a young man was a turning point in his life. Saint Louis' prayer of consecration to Jesus through Mary was the source of his papal motto, *Totus tuus*—Totally yours.

It is interesting to note that Saint Louis de Montfort actually predicted that after his death angry demons would come to hide the unpublished manuscript of *True Devotion to Mary* so no one could ever read it. He said, "I clearly see that raging beasts shall come in fury to tear with their diabolical teeth this little writing ... or at least to smother it in the darkness and silence of a coffer that it may not appear."[6] The manuscript was indeed lost for more than a century after his death.

However, the saint also predicted that his manuscript would be found and published, and its impact should greatly interest us as we talk about "saints in the making". He said the book's Marian spirituality would help form some of the greatest saints in the history of the Church. Father Gaitley likes to point out that he was drawn to the work because Saint Louis said it was the "surest, easiest, shortest, and the most perfect means" to becoming a saint.[7]

Father Gaitley does a tremendous job of making consecration to Mary more accessible to ordinary Catholics. He focuses on the Marian spirituality not just of Saint Louis de

---

[5] *33 Days to Morning Glory* (Stockbridge, Mass.: Marian Press, 2011).

[6] *True Devotion to Mary*, trans. Fr. Frederick Faber (Rockford, Ill.: Tan Books, 1985), 69.

[7] Ibid., 33.

Montfort but of four modern Marian saints whose insights on Mary are inspiring and practical in our day and age. In addition to introducing us to Saint Louis de Monfort, Father Gaitley invites us into the thoughts and practices of Saint Maximilian Kolbe, Saint Teresa of Calcutta, and Saint John Paul II. The book is short and to the point yet packed with an all-star lineup of modern Marian giants, and encourages us simply "to ponder in our hearts" throughout the retreat, just as Mary did as she contemplated God's extraordinary role for her humble life (see Lk 2:19).

Seeing Mary as Mother has always been sort of a given for me. I think I have largely taken her for granted. I assumed she was a consoling figure who tirelessly prayed and humbly offered joyful service to all of us, showering us with unending graces. When I hear the word "mother", this is automatically what I think of, and I realize that I have been greatly blessed in my life.

My own mother is everything I just described. I cannot ever remember my mother not joyfully serving. Of course, she raised four boys (five if you count my dad), and I do remember times when we were close to pushing her over the edge. However, as the years have passed, it has dawned on me what she sacrificed and how she has been a heroic witness to her Catholic faith, despite the moaning and groaning of her sons. She was steadfast in the face of ridicule; humble in the face of enormous odds and sometimes agonizing defeats (remember, four sons!); and she never once, that I can remember, put herself first, not even as a widow.

When my father was dying of cancer, my parents suffered through nights that I cannot imagine. My mother's faith and perseverance never wavered, at least not in any visible form. She showed us what "until death do you part" means, and she humbly followed my father to the cross just as Mary followed Jesus. She was and is rock solid. She continues to serve joyfully, never feeling sorry for herself, and never asking for anything in return. As I was growing up, she used to say something to me in the face of every game, track meet, exam, and trial, which has stuck with me my whole life: "Try your best, and let God do the rest." Is this not Mary's motto? The Scriptures say that when the angel Gabriel came to Mary and said, "Hail, full of grace, the Lord is with you!", Mary was "greatly troubled at the saying, and considered in her mind what sort of greeting this might be" (Lk 1:28–29). We can relate to Mary here. She realizes God is about to ask her to do something, and she knows that she is just a humble handmaid. Aren't we all greatly troubled when God gives us a task? Don't we all feel inadequate? Aren't we secretly thinking, "Please, Lord, pick somebody else"? However, Mary reminds us that we are the instrument, and God is the Master Builder. Just say yes, try your best, and let God do the rest.

After I left home, my mother entrusted me to God's providence. You would think that in some aspects, I would be set up for disappointment when discovering that not every woman imitates Mary the way my mother did. But wouldn't you know, I am now married to the most beautiful, selfless wife and mother I can possibly imagine. I enjoy the blessing to travel the country and try to inspire people to become saints, but my wife, Kristin, is the witness nobody sees. When we were married, our pastor, Father Mike Hohenbrink, in his homily, looked at me and said, "Your job is to get her to heaven." Then he looked at her and said, "Your job is to get him to heaven." I remember thinking, "That's just not fair—for her." I cannot believe she agreed to it, but she does an amazing job. She makes me want to be a saint.

So, I have no excuses for not becoming a saint. I was raised by one, and I am married to one. But more than that, I have a heavenly Mother who radiates beauty, humility, and joyful service. She also makes me want to be a saint, showering me with the graces to do so. Like all good mothers, she does not want me to become a saint just for my own sake—she wants me to make a difference in the world. She wants me to help others become saints. This is why consecrating ourselves to Mary is so powerful.

Her will is perfectly conformed to God's will, and from her perspective as the Queen of Heaven, she knows how to help us become saints. So we can give ourselves to her, *Totus tuus*, knowing she will take our small little sacrifices and effort and do what mothers do—fix them up nice and pretty and present them to the King. Remember those annoying things that mothers do to little boys—making them wear clean underwear and socks, spitting in their hair so it lies straight, and wiping the sleep out of their eyes. Perhaps it is annoying, but mothers know best. Mary is like a financial adviser. I do not know where to invest my money to get the most benefit, so I give it to a financial adviser, who knows the market better. Mary, as our spiritual sacrifice adviser, takes our sacrifices if we offer them to her, and she renders the most from them. She uses them where they are needed the most to help get souls to heaven.

The Bride

A couple of years ago I took all my kids fishing at a friend's pond. Marvin had invited us over on several occasions after I had mentioned to him that I would like to take my kids fishing sometime. One Sunday afternoon, we decided to give it a try. I was a little hesitant, but Marvin insisted that I bring the whole family. He had plans that day but came home to meet us when we arrived. After attempting to fish for about an hour, things started to unravel, as I had feared.

Having very little success in catching any fish, our children were frustrated. Our nine-year-old daughter had caught one bluegill. She and our five-year-old son were competitive in nature, so her brother, upon seeing his older sister catch a fish, was determined. He was not-so-safely trying to cast his own line over and over. Our seven-year-old daughter was extremely shy, and as Marvin was trying to assist her in casting her line, she stared blankly ahead, ignoring Marvin's existence, not answering any of his questions.

Our two-year-old was running all over the place as my wife chased her around the yard, with Marvin's dog in hot pursuit of both of them. I was trying to fish myself but was constantly interrupted by somebody who needed a hook baited.

Suddenly, everything fell apart. My wife had decided to try out the paddleboat on the other side of the pond to see if our two-year-old might sit still in a boat. Poor Marvin was trying to assist the two-year-old with her life jacket, not realizing she was going through a stage where she was very picky about the clothes she wore; she vigorously refused to put the jacket on. My wife, who had already entered the paddleboat, managed to get herself stuck on the safety rope in the water. At this point the two-year-old took off running, chased by the dog. Our son suddenly burst into uncontrollable tears because he could not catch a fish. Our oldest daughter was not helping by reminding him that she had caught a fish and maybe someday he could be as good at fishing as she was. Our second daughter was depressed at her own lack of success but sat silently with a scowl on her face, refusing to say a word, even as Marvin kindly asked if she would like some help. My wife was yelling at me to chase down the two-year-old, who had escaped, although I was finally getting a bite and did not want to leave my post when my bobber was going up and down.

It dawned on me what Marvin must have been thinking. After all, this was a man who had given up his Sunday afternoon to assist us at his pond, even though he had other plans. He offered us drinks, snacks, chairs, fishing poles, bait, life jackets, paddleboats, and anything else he could think of to make us welcome. If I were he, I would have said, "Put down your fishing pole and go grab your crazy two-year-old, teach your wife how to paddle a boat, teach your oldest daughter and son a little bit of sportsmanship, and sign your middle daughter up for mime class because she doesn't make a sound."

Reluctantly retrieving the two-year-old, who was now (combined with my wailing son) making an eardrum-piercing sound (I am pretty sure I saw a bird fall from the sky), I gave my wife a look that said, "We have to get out of here *now*!" I was so embarrassed. We packed up our things, which set my son off even more because he had to face the reality that he was not going to catch a fish. I had lost my temper and patience with all of them, trying not to scream angrily in front of Marvin. He could sense my frustration, and he came to my rescue by offering to allow the kids to feed the fish. This caught my son's interest immediately. His tears faded quickly as he got to throw food in the water, and it bought me enough time to get the van packed up.

As we were leaving, I told Marvin we were grateful for the opportunity, but figured he was relieved to get rid of us and must be frustrated that he had given up his Sunday. I had no intention of attempting to put him or myself through something like this again, believing he would be glad to see us go. However, do you know what he said before we left? "Please come back anytime. Our house is your house. If we aren't here, just come on over and make yourselves at home. There are drinks in the fridge, snacks in the cupboard—help yourself to whatever you need. You really made my day by bringing your family over. Your kids did just fine. Next time they can do some swimming, and we'll catch some fish and cook them over a campfire. Don't forget, those kids grow up fast, so enjoy the time you have with them now."

I was shocked. He had shared his home, his pond, his time, and his assistance with all of us crazy people, and yet he was saying that we had "made his day"? And you could tell he really meant it. I have read and studied Pope Francis' encyclical about evangelization called *Evangelii Gaudium* (The joy of the Gospel), and I realized that Marvin was the perfect example of what it means to evangelize. He was a great representation of what the Church, the Bride of Christ, is supposed to be.

The Church is supposed to welcome the lost into her home, those marred by brokenness and sin. She is supposed to go out of her way to meet people where they are and assist them in their trials. She is supposed to care for them, love them, and love being around them because they are brothers and sisters. Marvin never once mentioned Jesus, quoted Scripture, or gave us a theology lesson, but somehow he showed us who Jesus is, and it was attractive. It made me want to know where his joy came from. If I were not Christian, I would have wanted to ask him, What do you believe, and who is this Jesus that gives you such joy?

Some people clearly radiate joy because they know Jesus. My friend Joe is another example. I coached basketball with Joe, and he and his wife, Helen, always had a smile, a kind word, and a story about how God is good. People like this help us encounter God and get to know Him. You do not need a theology degree to evangelize. You need a relationship with God so filled with love that you cannot help but want to share His love with others. As Pope Francis sums up, "The saints were not superhuman. They were people who loved God in their hearts, and who shared this joy with others."[8]

It saddens me that sometimes our parishes lose this mission. As mentioned earlier, the root of the word "parish" is a Greek word meaning "somebody away from home". We are pilgrims, not tourists. We should not cling to our buildings and customs as if they are the destination. We spend a lot of time fighting over Mass times and locations and parish names, and a lot of things that can cause bitterness, especially in a time of priest shortages and consolidating parishes. The parish does not exist for itself. The goal is not just to get people to be members of the parish. The goal is to get people to the destination—heaven. The goal is to help form saints. The parish is not a business trying to please customers. It is a family trying to build disciples. We are one Church. So if you refuse to go to another parish because it is not *your* parish, then it is as if you are refusing to go to heaven, because that is the purpose and destination of *every* parish. The Church is like a huge ship sailing to a great destination, always moving, never standing still. She is trying to pull people out of murky waters and on board—not for the sake of their being on board but because the sure and final destination of this great ship is heaven.

---

[8] Twitter post, November 19, 2013, 6:19 A.M., https://twitter.com/Pontifex/status/402803391065100289.

That is why she must be founded on truth *and* love. As a doctor, I could have the best bedside manner in the world, but if I do not know what I am doing, I cannot cure diseases, and that should be why people go to a doctor. If you switch doctors every time a doctor tells you something you do not want to hear, you will end up seriously sick or dead. However, even if I am the best doctor in the world, nobody will come if I am mean, rude, and arrogant. The bedside manner is what draws people.

Marvin had a great "bedside manner" in our fishing adventure. But he was also firm about the rules—you have to wear a life jacket in the water, no throwing rocks, and you have to look carefully before casting your line. When my two-year-old screamed, Marvin did not loosen up on the life-jacket rule (which is what I was tempted to do).

Again, this is what the Church should look like. The goal is heaven. It does not do any good to welcome people to a "doctor" who does not know medicine, or a doctor who is afraid to tell people they are sick. My car mechanic can be the friendliest person in the world, but if he does not fix my car, I am not going back. Everyone is welcome to come home to the Church no matter what he has done or what he struggles with, but he is not welcome to come and try to change who the Church is instead of striving to change himself. You cannot get aboard the ship and then demand to steer it in a different direction or tell it to drop anchor and stop moving. It is not a cruise ship. It can and should be fun to be aboard the ship, but the fun and joy are rooted in knowing that it is going someplace eternally wonderful, and it is worth the work and effort to get there. More important, we are going to meet someone who is the longing of every human heart. It is worth throwing overboard those "possessions" that keep the ship from moving. Sadly, many people get angry and refuse to get on board because they want to bring those "possessions" with them, or they jump overboard because they refuse to let go of them. We must constantly be searching for new ways to get people aboard the ship but never forget or try to change the purpose and destination of the ship.

There is beauty in truth. There is beauty in love. There is beauty in holiness. The Bride of Christ is all these things. What is more beautiful than a bride?

Can You Prove That God Exists?

There are many reasons people do not know God and do not have an intimate relationship with Him and His family. One of the biggest stumbling blocks for people is finding proof that God is real. It is hard to have a relationship with somebody you do not know is real. Sherry Weddell, in her book *Forming Intentional Disciples*, notes that only 48 percent of Catholics are sure you can have a relationship with God.[9] So how do we know God is real?

Saint Thomas Aquinas gave several proofs of God's existence. The most basic of these proofs is that everything that exists had to come from something. If the universe began with the Big Bang, as many scientists believe, then who made the bang? If we go back far enough, we can come to the conclusion that there had to be an uncreated Creator, an unmoved Mover. Creation itself can help us to come to know God in the same way as studying a piece of artwork can reveal something about its artist.

Another argument you could use for the existence of God is the presence of miracles—those things that science alone simply cannot explain. I have read about

[9] *Forming Intentional Disciples* (Huntington, Ind.: Our Sunday Visitor, 2012), 44.

many miracles, but I have never experienced one myself. I have never heard an audible voice of God speaking to me, although I know people who have. I have never seen a vision of the supernatural or spiritual realm, although I know people who have. I was not among the seventy thousand eyewitnesses who saw the sun dance in the sky on October 13, 1917, in Fatima, Portugal, but I believe their testimonies. I have read about many Eucharistic miracles, but I have never seen a host turn to real human flesh and blood with my own eyes.

Very few people deny that Jesus was a real person in history, and Jesus claimed He was God. At the heart of our faith is the claim that Jesus, this real man who claimed to be God, rose from the dead. I did not see the resurrected Jesus, but I have read the stories of the disciples who did, and how each was willing to die for the truth of the Resurrection. Some were skinned alive, some were crucified, some were stoned, and some were tortured, yet none of them took back the claim that Jesus rose from the dead. The witness of the hundreds of martyrs who gave their life for this claim proves to me that He did rise from the dead. People do not die for something they know to be a lie.

I have never seen any of these miracles with my own eyes. However, I have seen many "miracles" that I believe prove God's existence. To me, every sunrise and sunset proves that God exists. My study of the human body, most especially the eye, proves that God exists. Every flower that blooms, and garden that grows, and bird that takes flight proves that God exists. When I see an athlete develop an amazing gift or hear a musician play a song that stirs my soul, it proves to me that God exists. My wife and children prove to me that God exists. Watching my children being born, and seeing them grow, walk, talk, and laugh, proves to me that God exists. As I look back at the kaleidoscope of my life, I begin to see a pattern emerging—a design, a plan that came together not by chance. I see God's fingerprints all over my life. In the end, it really just comes down to faith. As Albert Einstein once noted, there are two ways to live life: One is as if everything is a miracle, and the other is as if nothing is. To those who believe, everything is a miracle. For those who do not, nothing is. I know God is real, because I know Him. He is my best friend and my Savior. Deep inside there is a voice that is not my own. Often that voice has nudged me in the direction opposite of the one I wanted to go. But every time I have listened to that voice, my life has been blessed a hundredfold. I know that His way is better than mine. I know He loves me more than I love myself. I trust Him. God is real, and the kingdom of heaven is real. It is a kingdom worth fighting for, worth living for, worth becoming a saint for, and worth dying for.

> I love you, O my God, and my only desire is to love you until the last breath of my life. I love you, O my infinitely lovable God, and I would rather die loving you, than live without loving you. I love you, Lord, and the only grace I ask is to love you eternally.... My God, if my tongue cannot say in every moment that I love you, I want my heart to repeat it to you as often as I draw breath.
>
> —Saint John Vianney[10]

What worldly treasures are you holding on to because you are afraid to give them to God? Let them go. Your Father in heaven has so much more to give you.

For all the recommended resources for "Need to Know Him", go to the website: www.saintsinthemaking.com /need-to-know-him.html.

---

[10] Quoted in *CCC* 2658.

Chapter 5

T: THEOLOGY OF THE BODY

Color: Orange, for Health of Mind, Body, and Soul

The body, and it alone, is capable of making visible the invisible: the spiritual and the divine.

—Saint John Paul II

The Language of Love

Every parent knows the scary feeling of bringing home a firstborn child without an instruction manual. No matter how much you try to prepare, you never feel quite ready. There are so many questions and discoveries along the way. Before having my first child, I wondered how you teach children to talk. Do you have to teach them every word one by one? I was delighted to discover that children naturally pick up the language as they grow older. Almost like magic, they just start talking, although they do mix up words from time to time.

When my oldest daughter, Isabelle, was about six years old, my wife and I overheard a conversation she was having with my second daughter, Hannah, who was four years old. Isabelle had just started reading and writing, and she had started a little diary. One day she walked into the living room and found Hannah looking at her diary. Knowing that a diary is supposed to be private, Isabelle screamed at her, "Hannah! That is my diarrhea—you can't touch it!" You can imagine how the conversation flowed from there. Hannah replied, "I was just looking at it." Isabelle countered, "Diarrheas are private. If you want a diarrhea, you have to make your own. This is mine. I worked hard on it."

Now, as parents, we had several ways we could have reacted to this conversation. We could have screamed at Isabelle and told her to go wash her mouth out with soap because it is disgusting to be talking about diarrhea like that. We could have laughed at her and made her feel bad for messing up the words "diary" and "diarrhea". We could have just ignored it and let her continue believing that her little book was diarrhea. Or we could sit down with her and explain the meaning of the words to her. We did not have an instructor's manual on parenting, but we were pretty sure about what we needed to do. We explained to her that a diary is a book for writing your innermost thoughts—a place to record your secrets, fears, dreams, ambitions, and deepest desires. The diary is self-revelation. Diarrhea is, let's just say, not so sacred. It is actually a sign that something is wrong.

My point with this little story is that the loving thing to do was to tell her the truth about the meaning of those words. She did not mean to mix them up, and it would not have been loving to condemn her or make fun of her. However, it also would not have been loving to ignore the error and not to tell her the truth. John Paul II had this mentality in mind when he gave us his masterpiece, the Theology of the Body, at the beginning of his pontificate.

The body, he said, has a language. We are supposed to be speaking the language of love and truth with our bodies. It is a language that reveals who you really are, like a language you might find in a diary. However, our culture has slowly adopted a different language of the body. People were made to be loved and things were made to be used, but in our culture we tend to love things and use people. It is a language more like, shall we say, diarrhea.

John Paul II's Theology of the Body does not wag a finger at people. It does not condemn people or call them foolish. It invites us to let go of the language of lies and embrace a language of truth—a divine truth that is not shallow and superficial but instead deeply intimate. It does not seek to control or manipulate people, and it does not restrict our freedom. It liberates us. It is an invitation to let go of the diarrhea and embrace the diary. It is self-revelation and coming to know God in and through our bodies.

Perhaps one of the greatest victories for the enemy in the last century has been our confusion about the meaning of our bodies. Satan is the great plagiarizer. He takes what is true and beautiful, and he twists it into a counterfeit. He disguises lust as love, and we have taken the bait. Jesus said, "This is my body which is given for you" (Lk 22:19). The language the enemy suggests sounds eerily similar: "This is my body—don't tell me what to do with my body."

The Theology of the Body is explained in 129 talks given by John Paul II during the first few years of his pontificate, and the best way to sum up the entire teaching is this: God is love, and we are created in His image to love as He loves. If we can come to understand this, we can clear up a lot of confusion about the meaning of our bodies and begin to understand some of the challenging moral issues of our day, such as contraception, divorce, embryonic stem cell research, same-sex attraction, in vitro fertilization, pornography, fornication, abortion, and cohabitation. Although we will briefly address several of these issues, I cannot do justice to all of them in a single chapter.

Here are my four main objectives in presenting this introduction to the Theology of the Body:

1. To give you a foundation in the Theology of the Body so you can begin to ask honest questions and to dialogue with others about Church teachings on sexual morality in a healthy and respectful way.
2. To help you come to see the Church as a mother who always wants what is best for her children. Even if you do not agree with her, I hope you will see her motives as pure and good. Her teachings are never arbitrary; there are very good and logical reasons for them.
3. To help you understand that every person deserves to be loved, and begin to question what it means truly to love another person.
4. To discuss some of the most prevalent topics relating to the Theology of the Body and, in doing so, give you the tools necessary to discover why the Church teaches what she does in regard to natural and moral law.

God Is Love ...

If we could describe God in one word, I think it would have to be "love". The question is, What is love? This word gets thrown around a lot in our cultural language. From the time we are very young, we hear the message that God loves us, over and over, like the famous song "Jesus loves me, this I know, for the Bible tells me so ..." This is certainly accurate, but it does no good if we do not truly understand what love is. There are many forms of love and different ways to describe it. The culture and the Church really seem to be at odds over what love is, just as in chapter 1 we discussed the different perspectives on what true happiness is. One question I usually ask the teenagers I speak to is whether love is more of a choice or a feeling. Most of them will tell you that love is a feeling. Almost all elementary students will tell you it is a feeling. I am not too surprised, since our culture is constantly screaming to them that love is about feelings. Songs, movies, and romantic novels talk about two people "falling in love" or about "love at first sight". While feelings play a role in love, they certainly cannot be the essence of true love, or "agape" love, as we would describe God.

Because we use the phrases "fall in love" and "love at first sight", we tend to see love as something beyond our control, such as feelings and attractions, and focus only on the "eros", or romantic, side of love. We can become more and more attracted to a person, but attraction does not necessarily imply love. If I were to say, "I love steak" and "I love playing hockey" and "I love my wife", does the word "love" in all of these sentences mean the same thing? I hope not, for my wife's sake. When I say, "I love steak", am I saying, "I will lay down my life for this steak. I will guard and protect it with all that I am. No mold will ever come upon this steak"? No. When I say, "I love steak", I am really saying that I like what it does for me. It gives me pleasure; it tastes good. Loving steak is based on a feeling. I did not choose to like steak. When I was two years old, I did not sit down and decide which foods were going to taste good to me and which ones I was not going to like. Loving my wife is very different. Certainly, I am attracted to her, and my feelings for her grow stronger every year. In fact, I cannot help but be attracted to her, and I am glad about that. But loving her is something I choose to do.

Primarily, love is not a feeling or an attraction; love is a choice. Our feelings and attractions can evolve based on what we choose to love. For example, as a child I mostly desired junk food. As I grew older and personal health became more important, I became more attracted to food that made me feel good in the long term instead of food that just made me feel good instantly. When someone begins to value personal holiness and understands the mission to become a saint, I guarantee you that that individual becomes more attracted to others striving for holiness who help accomplish the mission. A person's inner beauty becomes more attractive than his outer beauty. In other words, love should master feelings; feelings should not master love. Feelings can lead to love, and love can lead to feelings, but feelings in and of themselves are not true love. Feelings come and go. Love should be constant.

The stereotypical image regarding love and feelings is the young woman dating the guy who treats her very poorly. Everybody knows he treats her poorly, but she will not break up with him. If her friends bring this reality to her attention, what does she say? "I can't help it; I love him." What she really means is that she is attracted to him and has strong feelings for him. If she loved him, she would not allow him to treat her the way he does.

Love is an act of the will. Every day we can choose to love or choose not to love, regardless of how we feel. Scripture says, "Love is patient and kind.... Love bears all things, believes all things, hopes all things, endures all things. Love never ends" (1 Cor 13:4, 7–8). Notice that every one of those qualities is an action. The passage does not say that love is warm and fuzzy and tingly. Do not get me wrong; feelings are important. Attraction and pleasure are good things. God gave us attraction and pleasure, and we should be attracted to our spouses. Romance is an important part of spousal love, and guys especially need to remember that keeping romance alive is in fact an act of love. We must remember, though, that feelings and attractions are by-products of love, and they may instigate love, but they are not love in the truest sense of the word.

Love comes from the spiritual heart and keeps us spiritually alive. It is the lifeblood of our soul. It is an essential part of the mystical body of Christ. The *Catechism of the Catholic Church* uses a quote from Saint Thérèse of Lisieux to bring this thought to life:

> If the Church was a body composed of different members, it couldn't lack the noblest of all; *it must have a Heart, and a Heart BURNING WITH LOVE.* And I realized that *this love alone* was the true motive force which enabled the other members of the Church to act; if it ceased to function, the Apostles would forget to preach the gospel, the Martyrs would refuse to shed their blood. LOVE, IN FACT, IS THE VOCATION WHICH INCLUDES ALL OTHERS; IT'S A UNIVERSE OF ITS OWN, COMPRISING ALL TIME AND SPACE—IT'S ETERNAL![1]

... And We Are Created in His Image ...

"God created man in his own image, in the image of God he created him; male and female he created them" (Gen

---

[1] *Autobiography of a Saint*, trans. Ronald Knox (London: Harvill, 1958), 235, quoted in *CCC* 826. Emphasis in original.

1:27). As human beings, there are many ways we can image God. Nothing else in creation is given this honor. When discussing the Theology of the Body, many people automatically think of marriage. The Theology of the Body is not just for married people; it is for anybody who has a body—every human being. The teaching is about the very meaning of our being and existence. It attempts to answer those age-old questions "Who am I?" and "Why am I here?"

Whether our vocation is to be single, married, or a celibate religious, we are called to image God in the way we live and love others. However, since the most common analogy used in the Scriptures to describe God's love for His people is that of bridegroom and bride, let us take a closer look at the vocation of marriage. The quote from Genesis 1 above specifically mentions making them male and female when speaking of the divine image. It is clear that males and females are equal yet different. It is the differences between male and female that call men and women to communion, as evidenced by God's first command, which is found in the following verse: "Be fruitful and multiply, and fill the earth and subdue it" (1:28). The husband is called to give himself to his wife, and she in return is called to receive that gift and give herself back to her husband. The love and communion between them becomes so real that it is life-giving. It is an exchange of love, which begets more love.

In a similar way, the whole story of salvation history is the story of a marriage. It begins with the marriage of Adam and Eve and ends in the book of Revelation with the story of the wedding feast of the Lamb. God is an eternal exchange of love. If we reflect on the Holy Trinity, we come to understand this a little better. The Father eternally gives Himself to the Son, and the Son gives all

He is back to the Father. The love between them is so real that it is another being—"the Holy Spirit, which proceeds from the Father and the Son", as we say in the Nicene Creed. Please keep in mind that every attempt to describe God ultimately falls short. The way a husband and wife love each other is analogous to this Trinitarian love, but we must remember that we are made in God's image; He is not made in ours. God, the first Person of the Trinity, is in no way sexual. He is not male or female. By His nature and transcendence He is "Father", but He is pure spirit. But the analogy of bridegroom and bride works well because God Himself uses it often in the Scriptures (see the book of Hosea for one example). In the fullness of time, God took on human flesh to show us the meaning of our bodies and the meaning of our existence.

Jesus is the Word made flesh (see Jn 1:14). He is love incarnate, and He came as a man and called Himself the Bridegroom (see Mt 9:15). He is God come among us in human form, with a body; and as a man He sacrificed Himself to sanctify His Bride, the Church. The Church is the mystical Bride of Christ, born from the water (think baptism) and blood (think Eucharist) that flowed from the side of Christ, just as Eve came from the side of Adam. Our eternal destination and purpose is "the marriage supper of the Lamb" (Rev 19:9). Marriage on earth is a sacrament, and a sacrament is a sign pointing us to something greater. Husband and wife are called to make visible the invisible mystery of God's life-giving love, just as all the sacraments do.

We must come to understand that God did not create us because He needed us. He did not create us because He needed somebody to fetch Him the remote or because He was bored and needed something to do. God is perfect love, lacking in nothing. He created us purely as an act of generous love. He created us to share in His divine love. That should be a comforting thought. We were purposely created by a loving Father to spend all eternity sharing His love. Until we understand this, we cannot find what we are looking for. As much as man and wife image God's love, they are only a sign of it. Marriage on earth points us to the marriage in heaven, and the goal of marriage on earth is to help us get to the real wedding in heaven, the marriage of the Lamb.

If you are married, or plan to be married, it is vitally important that you understand this. Your spouse, or future spouse, is not your ultimate fulfillment. No human being can ever be your ultimate fulfillment. The goal of marriage is to get your spouse to heaven, not to find everything you are looking for. A celibate priest or nun in many ways is skipping the sign on earth in anticipation for the real thing in heaven. A priestly or religious vocation requires the same sacrificial love that husband and wife require and images God's love just as much. It is a beautiful witness to something greater to come in a world that banks everything on the here and now. There are no marriages or sacraments in heaven, because once you reach your destination, you no longer need the signs.

Taking the marriage analogy a bit further, we know that with husband and wife, the two become one. This does not just refer to the marital embrace; it refers to the fact that the husband gives everything to his wife, and she in turn gives everything back to him. What belongs to the husband belongs to the wife, and vice versa. If we as the Church are the Bride of Christ, then we are called to become one with Him. How does this happen? In the Eucharist. That is why John Paul II called the Eucharist the sacrament of the Bridegroom and the

Bride. He said, "It is the Eucharist above all that expresses the redemptive act of Christ the Bridegroom toward the Church the Bride."[2] Just as Mary received the eternal life of God within her at the Annunciation, we receive that eternal life within us when we receive Jesus in the Eucharist. At the end of Mass, when the priest or deacon says, "Go forth", we are called to bear forth His life to the world. In other words, if we receive Jesus deeply in the Mass and become one with Him, His presence in us can transform the world. Saint Paul explained that experience as "It is no longer I who live, but Christ who lives in me" (Gal 2:20). We should say the same thing. When we leave church after Mass, we are supposed to be revealing Christ to the world, to become whom we eat. Everyone we encounter should encounter Christ in us. I can think of no greater way to image God than to be Christ to another person.

This is why the Church literally calls herself the mystical body of Christ. We are one body with many parts. Each part of the body is different but important. If the eye were to separate from the body, the eye would cease to function, and the body would suffer a great deal. The same is true with the body of Christ, the Church. Our role is important in God's plan for salvation. That is why we cannot fall for the lie of the culture—that what we do in the privacy of our own homes does not hurt anybody else. If we do not become the saints God created us to be, the whole Church will suffer. Another metaphor Jesus uses is the vine and the branches. As long as we stay connected to the vine, we will bear great fruit. As soon as we try to

[2] Pope John Paul II, Apostolic Letter *Mulieris Dignitatem*, August 15, 1988, no. 26, http://w2.vatican.va/content/john-paul-ii/en/apost_letters/1988/documents /hf_jp-ii_apl_19880815_mulieris-dignitatem.html.

remove ourselves from Christ and His Church, we will wither and die.

... To Love as He Loves

How does God love? If God is love and we are created in His image, we must ask this question. We can never give full justice to describing God's love in words. It is a great mystery. However, let us continue with the image of marriage to help us reflect on what it means to love as God loves.

The sacrament of marriage is a visible sign of an invisible mystery. We are called to love as God loves, and husband and wife are meant to show the world what God's love truly looks like. God is love. How do we imitate God's love in marriage? The words of the wedding vows describe the four qualities of God's love: Have you come here to enter into Marriage without coercion, freely and wholeheartedly? Are you prepared, as you follow the path of Marriage, to love and honor each other for as long as you both shall live? Are you prepared to accept children lovingly from God and to bring them up according to the law of Christ and his Church?

Free, total, faithful, and fruitful are how Jesus describes His love. In the Scriptures, He lays his life down freely because He has the power to do so (see Jn 10:18). In John 17 Jesus' prayer to the Father tells us that His love is total when He says, "Everything of mine is yours and everything of yours is mine" (v. 10),[3] and "The glory which you have given me I have given to them, that they may be one

[3] New American Bible.

even as we are one" (v. 22). At the end of the Gospel of Matthew, Jesus proclaims His faithfulness by saying, "I am with you always, to the close of the age" (Mt 28:20). Jesus also speaks of fruitfulness and His desire for us to live the abundant life when He says, "I came that they may have life, and have it abundantly" (Jn 10:10).

The words of the wedding vows describe God's love, and when the marriage is consummated, when the two become one, the words of the wedding vows become flesh. This is the language of the body that John Paul II spoke about. As we will see in this chapter, the marital embrace is supposed to be a renewal of wedding vows. It is the sign of the covenant of marriage and the unique expression of love between husband and wife.

Marriage Takes Three

My first year of college was not a good year. A disappointing year in sports, confusion about my vocation in life, and being dumped by my girlfriend because I was Catholic had me angry at God and the world. The last hurt the most. More than anything, I desired a wife and children, and I prayed every day that God would send me the right woman so that I could be happy. I had never had much luck on the whole dating scene, so when a woman finally did go out with me, I thought my prayers had been answered—but then I got dumped because of my faith. Where is the justice in that?

A couple of years later, though, I met my future wife, Kristin. Her beauty, smile, innocence, purity, and humility took my breath away. She is a better spouse for me than I had ever imagined. I joke (partly) that I married way up, and she inspires me every day to want to be a saint. I thought my prayers had been answered because of my persistence, much like the lady in Jesus' parable in Luke 18:1–8. God had given me the woman of my dreams, and in her, my ultimate fulfillment. At least, that is what I used to think—wrongly.

If there is one thing my wife has taught me, it is that God sent me this beautiful woman not to shut me up but to teach me that God is my ultimate fulfillment, not my wife. My wife illustrates this point when we teach marriage preparation to engaged couples. Drawing a picture of a triangle on the board, she tells the couples that marriage takes three. God is at the top of the triangle, and you and your spouse are at the corners on the bottom. From there, Kristin explains two possible paths the couple can take. If they choose to ignore God and go along the bottom because they want the other to be their ultimate fulfillment, it is possible they will crush each other under the weight of unachievable expectations. On the other hand, if they each choose to go up the side of the triangle toward God, they not only get closer to God but also get continuously closer to each other. This has been the case in my own life—the more I come truly to love Christ and His Church, the more I truly love my wife.

True love and chastity are incredibly difficult—some would say impossible—without God. That is why the enemy will do whatever he can to remove God from the picture. That is why a culture that has removed God from the picture does not believe that true love is possible. Without God, the Theology of the Body is an unrealistic teaching that simply cannot be lived, which is why the culture rejects it. However, if God is the foundation of my relationship with my wife, then my wife and I can image Him and reveal His love to the world by the way we love each other. Our lives and our bodies can be an offering to others, just as Christ offered His total self for us.

Superheroes

Our bodies are temples of the Holy Spirit, and we are called to glorify God in and through our bodies. This is really what living a life of chastity is about, whether we are married or celibate. Like the other virtues, chastity is a spiritual weapon that gives us power. It is not about repression or saying no to our sexuality. It is, in fact, about saying yes to the power we are given to reveal God's love to the world in and through our bodies. The Church's teaching on sex is not "Just say no." We need to help people understand that chastity is about saying yes to God's design for love and sexuality. What is at stake? Infinite happiness. We have the power to participate in the creation of human souls, and we are called to play a role in their salvation.

To that end, I have already mentioned how God often uses what we want to get what He wants. We should utilize the same logic when passing on the faith to others, especially young people. One powerful tool we can use is movies, and I think the *Spider-Man* movie trilogy starring Tobey Maguire is actually a tremendous reflection on the Theology of the Body. When Peter Parker, a skinny and weak teenager, is bitten by the genetically designed "superspider", he receives superhuman strength and ability. At the same time, many villains throughout the trilogy receive superhuman power as well. Peter Parker and each of the villains have to face the same question: How will I use my power?

Just like these characters, we each have God-given power and free will. Will we use the power for good or for evil? Will we use it to live the authentic truth of God's love or to follow after the enemy's counterfeits and deceptions?

The Search for Meaning in the Gift

When Peter Parker first becomes Spider-Man, he begins experimenting with his newfound abilities. From beating up a bully to experiencing the thrill of swinging from building to building through New York City, he tests the limits of what he can do. Soon after, to impress the girl he loves, Peter decides to use his power to win money in order to buy a car. Then, after discovering that his uncle Ben was shot and killed by a robber, he uses his power to find the robber and get revenge.

However, Peter discovers that using his gift to gain power, pleasure, wealth, and vengeance does not seem like the right thing to do. He begins to reflect on what his uncle Ben was trying to tell him in their final conversation in the original Spiderman movie: "These are the years when a man changes into the man he's going to become the rest of his life. Just be careful who you change into ... remember, with great power comes great responsibility." Peter realizes he has a gift, a gift not meant to be used for himself but for the good of mankind. He begins to play the role of hero and uses his gift to save others.

This is what chastity is all about: using our bodies and gifts not for ourselves but to help others. But that is not what the world preaches. Strip clubs, pornography, fornication, adultery, and all sins of the flesh seek to satisfy the self at the cost of another. Chastity seeks to make a gift of self for the sake of another. Easy, right? Of course not. Chastity is hard. It is a battle with several opponents we must be willing to face. This is another reason why we can use Spider-Man in teaching the Theology of the Body. Peter Parker faces the same three opponents you and I face—what the Church calls the world, the devil, and the flesh.

The World

Peter Parker quickly realizes that being a hero is not so easy. After all his sacrifices for the people of the city, he receives no recognition and is accused of being a criminal. The newspaper editor for the *Daily Bugle*, J. Jonah Jameson, does not have any superhuman powers, but I want to reflect on his connection to our own mass media. The media certainly can influence the way people see things, and in the *Spider-Man* movies, Jameson is determined to get the public to view Spider-Man as a menace instead of a hero. In fact, one reason Peter Parker decides to quit being Spider-Man for a short time is because nobody appreciates the sacrifices he makes to save others.

The strong influence of mass media is certainly true for our age. Consider the Catholic Church's teachings on love and chastity. If two people understand, appreciate, and follow the teachings of the Catholic Church before and during marriage, their chances of getting a sexually transmitted disease (STD) from each other are zero. Their chances of an unwanted pregnancy are zero (even if a child is a surprise, it is always valued as a precious gift). Their rate of divorce has been shown to be significantly less than

the general population.[4] Their chances of having children out of wedlock are zero. Their chances of negative
side effects from birth control pills or contraceptive sur-
geries are zero. Imagine a world with fewer STDs, fewer
unwanted pregnancies, fewer divorces, and fewer children
born out of wedlock. Each of these plays a part in poverty,
crime, and health-care crises, so to reduce the former is
to reduce the latter. People often claim that what they do
in the privacy of their own home does not affect anybody
else, but this simply is not true. What we do in the privacy
of our own home does affect everybody. This is not just
claimed by the Church. The report *Sexually Transmitted
Disease Surveillance 2013* by the Centers for Disease Control
and Prevention (CDC) says in its foreword:

> STDs are hidden epidemics of enormous health and eco-
> nomic consequence in the United States.... All Americans
> have an interest in STD prevention because all commu-
> nities are impacted by STDs and all individuals directly or
> indirectly pay for the costs of these diseases. STDs are pub-
> lic health problems that lack easy solutions because they
> are rooted in human behavior and fundamental societal
> problems.... Indeed, there are many obstacles to effective
> prevention efforts. The first hurdle will be to confront the
> reluctance of American society to openly confront issues
> surrounding sexuality and STDs.[5]

But despite the beauty and the benefits of the Church's
teachings, and their profound implication for our bodies,

[4] *What's Wrong with Contraception?* (Cincinnati, Ohio: Couple to Couple
League International); Mercedes Arzú Wilson, "The Practice of Natural Family
Planning versus the Use of Artificial Birth Control: Family, Sexual, and Moral
Issues", *Catholic Social Science Review* 7 (November 2002): 185–211.

[5] *Sexually Transmitted Disease Surveillance 2013* (Atlanta: U.S. Department of
Health and Human Services, 2014), Centers for Disease Control and Prevention website, https://www.cdc.gov/std/stats13/default.htm.

marriages, families, and sexuality, the culture and media portray the Catholic Church not as a hero but as a menace. She is often described and viewed as bigoted and uncompassionate because she does not condone certain behaviors (behaviors that the CDC has proven over and over to be dangerous and harmful). In addition, some people focus not on whether the Church's teachings are correct but on whether they are possible. Since they believe that the teachings on sexuality are impossible to live, they consider it cruel of the Church to expect people to adhere to them. So in regard to sexuality, the Church is seen as a judgmental villain, not a hero, and young people who try to live a chaste lifestyle are often ridiculed.

But this is the same Church that heroically helps those in need, providing relief to the poor, those in crisis pregnancies, and anybody who is suffering, as we will read about in the next chapter. When she performs the corporal works of mercy, she does not ask the people if they are Catholic; she asks if they are hungry or hurting. But she does not want just to relieve suffering; she wants to prevent it, and her teachings on sexuality aim to do that. So whether one agrees with the Church or not, she deserves respect when she teaches chastity instead of lust.

To those parents teaching their children right from wrong, to the brave doctors telling patients about the dangers of the sexual revolution, to the courageous priests willing to speak the truth even when it is not popular, and to the young people who suffer much ridicule to uphold the dignity of their bodies, I say: Continue playing the part of hero. Even when people mock you, condemn you, and accuse you of many things; even when newspaper reporters like J. Jonah Jameson twist the facts to turn even those people you are trying to save against you, continue speaking and living the truth anyway. Do not quit being

"Spider-Man", because we all need heroes. Eventually, people will come searching for the truth when they are left feeling empty by all the temporary pleasures they thought would make them happy. If you are there to show them true love and authentic truth, they will want what you have and come to see you as the hero you are.

The Devil

Satan, in his cleverness, knows that God is truth and love and that our hearts are restless without Him. Satan also knows that he cannot create his own truth, so he takes a different tack—he simply takes the real truth, twists it, and presents the twisted version as the actual truth. This is genius. He creates counterfeits that contain traces of the truth, which makes his lies and deceptions more attractive and believable. For example, he takes love and distorts it into the counterfeit of lust. He uses the beauty of God's creation to attempt to make us forget about the Creator. He is the deceiver, the father of lies, and he will always try to make a deal with you, a truce with you. Going back to Genesis 3, we see how the devil (the serpent) uses temptation and deception to convince Adam and Eve that their happiness lies in grasping at the things of this world instead of trusting a loving God to provide them with everything they need to be happy.

We see a parallel in the first *Spider-Man* movie with its villain the Green Goblin. He offers Spider-Man a truce, encouraging him to imagine how much power they could have if they worked together. The Green Goblin starts off as a good man with good intentions but decides to use his power to gain wealth, power, honor, and pleasure—in other words, accomplishments only for himself. He tells Peter that only fools are heroes and that people are not worth saving. Despite the fact that the people do not appreciate Spider-Man, Peter decides to help them anyway and uses his power to do good.

At one point, though, Peter Parker begins to ask the question the enemy wants him to ask: What's in it for me? Being Spider-Man instead of pursuing worldly goods has kept Peter poor and living in an old, run-down apartment. This is one reason that Peter decides in *Spider-Man 2* that he does not have to use his power. He can just be a "normal" person and live a comfortable life.

This choice to repress his powers unfortunately reflects the caricature of Church teaching about the meaning of the body and sexuality, in which the message is "Just don't do it", as if sex were wrong and dirty—that is, as if young people were being told just to take a cold shower and pretend they did not have desires or feelings. This is like telling Spider-Man not to use his powers. Our sexuality is a gift. It should not be repressed or seen as a curse. Again, it gives us the power to help create souls and the power to help save souls.

As I said before, though, Satan is a genius. If we take his bait and fall for his lies, his strategy changes from deceiver to accuser. He begins to convince us that we are no longer worth saving and that God could not possibly love us now. How often does guilt weigh us down when we get into a cycle of sin? Once we have used others or allowed ourselves to be used as an object, we begin to feel hopeless. We become numb to sin because it just does not seem to matter anymore; we have fallen too far. The enemy whispers, "God does not love you. If He loved you, then why are you alone? Why do you suffer? Why did He let you fail? And if you loved Him, how could you have committed such horrible sins?" Can you hear that voice? That is why the crucifix is so essential. The crucifix is the rebuttal to all the enemy's accusations. When you hear the voice of the enemy, tell him to go to hell, and cling to that crucifix. You can see that God loves you! No matter what you have done, Christ shed His blood for you because He loves you and knows you can always be made new in Him.

The Flesh

As challenging as the world and devil are in this battle of chastity, the greatest battle lies within. In *Spider-Man 3*, Peter comes face-to-face with his own dark side. He is taken over by a "black suit" that turns him into something ugly. In the movie trailer, when he puts it on, you hear him say, "The power ... it feels good ... you can lose yourself to it." The black suit makes him aggressive, mean-spirited, and vengeful. After finally realizing that even Spider-Man needs help sometimes, where does Peter Parker go to find help? To a Catholic church! You can see him tearing off the black suit in the bell tower of the church. This is fitting, since it is the Catholic Church, through the power of Jesus Christ, that has freed so many from a life of sin and addiction.

The best quote of the movie series comes at a funeral near the end of *Spider-Man 3*. Peter says, "Whatever comes our way, whatever battles are raging inside of us, we always have a choice. It is the choices that make us who we are, and we can always choose to do what is right."

Regardless of who our parents are; regardless of our laundry lists of sins; regardless of our salaries, the schools we went to, whom we are dating, or how many points we scored in the big game, we always have a choice. No force on earth, or in hell, can take our will from us. We are always free to choose either the "saint inside of us" or the "Satan side of us". Choose wisely.

Mother Knows Best

We have laid the foundation of the Theology of the Body, and we have studied the opponents we face in the battle to live chaste lives. Now we must apply the teaching to some of the pressing moral social issues of our day. These issues can be extremely challenging, and I am well aware that this chapter is probably the most difficult for many to accept and agree with. I have found that teaching the Theology of the Body in a culture where it is extremely countercultural can be frustrating and difficult, and sometimes it seems safest and easiest just to avoid these topics all together. However, we cannot do that. As parents, catechists, friends, and citizens of a great country, we must find a way to dialogue about these issues in a healthy way. The Theology of the Body really is a beautiful teaching—it is the diary we spoke of earlier, but we must remember that teaching it in truth *and* love is vitally important. We should aim not to win arguments but to win hearts.

Before we can have a discussion and pass this teaching on to anybody, we must have a common ground, and I believe I know what that common ground is: Most people truly want to do what is best for others and believe that others deserve to be treated with love and respect. The frustrating thing is that although the Church also believes this, she regularly gets accused of bigotry or discrimination. People fail to understand that the Church is our mother, and parents always want to do what is best for their children, even if doing so sometimes results in resentment from their children who misunderstand. For example, if my children are playing with a lighter and setting things on fire, I am going to take the lighter away even if I know they will throw a huge tantrum and accuse me of being mean and unfair. I would rather they hated me than I see them get hurt or hurt others. The Church, as our mother, is always going to encourage us to do what is best for us, even when it is hard.

Imagine that someone comes up to you complaining about a pain in his hand. You look at it and notice a very large pin stuck in it. As you go to take it out, he stops you and says, "Ignore the pin. Just give me some pills for the pain." Seems silly, right? As a doctor, though, I regularly see what has been called a "treat the symptoms without treating the disease" mentality. When most people have a fever, a head that hurts, a body that aches, or a nose that runs, what is the first thing they do? They run to the drugstore to get medication to reduce the fever, numb the pain, and stop the runny nose. But what do all these symptoms mean? Do they mean your body is not working correctly? Actually, they mean your immune system is doing its job. The fever is actually a sign that the body is fighting the infection. A runny nose is your body's way of flushing out the virus. The problem is not the runny nose, achy body, and fever (though sometimes medication is necessary to make the symptoms more tolerable). The problem is an intruding virus that was able to attack your body probably because it was worn down, out of shape, or unhealthy. Yet many people treat the symptoms without getting the rest, exercise, or good diet needed actually to get rid of the underlying cause.

The same mentality is demonstrated when it comes to sexual morality. There are signs of sickness everywhere in our culture—high rates of divorce, depression, pornography use, crime, abuse, STDs, out-of-wedlock pregnancies, and abortions. These are all symptoms that something is wrong.

Yes, we need to treat those symptoms and help relieve the suffering that exists; but if we do not start changing the behaviors that cause the symptoms, the symptoms will not only remain but get worse. Choices have consequences, and these statistics are not cases of things that happen to victims just by chance. When we act against nature, bad things happen. Instead of trying just to minimize consequences, we have to get to the root of the problem.

Is addressing the root easy? Painless? Of course not. Because of man's sinful nature, true love involves suffering, which makes it difficult to teach the Theology of the Body in a world that rejects any meaning in suffering. But can't God use even suffering as a catalyst to help us make better decisions? For example, if my children touch a hot burner, I want it to hurt so that they yank their hands away before their bodies are permanently scarred and so that they remember never to do that again. If they cannot feel pain, they will certainly end up destroying themselves. As a culture, we are destroying ourselves, and we continue simply to put anesthetic on the pain as we continue doing the same things.

As we go through these different issues, I hope you can see the Church as the loving mother who does not want to see her children suffer instead of as an overbearing parent trying to keep her children from having any fun. Her teachings are not to be followed simply because she says so but because they come from God, the perfect parent, who created you and knows what brings you true joy and happiness.

Chastity outside of Marriage

We have discussed how love means choosing what is best for your beloved and how sexual intimacy is supposed to be the expression of wedding vows. Two people who are not married may in fact love each other, but sexual intimacy between them would be lying with their bodies. There is a great power in this sacred act, and as we have noted above, with great power comes great responsibility. Until you make the vow to give everything to the other person freely, totally, faithfully, and fruitfully, then you have not vowed to take responsibility for the power you have been given. If people are not willing to take responsibility for the act and make a total gift of self until death, then poverty, abortion, infidelity, and fatherless children will often result.

We can go back to our favorite web-slinging hero to see a willingness to sacrifice for love. At the conclusion of the first *Spider-Man* movie, Mary Jane, whom Peter is in love with, finally confesses her love for him. Peter's response is something that would probably shock most people: He tells her they can be only friends. He says this not because he does not love her anymore but because he loves her more than ever. Spider-Man will always have enemies, who will go after the people he loves. So Peter decides to protect Mary Jane from evil by not going out with her. His decision was not based on his libido or what would make him *feel* happier. It was based on love, which *chooses* what is best for the beloved.

This mentality is heard in an insightful statement from *Spider-Man 2*: "Sometimes, to do what is right, you have to give up the things you want the most." Young people often desire more than anything to be sexually intimate with a boyfriend or girlfriend. However, the earlier they start having sex, the more likely they are to experience depression and engage in high-risk behaviors.[6] Depression

---

[6] Denise D. Hallfors et al., "Which Comes First in Adolescence: Sex and Drugs or Depression?", *American Journal of Preventative Medicine* 29 (2005): 3.

and high-risk behaviors can put them at more risk for living in poverty, acquiring STDs, having children out of wedlock, enduring broken relationships, and performing poorly in school. Meg Meeker, a well-known pediatrician, speaks and writes often about the correlation of teen sexual activity and all these dangers. I strongly encourage all fathers to read her book *Strong Fathers, Strong Daughters* to open their eyes to the dangers young people face.[7]

The spiritual harm sin does is its most destructive side effect, but it is important to point out the emotional and physical dangers to young people. It is never loving to have sex with your boyfriend or girlfriend, because it is never loving to lie, and your body is making promises it has not vowed to keep. If you love the other, you will learn to express your affection through different means until you have made those sacred vows. This is part of what separates the world's idea of love from genuine love.

The idea of sacrificing for the good of the other is also true concerning those who experience same-sex attraction. This hot-button issue can be difficult to talk about because it is emotionally charged. After all, many of us love people who experience same-sex attraction. Since those who experience same-sex attraction simply want what everybody else wants—to love and be loved—the Catholic Church's teaching against homosexual acts can seem harsh and lacking in compassion. But a lot of the hatred directed toward the Church regarding this matter is due to misinformation or ignorance.

The Catholic Church does not teach that experiencing same-sex attraction is sinful. Homosexual tendencies are disordered desires, and because of concupiscence—the tendency to do wrong because of original sin—everyone has disordered desires. In this context, "disordered" means

<hr />

[7] *Strong Fathers, Strong Daughters* (New York: Ballantine Books, 2007).

that something is not being used for the purpose it was made. For example, if I use a hammer to try to cut my hair, that is a disordered use of the hammer. Now consider our reproductive organs. Each is designed so that it can unite with the reproductive organ of someone of the opposite sex in an action with life-creating potential. Two people of the same sex cannot fulfill the design—and therefore the purpose—of their reproductive organs with each other in either the unitive or the procreative aspect. This truth may seem unloving. After all, if two people of the same sex love each other, shouldn't they be able to express that love however they like? But let us look at how science confirms the negative effects of not using our reproductive organs according to their design. According to both the CDC and the Gay and Lesbian Medical Association, those who engage in same-sex acts are much more likely than heterosexuals to be promiscuous, engage in high-risk behaviors, be depressed, acquire STDs (some of which are deadly) because of these high-risk behaviors, and abuse drugs and alcohol.[8] Those are not behaviors that describe love.

The response of the medical world is simply to offer more protection against STDs in the form of condoms and very expensive drugs, such as Truvada, a drug designed to be taken as a daily pill to prevent HIV infection in people at high risk, such as males who engage in homosexual acts. (This drug would cost in the neighborhood of $1,500 a month, yet insurance companies often cover 100 percent of the cost for those who choose to live this high-risk lifestyle.) The CDC quote mentioned earlier admitted that

[8] "Ten Things Gay Men Should Discuss with Their Healthcare Provider", GLMA Health Professionals Advancing LGBT Equality, http://glma.org/index.cfm?fuseaction=Page.viewPage&pageID=690. GLMA also provides the top ten things to discuss with your health-care provider for lesbian, bisexual, and transgender persons.

STDs are "public health problems ... rooted in human be-havior", yet we are unwilling to admit that these human behaviors are dangerous, and therefore we are unwilling to get to the root of the problem.

If you are encouraging the people you love to act out on their same-sex attraction, I think it is important that you ask why those high-risk behaviors are so common and therefore whether it is loving to tell them to embrace their desires. Are they allowed to love? Of course they are. They need and deserve to love and be loved. But love is not synonymous with sexual intimacy.

So what does this mean for people who experience same-sex attraction? As the *Catechism of the Catholic Church* explains:

> The number of men and women who have deep-seated homosexual tendencies is not negligible. This inclination, which is objectively disordered, constitutes for most of them a trial. They must be accepted with respect, compassion, and sensitivity. Every sign of unjust discrimination in their regard should be avoided. These persons are called to fulfill God's will in their lives and, if they are Christians, to unite to the sacrifice of the Lord's Cross the difficulties they may encounter from their condition.
>
> Homosexual persons are called to chastity. By the virtues of self-mastery that teach them inner freedom, at times by the support of disinterested friendship, by prayer and sacramental grace, they can and should gradually and resolutely approach Christian perfection.[9]

Is the self-mastery asked of those who experience same-sex attraction easy? Not at first, just as it is not easy for heterosexuals to practice self-mastery at first. But once

[9] *CCC* 2358–59.

again, because true love in a fallen world is never easy, it requires a willingness to sacrifice. This is why the Catholic Church's teaching is so liberating for those who experience same-sex attraction. Just like everyone else, they have a particular cross to carry, and just like everyone else, they are destined to be saints. It is not homosexual versus heterosexual; it is being chaste versus being unchaste. The good news is that whether we have homosexual desires or heterosexual desires, we are not doomed to act on our disordered desires. Our desires do not define who we are, and Christ gives us strength to choose what is best for ourselves and those we love. So please start evaluating and, if applicable, criticizing what you hear from a homosexual agenda that is so adamant about normalizing homosexual behavior that it ignores facts that can really hurt our friends and family. The motive of the Church's teaching is not to discriminate against or judge those with same-sex attraction. The Church wants what is best for them, whether they believe that or not.

Chastity within Marriage

Many people understand the idea of being chaste outside the context of marriage, but what does chastity have to do with two people who are already married? Simply put, saying, "We are now married, so we don't need to be chaste anymore. Yay!" is the same thing as saying, "We are now married, so we don't have to love each other anymore. Yay!" Part of the problem is that people often mistakenly interchange the words "chastity" and "abstinence". For example, the "chastity" entry at Vocabulary. com reads, "If you practice chastity, it means you aren't having sex of any kind, perhaps because you're waiting until you get married, or maybe because you believe sex is evil." What a laughable definition of chastity, and one the Church strongly disagrees with.

YOUCAT, the Catholic Church's catechism for teens, says this about chastity: "A chaste love is a love that defends itself against all the internal and external forces that might destroy it.... Chastity and continence are not the same thing. Someone who has an active sex life in marriage must be chaste, too. A person acts chastely when his bodily activity is the expression of dependable, faithful love."[10]

Remember that the body is supposed to make visible the invisible reality of God's love, since we are made in His image. Sexual activity is supposed to be a renewal of wedding vows, where the vows expressed verbally on your wedding day become expressed physically. The body says in the act, "I will freely give all of myself to you and will faithfully be with you until death. I give you everything—my fatherhood, my motherhood, my talents and abilities, my time, my very life." Chastity is expressing love in our minds and with our bodies, whether that is by practicing self-discipline before marriage or by properly engaging in the marital embrace after the wedding.

One reason marriage is on the decline is that people no longer understand the covenantal nature of marriage. Marriage is viewed as a contract, an exchange of goods, where each person promises to provide happiness and pleasure in exchange for happiness and pleasure from the other. What happens when someone decides that the marriage no longer brings him happiness or pleasure? He "voids" the marriage, just like he would void a contract where the other side does not uphold his end. But marriage is much more than a contract; it is a covenant. A covenant is not

---

[10] *YOUCAT* (San Francisco: Ignatius Press, 2011), 404.

an exchange of goods ("I'll give you pleasure if you give me pleasure") but an exchange of persons ("I am yours and you are mine"). This is why marriage images God's love; He gives us His very self freely, totally, faithfully, and fruitfully and asks us to do the same for our spouses. The marital embrace is meant to make that covenantal love visible. So why is fornication sinful? It replaces the solemn, deep, covenantal love that sex is meant to convey with a shallow, contractual distortion based on pleasure. Or in the words of Jason Evert: It is not that sex outside of marriage is going too far; it is that it is not going far enough.

While marriage is essential for the full expression of love in the marital embrace, it is no guarantee that every sexual act in marriage is an expression of love. After marriage, chastity can still be a struggle, and the body can still speak lies. Some lies are obvious: Adultery shares an action meant for the spouse with someone who is not the spouse, and pornography trains us to see the other as an object to be used, ruining countless marriages. Both of these lack the aspects of being free, total, and faithful.

While most people still see adultery and using pornography as obviously nonloving, there is another example of a lie with the body that may be more challenging to understand and accept. The Church's teaching against contraception can be a tough pill to swallow (pun intended).

First, a little history. Every Christian denomination taught that contraception was immoral up until the 1930s, when the Anglican church accepted it first in limited circumstances, and then more generally. Since then, every Christian denomination except the Catholic Church has followed suit and changed its stance on the morality of contraception. It is the Church's teaching on contraception that many Catholics struggle with the most, but perhaps it is through this teaching that the Church has proven her authenticity the most. In the 1960s, when the contraceptive pill was becoming popular and widely available, everybody thought that the Church would finally "get with the times" and change her stance on contraception. However, Pope Paul VI shocked the world in 1968 with the encyclical *Humanae Vitae* (Of human life), in which he reinforced the Church's consistent teaching that contraception is immoral and gave some stern warnings about what would happen if the world embraced a contraceptive mentality.

Carefully read these prophetic words Pope Paul VI wrote in 1968 about the consequences of contraception:

> Let them first consider how easily this course of action could open wide the way for marital infidelity and a general lowering of moral standards. Not much experience is needed to be fully aware of human weakness and to understand that human beings—and especially the young, who are so exposed to temptation—need incentives to keep the moral law, and it is an evil thing to make it easy for them to break that law. Another effect that gives cause for alarm is that a man who grows accustomed to the use of contraceptive methods may forget the reverence due to a woman, and, disregarding her physical and emotional equilibrium, reduce her to being a mere instrument for the satisfaction of his own desires, no longer considering her as his partner whom he should surround with care and affection.
>
> Finally, careful consideration should be given to the danger of this power passing into the hands of those public authorities who care little for the precepts of the moral law. Who will blame a government which in its attempt to resolve the problems affecting an entire country resorts to the same measures as are regarded as lawful by married people in the solution of a particular family difficulty?

Who will prevent public authorities from favoring those contraceptive methods which they consider more effective? Should they regard this as necessary, they may even impose their use on everyone.[11]

So Pope Paul VI predicted that with widely available contraception, infidelity would increase, young people would be much more tempted into sexual immorality, men would lose respect for women, and countries would use it to control entire populations (think of China). Everything he said came true—and more. Since 1968 the rates of divorce, abortion, STDs, and domestic violence have all skyrocketed. Some argue that it is just a coincidence, but these tragedies logically follow from the mentality that contraception creates. Instead of being "behind the times", Pope Paul VI demonstrated that the Church understood what "the times" had in store for us if contraception became widely available.

Even those who disagree with the Church should admire her courage in being consistent with her teaching despite its lack of popularity. Truth is not decided by popular vote. Pope Paul VI went on to admit that the teaching on contraception would be hard for people to accept, but the Church has no authority to speak against the true moral and natural law. I love the following quote from *Humanae Vitae*, where we see the humility of the Church:

But it comes as no surprise to the Church that she, no less than her divine Founder, is destined to be a "sign of contradiction." She does not, because of this, evade the duty imposed on her of proclaiming humbly but firmly the entire moral law, both natural and evangelical. Since the Church did not make either of these laws, she cannot be their

[11] *Humanae Vitae*, 17.

arbiter—only their guardian and interpreter. It could never be right for her to declare lawful what is in fact unlawful, since that, by its very nature, is always opposed to the true good of man.[12]

To clarify, the Church does *not* teach that contraception is wrong simply because it is unnatural. After all, pharmaceuticals are unnatural, but we do not consider it immoral. For those that object that if medicine is OK, then the pill should also be, please keep in mind that contraception is not medicine. Medicine is meant to help the body work the way it was designed to. In other words, it fixes something broken. Contraception, on the other hand, tries to break something that is working. In addition, the list of possible side effects of the contraceptive pill are extensive, including stroke, blot clots, and cancer. The contraception pill is actually classified as a Group 1 carcinogen by the World Health Organization. Knowing this, husbands need to ask themselves a serious question: Is it loving to ask my wife, even if she is willing, to take such a pill? Ironically, our country has had a health-care mandate to provide these carcinogens free of charge to perfectly healthy women. Once again, this an attempt to make their own "natural law", with bad consequences.

While the obvious physical dangers of the contraceptive pill should give us pause, the ultimate reason contraception is considered immoral is that it violates the wedding vows, and every act of the marital embrace must be faithful to the vows we express at the altar. The marital embrace must be a free gift of self, a total gift of self, with each spouse faithful to the other, and ordered toward procreation. Regarding the last aspect, some argue they can be open to life

[12] Ibid., 18.

and therefore fulfill their wedding vows without *every* act being ordered toward procreation, but try that logic with the other parts of the vows. It is like saying, "I can be faithful to my wife and therefore fulfill my wedding vows without *every* sexual act being with her."

We cannot separate unity and procreation. Every sexual act must be open to unifying the couple *and* also must be open to the fruit that can come from that unity. Rape can be ordered toward procreation, but it is no way unitive. In the same way, a contraceptive act may be in some ways unitive, but it is not ordered toward procreation. (Note: This is NOT equating the sinfulness of rape with that of contraception.) When we have a contraceptive mentality, it affects how we view a new life that may result from the act despite our best efforts to prevent it. The new life is viewed as something that went wrong. That is why contraception does not reduce abortions; it leads to them. Abortion has skyrocketed since contraception became widely available, and the U.S. Supreme Court has even ruled that abortion is necessary because contraception can fail.

The separation of the marital embrace from the conception of children is why contraception is really at the root of all these issues of sexual morality. It is much more difficult to argue against homosexual acts on the basis that the acts are intrinsically sterile when you are artificially sterilizing yourself at the same time. (In fact, supporters of giving the drug Truvada to prevent HIV infection in homosexual men argue that it is no different from giving contraceptive pills to women.) It is more difficult to speak about the awe and responsibility that comes with the act when you remove its most powerful and awe-inspiring function. Once you separate procreation from the sexual act, it is a slippery slope, a slope we are sliding down as a culture. The act becomes a simple form of recreation, with the possible hazards of pregnancy and disease, so "Protect yourself" becomes the mantra. It is like the culture is saying, "If you drive a car, wear a seatbelt. If you play football, wear a helmet. If you have sex, wear a condom." We have taken the sacred and turned it into something trivial and without meaning. Again, an act that forces you to protect yourself from danger is not an act of true self-giving love.

Yet, condemning contraception does not mean we are obligated to have as many children as biologically possible. The Church fully supports and encourages the responsible spacing of children through Natural Family Planning (NFP), which is scientifically proven to be 98 to 99 percent effective, just like the pill.[13] (Even the package insert for the contraceptive pill references the effectiveness of NFP.) It involves abstaining during the fertile periods of a woman's cycle, and there are several different methods to help track the cycle, even if it is irregular. There is a "downside" to NFP, which I assume is why many people do not consider it. It is hard at first—usually not hard to figure out but just hard to do. This is because it involves self-discipline and sacrifice. However, love is not afraid of those things; love *is* those things. After all, if you cannot abstain for seven to ten days out of the month for your spouse's or family's sake, then are you really free? In addition, there are many benefits to NFP. It works with the woman's natural fertility cycle. If pregnancy is desired,

---

[13] "The Effectiveness of a Fertility Awareness Based Method to Avoid Pregnancy in Relation to a Couple's Sexual Behaviour during the Fertile Time: A Prospective Longitudinal Study", *Human Reproduction*, doi:10.1093/humrep/dem003, cited in European Society for Human Reproduction and Embryology, "Natural Family Planning Method as Effective as Contraceptive Pill, New Research Finds", reprinted in *ScienceDaily*, February 21, 2007, http://www.sciencedaily.com/releases/2007/02/070221065200.htm.

NFP can help couples conceive. It builds communication between the spouses and fosters teamwork. There are no harmful side effects. Jason Evert recorded a talk titled "Green Sex" that goes through all the advantages of NFP, and I highly recommend it.[14] Jason Evert's presentations to adults and teens are entertaining, relevant, packed with research and statistics, and in no way judgmental.

In addition, I highly recommend Christopher West's materials, including his book *Good News about Sex and Marriage*.[15] While this book answers pretty much any question regarding the Theology of the Body, let me touch on perhaps the most common question regarding contraception and NFP: What is the difference? After all, making yourself infertile or simply waiting until you are naturally infertile both have the same result—no baby. Christopher West answers this question with some of his own. What is the difference between an abortion and a miscarriage? Both result in a dead baby. What is the difference between killing Grandma and just waiting for her to die naturally? Both result in the same dead grandma. I hope you can see that there is a monumental difference in these two acts that end with the same results.

Can NFP be abused? Yes, if the couple decides not to have a child for purely selfish reasons. That is why it is up to the couple prayerfully to use their reasoning to determine if they have a serious reason to abstain; but it is important that children are always seen as a blessing, even if one comes as a surprise when we do not feel ready. After all, children are one of the main purposes of marriage, and we promise to "accept children lovingly from God" in the vows.

---

[14] "Green Sex", CD, available from the Chastity Project, http://www.chastityproject.com.

[15] *Good News about Sex and Marriage* (Cincinnati, Ohio: Servant, 2004).

Ironically, it is often the fruit of the spouses' love who teaches us what love really is. Having children is indeed difficult; nobody can deny that. Having children requires a huge dying to self, a huge sacrifice, and a lot of suffering. Once again, love is not afraid of those things; love is those things. Children teach us to die to self, to serve, and to lay down our lives for others in sacrificial love. Perhaps that is why we so often avoid them and why the Church's teaching against contraception seems like such a cross. Raising my children has no doubt been the greatest challenge of my life but also the greatest blessing. There will be suffering, but there will be great fruit from that suffering.

This does not mean that a couple who is unable to conceive a child because of unintentional infertility due to age, sickness, etc., has any less of a marriage. We are called to be open to life, and a couple infertile because of the reasons mentioned above can be just as open to life as a couple who has ten children.

However, when we purposely make the sexual act sterile, create human life in a petri dish, or engage in sexual acts that are intrinsically infertile (such as those between two men or two women), we push God out of the picture and try to become God ourselves, creating our own relative truth about what is good and what is evil. If we remember the story, that was the very first temptation the serpent used—to eat from the tree of knowledge of good and evil.

The Dignity of Human Life

The basis for the Church's teaching on the dignity of human life is that every life is valuable, every person is made in God's image, and our bodies are temples of the

Holy Spirit. No matter how small or weak we perceive a human life to be, that person deserves to be cherished, not based on what he can do but because of who he is—a child made in the image of the Most High God. This will help us understand why embryonic stem cell research and in vitro fertilization are immoral. These are some tough issues that get to the heart of human suffering.

Going back to the Spider-Man characters, I cannot help but think of the villain Sandman, whose daughter is very ill. He cannot afford the medical bills, so, desperate to help his daughter, he becomes a thief who ends up killing Peter Parker's uncle Ben.

It is hard not to feel sorry for the Sandman. After all, he is a parent who just wants to help his daughter. Unfortunately, he is willing to harm others to try to help her. At the end of the movie, he tells Peter he is sorry for killing his uncle. The Sandman does not expect forgiveness; he just wants Peter to understand, telling Peter he "did not have a choice". Peter does forgive him but also reminds him that we always have a choice.

The Catholic Church's teachings on embryonic stem cell research and in vitro fertilization can seem hypocritical at first glance. The Church is always promoting openness to life but rejects some technologies that can help those suffering from debilitating disease or that can help couples who are unable to have children. Just like the Sandman's situation, those who suffer from handicaps or infertility seem to have no choice but to do whatever is necessary by utilizing modern technology.

But also like the Sandman, they are willing to hurt other people (though probably unknowingly). We must remember that every human life is sacred, and that is why the direct destruction of human life that takes place in embryonic stem cell research and in vitro fertilization makes those actions immoral. The Church fully supports adult stem cell research, which is currently far more successful than the embryonic version, and the Church supports any medical technology that helps infertile couples be able to conceive, so long as life is not being destroyed in the process and it does not separate the generation of new life from the marital embrace. We cannot separate the unitive and procreative aspects of life-giving love.

Abortion is one of the ultimate examples of losing respect for the value of human life. As with many other issues, advocates for abortion claim it is done to relieve human suffering. Sometimes, they say, the suffering that is relieved is that of the mother; other times it may be that of the child, who would be brought up in a dangerous environment or with significant disabilities. After all, if a child is conceived in a mother who is not ready for a child, why bring the child into the world knowing that the baby will suffer along with the mother? Again, the mystery of human suffering is the key to understanding this. We all suffer in a fallen world. The answer is not to destroy the child. Perhaps the child is God's answer to the problem.

As an example, I once heard a young mother's testimony about when she became pregnant in college. Her roommates pleaded with her to have an abortion, so that her bright future would not be ruined. She contemplated the decision for a long time and in the end decided to keep the baby. She went on to explain how Jesus had helped her through the process. He is the Good Shepherd, she said, and sometimes shepherds have to go after lost sheep. The young woman believed that the pregnancy was Jesus' way of helping her realize how far she had wandered and how much she needed Him. She was making very poor moral choices, and spiritually her life was spiraling in the wrong direction. Having a baby changed everything for her. The baby became her whole life, and she realized that even though her baby brought suffering along with joy, the child had saved her from wandering away from Jesus. She said she could not imagine her life without her child, and she now works for a pregnancy crisis center to help other young mothers. But even if every situation does not have the happiest of endings, we must always remember that every life is beautiful and every child is a child made in the image of God. Regardless of how much suffering we endure in this life, it is nothing compared with the eternal joy we are destined to experience in heaven.

"Frozen" by Rules?

The culture projects its views and propaganda on our children from the time they are very young, so we must find ways early in our children's lives to root them in the truth about who they are and the meaning of their bodies. I have searched for ways to give my small children a foundation in the Theology of the Body. For example, I have three young daughters, and like every other little girl in America, they love the movie *Frozen*. (I personally found it a little tiring after my 472nd viewing with them.) I am usually skeptical of movies, but with the right pair of lenses we can catch a tremendous glimpse of the message behind Saint John Paul II's Theology of the Body in this particular movie. The theme song you could not get away from is "Let It Go", and left alone, this song can do considerable damage. With relativistic lyrics like "No right, no wrong, no rules for me, I'm free!" you would think it is the antithesis of the Theology of the Body. However, this song is not the climax of the movie, and if our children can see the consequences of what happens when you just "let it go", they will see that none of us is an island and that our choices always affect others.

The movie portrays dangers of extremes in feelings and attractions: repression and "letting go of right, wrong, and rules". Elsa was born with the power to create and control snow and ice. Since she has trouble controlling her powers and is told they are driven by emotion, her parents raise her with the motto of "Conceal, don't feel."

Predictably, Elsa gets to the point where she cannot repress them anymore and accidentally freezes the entire kingdom. Afraid of harming others with her power, Elsa runs away to the mountains, where she quickly transitions to the mind-set in the theme song. She eventually sees that the total freedom she craved did not bring the joy she had hoped. In the end, she realizes it is the properly directed use of her powers that brings joy both to her and to others.

This is the lesson the Church wishes to convey. What is the answer to temptation and disordered desires? What is the advice that should be given to people who are trying to save sex for marriage, who experience same-sex attraction, or who desire to watch pornography? The answer is not repression—and the answer is not "Let it go." Instead, the answer is true love, a love that has properly directed desires and actions.

We have already discussed how true love is a choice. The act of "true love" in *Frozen* is not a romantic kiss but an act of self-sacrifice. True love is, as Saint Paul describes, "to present your bodies as a living sacrifice" (Rom 12:1). Elsa discovers that her powers are not evil but were simply controlled by fear and pointed in the wrong direction— exactly what lust does to our feelings and attractions. Lust sacrifices others for the sake of self. Love sacrifices self for the sake of others. The lustful desires we have do not define who we are, and we are not doomed to act on them. With Jesus' help, we can reorient those desires toward love and use our gifts for good and not harm.

Frozen is just one example of how we can use what our children listen to, watch, and read to help them understand the value of their bodies, feelings, and love. Remember, though, that simply because something can be used as a tool to teach a valuable lesson does not mean we should always allow our children to be exposed to it. Be prudent in what you allow your children to experience, and be willing to experience it with them, so that you can better use it to communicate what is right, good, and just—to teach them that "with great power comes great responsibility."

This Is My Body

Reflecting on movies is great, but movies cannot compare with real-life stories. Before we close our reflection on the Theology of the Body, I would like to introduce you briefly to four very young saints whose powerful and heroic witness to courage and love can help us on our journeys. Saint José Sánchez del Río was martyred in 1928 during the Mexican Cristero War for aiding the Cristeros in their fight for religious freedom. Since he was only fourteen years old, government officials did not plan on executing him but instead forced him to watch other prisoners being hanged and gave him the option of returning home if he would simply utter, "Death to Christ the King." José had a deep love for Jesus Christ and refused to dishonor his King with those words. After slicing the bottoms of José's feet with a knife, enemy soldiers made him walk to the cemetery and forced him to look at his own grave before giving him one more chance to renounce his Lord and Savior. With an amazing courage, José shouted, "Viva Christo Rey! Viva Christo Rey!" which means "Long live Christ the King!" He was shot, but before he died, he used his own blood to draw a cross in the sand. José was martyred because he understood that it is better to die with God than to live without Him. His story is beautifully portrayed in the movie *For Greater Glory*.

Saint Maria Goretti was a victim of attempted rape when she was eleven years old. Refusing to give in, she was murdered by her nineteen-year-old attacker, Alessandro, whose farm her poor family worked on. After resisting and imploring Alessandro, "Do not touch me; it is a sin!" he stabbed her fourteen times. A day later she died in the hospital but not before forgiving Alessandro and praying for God to have mercy on him. Alessandro had a dream in prison that Maria was handing him a bouquet of lilies, and he had a conversion. He became very remorseful for his crime and was a model prisoner. After being released from prison early on good behavior, he joined the Franciscan Third Order.

Saint Agnes is another great example of a young virgin martyr. Even at the young age of twelve, Agnes was so beautiful that men came to ask for her hand in marriage. She denied their requests because she had consecrated herself to Christ. She lived at a time when it was illegal to be Christian, and one of the men she turned down was so filled with anger that he turned her in to the emperor Diocletian to be executed for being a Christian. Agnes was given many opportunities not only to save herself but to relish the luxuries of life if she would just renounce Christianity. But she was so strong in her convictions that her executioner was trembling at the thought of killing her. Diocletian urged many men to seduce her, but she cried out, "You may stain your sword with my blood, but you will never profane my body that I have consecrated to Christ." Then she turned to the nervous executioner stunned by her courage and said, "I already have a spouse, and I will not offend Him by pretending that another might please me. I will give myself only to Him who first chose me. So, executioner, what are you waiting for? Destroy this body that unwanted eyes desire." Saint Ambrose, the great bishop of Milan, said this about Agnes: "But maidens of that age are unable to bear even the angry looks of parents, and are wont to cry at the pricks of a needle as though they were wounds. She was fearless under the cruel hands of the executioners."[16] Agnes hurried to the place of her execution more joyfully than a bride goes to her wedding. Agnes is a great role model, especially for young women in our culture today.

As great as the stories of Blessed José Sánchez del Río, Saint Maria Goretti, and Saint Agnes are, the greatest saint story I have ever heard is that of Saint Philomena. I believe she must be one of the Catholic Church's best-kept secrets, and her story needs to be told. Like Agnes, she was also martyred by the haughty Diocletian, whom she refused to marry because she had consecrated herself to Jesus Christ, but not before performing many miracles that converted onlookers to Christianity. While this is remarkable in itself, it is after her death that things get even more interesting. Philomena's grave and story were not discovered until 1,500 years after her death! She was canonized solely based on the amazing power of her intercession, as hundreds of miracles began occurring as a result of prayers to her and veneration of her relics. On top of all

[16] Saint Ambrose, *Selected Words and Letters*, in The Nicene and Post Nicene Fathers of the Christian Church, vol. 10 (New York: Christian Literature Company, 1890–1900), 847.

the miracles, Saint Philomena was appearing to three different people in different locations giving them the story of her life. The three stories matched, even though the three people did not know each other or know about one another. The story given in Philomena's own words 1,500 years after her death is officially approved as authentic by the Catholic Church, and it is absolutely amazing.

Our young people need authentic witnesses to learn from and to model, especially in regard to chastity and courage. Saint José Sánchez del Río, Saint Maria Goretti, Saint Agnes, and Saint Philomena are powerful intercessors for young people and all of us. Each of these young martyrs, all younger than fifteen at the time of their deaths, took to heart the words of Jesus Christ, "This is my body which is given for you" (Lk 22:19). They not only believed in that love but echoed the same words back to their Savior in response to that love: "This is my body which is given for you."

Saint Maria Goretti, pray for us. Saint Agnes, pray for us. Saint José Sánchez del Río, pray for us. Saint Philomena, pray for us. Saint John Paul II, pray for us. Help us to see ourselves as sons and daughters of the Most High God, heirs to the kingdom of heaven, brides of Christ, saints in the making, and children of light. Help us to offer our bodies as living sacrifices, as you did, so we may reveal the love of God to the whole world.

For all the recommended resources for "Theology of the Body", go to the website: www.saintsinthemaking.com /theology-of-the-body-resources.html.

Chapter 6

S: SACRIFICE AND SERVICE

Color: Yellow, for Brightening Someone's Day

Let us never forget that authentic power is service, and that the Pope too, when exercising power, must enter ever more fully into that service which has its radiant culmination on the Cross.

—Pope Francis

A Missionary Church

Saints in the Making University (SIMU) will offer you many great resources to learn your faith and teach it to others. But SIMU is about more than books and resources. SIMU is about living the faith. Sooner or later, we must get out of the books and go be the hands and feet of Christ. We must go out into the world and encounter Christ in the poor, the afflicted, the hungry, and the lost. Once we encounter the living God, we discover we have been given a mission. Christianity is missionary in nature. Everyone in the story of salvation history who encounters God is given a mission, no matter how unworthy he appears to be.

Upon seeing the Lord seated on a high and lofty throne, the prophet Isaiah said, "Woe is me! For I am lost; for I am a man of unclean lips, and I dwell in the midst of a people of unclean lips; for my eyes have seen the King, the LORD of hosts!" (Is 6:5). When Moses encountered God in the burning bush, he "hid his face, for he was afraid to look at God" (Ex 3:6). When God told Moses to go to Egypt and free his people, Moses objected, "I am slow of speech and of tongue.... Oh, my Lord, send, I pray, some other person" (Ex 4:10, 13). When Gideon was told by the angel of the Lord to lead an army against the Midianites, Gideon responded, "Please, Lord, how can I deliver Israel? Behold, my clan is the weakest in Manasseh, and I am the least in my family" (Judg 6:15). When Jeremiah received his call to be a prophet, he said, "Ah, Lord GOD! Behold, I do not know how to speak, for I am only a youth" (Jer 1:6). When Peter saw the power and authority of Jesus, he said, "Depart from me, for I am a sinful man, O Lord" (Lk 5:8).

Every one of these significant characters in the story of salvation history saw himself as unworthy, and yet, Isaiah and Jeremiah went on to become great prophets; Moses became a great leader who led the Israelites to freedom from bondage and taught them the law of God; Gideon defeated a powerful army even though he was greatly outnumbered; and Peter went on to become the rock on which Christ would build His Church. Do you see what God did with these men? Despite their insistence that they did not have what it takes, God proved that the only thing they needed was faith and obedience. Their strength came from God, who was not afraid of their weakness and sin. In fact, their weakness and sin were proof of His power. It was almost as if God was saying to each of them, "I know you are weak, and I know you are sinful. But I've got a job for you."

In his documentary *Catholicism*, Father Robert Barron uses the story of Peter in Luke 5 in his introduction to the saints.[1] Father Barron points out that Peter was most likely a very successful fisherman. Jesus, uninvited, got into Peter's boat and then brought in a catch the likes of which Peter had never seen. This represents the invasion of grace. All it takes to become a saint is to allow Jesus to get in your boat. If you allow Jesus to live through you and guide your life, He will make you a fisher of men and your life will bear fruit beyond your wildest imagination.

Actions Speak Louder than Words

Serving others is not about what you alone can do by your power. It is about what God can do through you. Our discussion of the Theology of the Body shows us that love is a choice; it is an act of the will. After Jesus rose from the dead, he asked Peter three times, "Simon, son of John, do you love me?" Each time, Peter answers yes, and after each yes, Jesus gives him something to do: "Feed my lambs", "Tend my sheep", "Feed my sheep" (see Jn 21:15–18). Jesus is telling Peter, "Do not just tell Me; show Me." I mentioned that my father was not good with emotions. He never told his sons he loved them until he was dying. Now, people do need to hear these words, so do not mistake what I am about to say. I tell my wife and children I love them every single day, as every parent should. However, even though my father never said

---

[1] *Catholicism* (Skokie, Ill.: Word on Fire, 2011), disc 4, episode 8, DVD.

it, I never doubted that my father loved me because he showed me. I would rather have a parent who showed his love than a parent who just said he loved me. Love is an action. If you say, "I love you", every day, but never show your love through action, it is like saying, "I'll take out the trash today", but then never doing it. It would be better not even to say it.

Jesus gave us this lesson in the parable of the two sons (see Mt 21:28–32). When given the order to work in the vineyard, one son said he would and the other said he would not. However, each of them changed his mind, and the son who said he would not, did, and the son who said he would, did not. It was the son who did what he was told who *did* the father's will, not the one who *said* he would. As Christians, we cannot just say we love God. If we truly love God, we will "feed His sheep". Nobody will really listen to what you tell him if you are not willing to practice what you preach. In his encyclical *Evangelii Nuntiandi*, Pope Paul VI said, "Modern man listens more willingly to witnesses than to teachers, and if he does listen to teachers, it is because they are witnesses."[2]

The Little Way

There are many blessings that have brought me great joy and satisfaction in my life—winning a state championship; graduating as an eye doctor; fixing up an old house and making it into a home; getting my books published; running marathons; and most important, getting married and having children. While these are the things that have brought the most joy, I realize they are also the same

[2] *Evangelii Nuntiandi*, 41.

things that have required the most sacrifice and suffering. True love in a fallen world involves sacrifice. If you forget that, just look at a crucifix.

The most important things in life rarely require one huge sacrifice but instead require many small sacrifices. We can see a great witness of this truth in the life of Saint Thérèse of Lisieux. Saint Thérèse, a Doctor of the Church, taught us in her autobiography about her "little way". Very few people had even heard of Thérèse of Lisieux at the time of her death in 1897, but because of her autobiography, her fame quickly spread. People were drawn to Thérèse's little way because in her life we discover that we all have what it takes to become saints.

Saint Thérèse knew that compared with the great saints of the past, she was a "humble" grain of sand among great mountains.[3] She called herself a "little flower", and she decided that her path to heaven would be based not on being bigger but on being like a little child whom Jesus could carry to heaven. She decided she would do the small things in life with extraordinary love. This is our path to heaven. We can serve others through small acts of great love.

A Great Treasure

To serve others the way God wants us to, we must first come to view others the way God views them. Jesus tells us:

> The kingdom of heaven is like treasure hidden in a field, which a man found and covered up; then in his joy he goes and sells all that he has and buys that field.

[3] Saint Thérèse of Lisieux, *The Autobiography of Saint Therese of Lisieux: The Story of a Soul*, trans. John Beevers (New York: Doubleday, 2001), 113.

Again, the kingdom of heaven is like a merchant in search of fine pearls, who, on finding one pearl of great value, went and sold all that he had and bought it. (Mt 13:44–46)

For most of my life, I understood these parables only in the traditional way, as most people do. The kingdom of heaven is the treasure and the pearl, and we are the man or the merchant who should sell everything we have to obtain the kingdom.

However, there is another way to look at this story. God is the merchant, and we are the treasure. Jesus Christ paid the ultimate price; He gave everything He had, including His very life, to obtain salvation for our souls. He loves us that much. To God, we are His sons and daughters, heirs to His kingdom, and we are destined to be part of the kingdom of heaven. In His eyes, every human being is worth dying for. This means you are a great treasure and you were purchased at a very high price. "Do you not know that your body is a temple of the Holy Spirit within you, which you have from God? You are not your own; you were bought with a price. So glorify God in your body" (1 Cor 6:19–20).

Everything you have is a gift from God. He gave you these gifts for a reason, to do with them what He did with them. "You shall love the Lord your God with all your heart, and with all your soul, and with all your mind.... You shall love your neighbor as yourself" (Mt 22:37, 39). These two greatest commandments go hand in hand, for Jesus also said, "As you did it to one of the least of these my brethren, you did it to me" (Mt 25:40). So what are some concrete ways we can use our gifts to serve others? As always, we have great guidance from our Church, which outlines the corporal and spiritual works of mercy for us.

The Corporal and Spiritual Works of Mercy

The corporal works of mercy are

to feed the hungry;
to give drink to the thirsty;
to clothe the naked;
to give shelter to the homeless;
to visit the sick;
to visit the imprisoned; and
to bury the dead.

The spiritual works of mercy are

to instruct the ignorant;
to counsel the doubtful;
to admonish sinners;
to bear wrongs patiently;
to forgive offenses willingly;
to comfort the afflicted; and
to pray for the living and the dead.

In many ways, the corporal and spiritual works of mercy are our way of living out everything we discussed in the first five classes. They are about

1. sharing the good news of salvation with everyone we encounter (Saving Grace);
2. using the gifts and talents God gave us to serve others and glorify Him (Athletics);
3. reliving the life of Christ as we play our role in salvation history (Instructor's Manual);
4. loving God with all our heart, all our mind, and all our soul (Need to Know Him); and

5. offering our bodies as a living sacrifice (Theology of the Body).

The Corporal Works of Mercy

Feed the Hungry

One-third of the world is suffering from hunger. Yet, in the United States, over one-third are obese, many from overeating. There is a disconnect here. While the solution to world hunger is not always as simple as it seems, there are many ways we can practice the corporal work of mercy to feed the hungry. Many programs work overseas to help support people of lesser means.

However, feeding the hungry is more than sending a donation to a faraway land once a month. People in our own neighborhoods are hungry as well. It is important that we become aware of the humanity around us. If your own brother or sister were starving, I think you would step in and do something right away to help him or her out. We are all brothers and sisters, and nobody in our neighborhoods should go hungry. I encourage you to get involved at your local food pantry or homeless shelter to see how you can help. Do not just donate money or canned goods occasionally, but volunteer your time so you can actually encounter your brothers and sisters face-to-face. The adage "Out of sight, out of mind" often holds true.

During my first semester of college I was assigned to a place called the City Mission as a service project for a class. The mission provided temporary food and shelter to those in the community who were in rough times, between jobs, or trying to get their lives back together. It was an eye-opening experience to see so many people lacking basic things most of us take for granted. Our current pastor spent many years in Africa ministering to people from undeveloped lands. You can see how that experience affected him and gave him a heart for the poor and needy, and he has done a tremendous job opening the eyes of our community to the hunger around us. He started a monthly food collection at our parish for the local shelters and food kitchens. My family recently had the opportunity to deliver those monthly donations, and it was a great learning experience for my spouse and me and our children, not only to encounter those places people go when they have nothing, but to witness the outpouring of generosity from our parish community. Our potential in Catholic parishes to relieve the suffering around us is tremendous when we work together.

Donating our time and money to food pantries and homeless shelters is not the only way to feed the hungry. There are many ways to reach out to those who may be struggling. August 6 is the anniversary of my father's death. It is a special day for us, and I always take that day off work. My dad's favorite thing to do was to take us out to eat. He loved eating out, and he absolutely refused ever to let any of his children pay the bill for a meal, even when we were older and had families of our own. On the five-year anniversary of my father's death, I decided to take my own family out to lunch. I was going to be the dad and pay for the meal. My dad's favorite restaurant was Big Boy. I never really liked Big Boy, but since this was the anniversary of his death, I considered bringing my family to Big Boy. I do not believe I had been there since he died. After thinking about it, though, I decided I did not want to go to Big Boy and took my family someplace else. Pulling up to the other restaurant, we discovered a sign on the window: "Closed due to kitchen fire". Reluctantly, I took that sign as a "sign" that I was supposed to go to Big Boy, so that is what we did.

When the hostess seated us at our table, I remember consciously noticing a man sitting in the booth next to us. He was all alone at eleven in the morning on a weekday, and I was curious about his story and why he was there. Not long after we sat down, he finished his meal and left. I watched him leave. He never looked at us or said anything to us as he was leaving. About five minutes later, the waitress came back and said, "That guy back there just paid your bill." It absolutely knocked the wind out of me. That man had no idea who I was or why I had brought my family there that day. But he touched my life in a way that I will never forget, simply by paying for our meal. I was hungry that day for so much more than food. I was hungry for consolation, and hungry for the presence of my father. My dad was one of those guys who would always win at everything, and in a way it was almost as if he were there saying, "I'm still not going to let you pay."

Paying for a meal is a powerful way to make somebody's day—anybody's day. I realized at that moment the power we all have and how our gifts are meant to be paid forward. Not wanting to let my dad "win" again, I decided to add up what our bill would have been, and I left it all as a tip for the waitress. I left the money on the table and wrote on the receipt, "Have a great day!" As we were leaving, I could not help but look through the window as she went to clear the table, and the look on her face was priceless. I wonder about her story too, but that is for God to know. Be generous, and God will use you to feed the hungry. Set aside some money each month to make somebody's day by feeding the hungry. When the time seems right, pay somebody's bill at a restaurant or a grocery store. Try to do it anonymously. Write the person a note. The last time we paid someone's bill, it was for a young couple who were dating, whom we had just seen at Saturday evening Mass.

It was so refreshing to see a young college couple at Mass. We wrote on their receipt, "Become saints."

If you set aside a little bit of money to make somebody's day, your life will flood with passion and purpose. There is great joy in looking for an opportunity to feed the hungry through the everyday people you encounter.

Finally, there is one more way that I recommend you feed the hungry—the most powerful way: fasting. We have all heard somebody make the remark "There are starving kids in Africa, and you are wasting your food", when we do not clear our dinner plate. It is true that we should not waste food. However, that means we should take smaller portions, not devour as much food as we can so it "doesn't go to waste". Gluttony does not cure hunger.

Our culture often promotes gluttony. If you walk into a movie theater, what do you immediately smell? Popcorn! And boy, does it smell good. It is almost like the theater workers spray those fumes in the doorway (maybe they do). On the way there we say, "We are on a tight budget—no popcorn tonight", but then of course one whiff of that popcorn and we think, "I'll have just a little." At the snack counter, you say, "We would like a small popcorn and a small Coke." The lady behind the counter points at a bowl about the size of a Dixie cup and says, "The small is six dollars. But you can upgrade to the large tub [literally a tub] of popcorn, which is six fifty, and you will get free refills! Same thing with the Coke. You might as well get the tub of popcorn and the liter-size Coke for fifty cents extra." You think to yourself, "What a good deal! I want to get my money's worth. After all, there are starving kids in Africa, and I do not want to spend all that money on such a small portion." Of course, you have to eat and drink all that so you can get a refill and really get your money's worth!

We should learn the virtue of moderation and ask God to give us only what we need. This prayer from Proverbs is beautiful: "Two things I ask of you; deny them not to me before I die: Remove far from me falsehood and lying; give me neither poverty nor riches; feed me with the food that is needful for me, lest I be full, and deny you, and say, 'Who is the LORD?' or lest I be poor, and steal, and profane the name of my God" (Prov 30:7–9).

My point is that there is value in fasting and moderation. Some people should not fast due to health conditions, but for most people, research has shown that intermittent fasting as our Church recommends can be healthy for us.[4] Fasting does several things to help others in need. First, Jesus Himself said that some demons can be cast out only by "prayer and fasting" (Mt 17:21). Making a sacrifice can help others. It also helps us develop a stronger will. It helps us to hear God's voice clearly, as opposed to our own voice (if you hear a whiny and complaining voice, that one is yours). Giving up food for a short period of time gives us a taste (pun intended) of what it is like to be hungry. It is much easier to have compassion for others if we feel those hunger pains ourselves from time to time. As one option, I recommend you fast on Wednesdays and Fridays, with no meat and no food between meals. Recently, I joined a group called e5 Men (www.e5men.org). Based on Ephesians 5, it is a group of men around the world who do a twenty-four-hour bread-and-water fast for their wives and all women the first Wednesday of every month. It is another way "to put food on the table" as we are called to do, but in a much more profound way.

[4] Kris Gunnars, BSc, "10 Evidence-Based Health Benefits of Intermittent Fasting", *Healthline*, August 16, 2016, http://www.healthline.com/nutrition/10-health-benefits-of-intermittent-fasting#section11.

Whatever mode of fasting and moderation you choose, be sure to develop the self-discipline to do it with joy. Don't let others know you are fasting. If you aren't able to do it without being so irritable that your family and friends suffer from being around you, then you can do more harm than good.

Give Drink to the Thirsty

When I train for marathons, I usually do my long runs on Saturday mornings during the summer—a fourteen-mile loop on the country roads around my home. It is a scenic run, connecting all three church buildings that have been formed into our one parish. Those churches are usually my only relief for water. I try to start my runs as early in the morning as possible to avoid the summer heat, but some days the heat is unavoidable. At times the hot summer sun gets the best of me, and I find myself exceedingly thirsty with many miles until I can get to any water. I feel the pain of being thirsty to the point of feeling as if I cannot go any farther. It is one of the most painful, helpless feelings. Reaching those churches to refill my water bottle is such a great relief, but I cannot help looking up at the crucifix and seeing Jesus hanging there with those words echoing off of his lips: "I thirst" (Jn 19:28).

Jesus thirsts for souls, and so should we. He thirsts to relieve the pain and suffering of His children, and so should we. I have come to realize that there are hundreds of millions of people all over the world who do not have access to clean water and who feel this kind of thirst every day. If you do not have food, you will die. If you do not have water, you will die sooner. Water is a basic human need, and in the United States we take water for granted. It is about the only thing left that you can usually get for "free".

As with giving food to the hungry, there are many helpful organizations you can utilize to give drink to the thirsty. Many people donate money to make it possible to dig wells and to provide access to water, and some even go on mission trips to do the work themselves. One young man from our parish recently shared his experience of doing so, an experience that I am sure he will never forget. When you give somebody a cup of water, you relieve his thirst for a moment. When you give him a well, you relieve his thirst for a lifetime.

Clothe the Naked

Nobody should be without proper clothes. We Americans have so much "stuff" that it is embarrassing. As someone who hates laundry and also has four kids, I cannot keep up with it. It always seems there are clothes everywhere but I have nothing to wear. I really think we should go back to *Little House on the Prairie* days. The family members each had one outfit for the week and had some nice Sunday clothes. That's it. How much simpler would that be? Smelly, but simple. This may sound absurd in our culture, but in actuality, that is the radical nature of the Gospel. "He who has two coats, let him share with him who has none; and he who has food, let him do likewise" (Lk 3:11).

As our children have grown, many people have been generous, passing on their children's clothes to us. Part of the problem with kids' clothing is finding something that fits, because kids are constantly changing sizes. Recently, we realized we had boxes and boxes of clothes given to us by family and friends. The sheer amount was clogging up our house, and we simply decided to pick a couple of outfits for each child and pass the rest on. We all need to go through our closets and get rid of our excess. Do we really need to keep that sweater from high school that might come back in fashion one day? (I still have clothes I wore in high school, although my wife is making me move on and update my wardrobe.) I recently realized I had three winter coats that I had never worn. Those coats could be saving somebody's life if put in the right hands.

It is OK to buy some nice clothes from time to time, but each time we should donate something else where it can be used. It is actually quite liberating. Remember, it is not your stuff. If you have two shirts, the first one is yours. The other one belongs to the poor. In our excess, we need to make sure everyone is taken care of. Crisis pregnancy centers, homeless shelters, domestic violence shelters, and city missions can all tell you what they need. Provide it to them.

Give Shelter to the Homeless

If you have never been to a homeless shelter, seek one out. You might be surprised by how much potential you have to help those who do not have a place to call home. It is our duty to seek them out and help them. In Pope Francis' encyclical *Evangelii Gaudium*, he reminds us that the poor should have a special place in our lives. He writes:

> God's heart has a special place for the poor, so much that he himself "became poor" (2 Cor 8:9). The entire history of our redemption is marked by the presence of the poor. Salvation came to us from the "yes" uttered by a lowly maiden from a small town on the fringes of a great empire. The Saviour was born in a manger, in the midst of animals, like children of poor families; he was presented at the Temple along with two turtledoves, the offering made by those who could not afford a lamb (cf. Lk 2:24; Lev 5:7); he was raised in a home of ordinary workers

and worked with his own hands to earn his bread.... He assured those burdened by sorrow and crushed by poverty that God has a special place for them in his heart: "Blessed are you poor, yours is the kingdom of God" (Lk 6:20).[5]

This is why Pope Francis says he wants "a Church which is poor and for the poor". He says, "They have much to teach us. Not only do they share in the *sensus fidei* [sense of faith], but in their difficulties they know the suffering Christ."[6]

I was recently struck by a news story about a controversial piece of art that has been placed in front of different churches around the country. It is called *Homeless Jesus*, by artist Timothy Schmalz, and it is a very real-looking statue of a park bench with a homeless man lying down covered in a blanket. If you approach the statue to take a closer look, you will see that the man is Jesus with His nail wounds. Many have walked by, some have called the police, and some have been scandalized, especially when the statue is placed in a "rich" neighborhood. I am sure the statue has caused many people to stop and think. The next time you see a homeless person, before you immediately stereotype him as a drug addict or a troublemaker, remember that it is Jesus in disguise.

Where you live, homelessness may seem like a faraway problem that can be helped only by sending a check overseas. There are certainly ways to help give shelter to people in faraway places, but there are also opportunities to help in your own area if you seek out the needs of those around you.

I have never been homeless, but I have had others allow me to live in their homes on several occasions when I was in college. They showed me a generosity that I will not forget. Sometimes the "homeless" seeking shelter are our own friends and family members, and because I was shown compassion and was welcomed into other people's homes during difficult financial times, it encouraged me to do the same for others after I was married.

We cannot cling to our own security. We must seek out those less fortunate, even if it makes us uncomfortable. As Pope Francis says, "I prefer a Church which is bruised, hurting, and dirty because it has been out on the streets, rather than a Church which is unhealthy from being confined and from clinging to its own security."[7]

Visit the Sick and the Imprisoned

I would like to discuss the next two corporal works of mercy together because they both involve visiting people when they feel trapped and need healing, even if they are trapped and hurting for different reasons. It is in bad times that we discover true friends. The world is noisy, fast-paced, and obsessed with productivity. To visit those in the hospital or in a prison is to value them based on who they are, not what they have or what they can do. It is not fun to visit people when they are hurting, but it is a great act of mercy. At those times, they need other people the most—they need their presence and to know they care.

I work in nursing homes for my career as a mobile eye doctor. Each day I treat people who in many ways are chronically sick. They often feel like prisoners because, in a world obsessed with doing and having, they cannot do much of anything, and they do not have much of anything.

[7] Ibid., 49.

They have lost their independence and can no longer take care of themselves. They cannot go anywhere without somebody to take them. They have lost their homes and the majority of their possessions. Many are widowed and alone. Many are constantly hurting, physically and emotionally. Many wonder why they are still alive. In the next corporal work of mercy, burying the dead, we will talk about how life is short and fragile. However, sometimes life can be brutally resilient. Both the fragility and the resiliency of life can cause enormous suffering, and both are opportunities to provide corporal works of mercy.

Because of my career, I can recognize the value of a simple visit. Of course, prison ministry, which involves going into actual prisons, is a powerful experience. Those who have hit bottom are often very open to hear the good news of Jesus Christ. The hope of Jesus is often the only thing they have left. They are searching for mercy and compassion. They want a second chance, and they can find it in Jesus Christ. They often need somebody to bring them this hope and good news and speak to them of the greatest and truest freedom—the freedom from sin and death. If you ever have the opportunity to do prison ministry, I strongly suggest you give it a try. It is not for everybody, but for those who are called, it is very fulfilling.

On a speaking trip to Hutchinson, Kansas, I had the opportunity to speak at a maximum-security prison. One of the prisoners had read my book and found out I was coming to the area, and he arranged the visit. It was an experience I will never forget. It was rather intimidating going through all the security, with huge sliding doors and a gigantic barbed wire fence, escorted by a guard. I did not know what to expect. I knew that many of the men were in there for life, and I wondered what kind of perspective they had on the Catholic faith.

What I discovered speaking to those men was that most seemed genuinely interested in their faith. (However, some admitted afterward that somebody had dragged them there by bribing them with punch and cookies. One prisoner said he had planned on grabbing a cookie and leaving after five minutes but decided to stay for the whole talk after hearing the first five minutes. That is one of the greatest compliments I could get.) They asked some really good questions. I realized that many of those inmates are actually freer than a lot of people in the outside world. The world is full of distractions and noise and "false gods" that make us forget about how much we depend on the real God. In prison, the need for God becomes painfully clear, especially for those in for life. I asked those men to pray for me, as I would be praying for them. Their prayers are powerful, and their conversion is powerful. Their potential to be great saints is enormous. Let us not forget that Saint Paul was a murderer, Saint Peter was a coward, Saint Francis and Saint Ignatius were arrogant. I recently read the story of Blessed Bartolo Longo, who was a satanic priest before his conversion! The reality is that God is attracted to our weakness and sin—not because He likes sin but because He likes being a Savior. He likes to demonstrate His power through our weakness.

Whether or not we can go into prisons, we can all go to the sick and the homebound. As I see patients in nursing homes, a recurring theme in each diagnosis list is depression. They are lonely and often feel forgotten. Your potential to make a difference in a nursing home is unfathomable. One daughter whose mother was in a nursing home told me about a grumpy old man she would see when visiting her mother. He always had a frown, he was always inconsiderate to the nursing aides, and he never participated in any activities. One day her family decided that the next time they went to visit her mother, they would bring the old man a card and some flowers, just to say they cared. After doing so, the nursing staff said the old man was a different person. He began participating in activities and was much kinder and more considerate to those around him.

If you have children, bring them to nursing homes. Souls are healed by being with children, and in many ways, so are the body and the mind. Children bring life and joy, and their mere presence can make somebody's day in a nursing home.

When I think about the corporal work of mercy of visiting the sick, I cannot help but think of Blessed Pier Giorgio Frassati. Growing up in Italy with some of the wealthiest parents in the country, he had all the material possessions he could ever want or need. His parents were not religious, and he developed a deep love for the Catholic faith without their support or encouragement. Because he deeply loved Jesus and Mary, he developed a deep love for the poor and the sick. He was a very popular, handsome, and athletic young man, and a great leader among his college friends. He would take them on mountain hiking adventures and spend time with them in the pool hall, and he was always speaking of his faith and sharing his joy with them. Sometimes he even gambled in the pool halls: he told his friends that if they won, he would give them money, but if he won, then they would all go and spend a holy hour with Jesus. When he won, his friends listened to him, and he brought them to the church, where they usually just sat and watched him pray.

Even though he was a popular young man, his deep love for the poor consumed much of his life. Whatever money his father gave him he used to help the poor and the sick. He would visit with them, buy them medicine and supplies, and treat them in whatever ways he could. He often did this secretly, using his lay Dominican name, Jerome, since Frassati was such a well-known name because of his father. At twenty-four years old, he contracted polio from one of the sick people he had been visiting, and quickly the disease took his life. Even in his dying moments, his last concern was for the poor and the sick he was serving: he asked for a pencil and paper and scribbled a message to a friend not to forget the injections for Converso, a poor man he had been supporting by purchasing his medicine.

Pier Giorgio died at age twenty-four in 1925. At his funeral, his parents were astonished to see thousands of people line the streets, most of whom were the poor people he had been supporting. In 1981 his body was exhumed and found to be totally incorrupt. He was beatified in 1990 by Pope John Paul II, who called him the "Man of the Eight Beatitudes". Pier Giorgio Frassati is a great role model for all of us, especially young people. He was full of life, energy, enthusiasm, joy, and love for God and neighbor. Father Tim Deeter is a man who has studied Pier Giorgio's life extensively, and I strongly encourage you to listen to his talk "Blessed Pier Giorgio Frassati: Man of the Beatitudes".[8]

Bury the Dead

Funerals change people. Every time I have gone to a funeral, it has deeply affected my life. My family recently read a book together called *Life's Greatest Lesson* by Allen Hunt, written from the perspective of a ten-year-old boy who goes to his grandmother's funeral and realizes the

---

[8] *Blessed Pier Giorgio Frassati: Man of the Beatitudes* (Sycamore, Ill.: Lighthouse Catholic Media, 2009), CD.

impact she had on the world.[9] Throughout the book, the boy's grandfather tells him stories of what his grandmother did to earn such admiration from so many people who came to her funeral to pay their respects. The book is well written and easy to read, and my children loved hearing the story as much as I did.

We should always honor and respect with a proper burial those who go before us. This is a perfect example of how offering a work of mercy to others ends up greatly affecting our own lives. Every life is a story—a story with a great lesson. Every funeral is a reminder that we are dust and to dust we shall return.

Since my father passed away in 2008, I have spent a lot more time in cemeteries. Seeing the name of somebody you love on a tombstone changes you. My own name is on the back of my father's stone, and each time I visit him I hear his voice: "I've run my race; now you must run yours. Don't waste the opportunity that lies before you. Life is short." I do not hear this voice just at my father's stone; I hear it echoing through the whole cemetery. Every tombstone I pass by makes me long to know that person's story. Some of them lived one hundred years—some only two. Some never made it out of their mother's wombs.

I see the tombstone of the three-year-old boy who is the son of one of my good friends. I have little children, and I cannot help but squeeze them tight after visiting the tombstone of little Thomas. I see the tombstone of the soldier who took his own life, and contemplate the terrible darkness and suffering he faced in this life, and the void his family now faces. I see the teenager whose car was struck by a train, and the young man whose life was taken by a drunk driver. I see my grandparents' grave, my grandfather

[9] *Life's Greatest Lesson* (North Palm Beach, Fla.: Beacon, 2013).

having been there for twenty-two years, recently joined by my grandmother, who had been a widow for more than twenty years.

The tombstone in front of my father's belongs to two brothers with whom I went to school. They died together in a farming accident. Not far away is the tombstone of a teenage boy. I discovered that he had gotten his girl-friend pregnant in high school. He got his life together after they had that child, and shortly after high school he proposed to the young lady. They bought a house. He was moving some furniture when he fell off the back of the truck and died. I see his cross on the side of the road when I return home.

My friend Chris was an all-star athlete in high school. I remember jumping into Chris' arms at center court after knocking off the defending state champions in the first round of the state basketball tournament during my junior year. Chris was a solidly built young man with a contagious smile, an all-state linebacker with a college football schol-arship. A year after our tournament victory, he drowned in a lake on his college campus. He was as strong as an ox and seemingly invincible, but he was gone, just like that.

My friend Ryan always had a locker and a seat next to me in school since we both had last names that started with *W*. I remember sitting next to Ryan again at our ten-year class reunion. He introduced me to his wife and brand-new baby. A year later, Ryan died of leukemia.

The parish next to ours has Eucharistic adoration twenty-four hours a day. During the last quarter, I signed up for the midnight shift. I would spend an hour with Jesus every Tuesday night after my kids went to bed. The lady who signed up for the hour after me had never signed up for adoration before. Her name was Debra. She always came with a smile, and usually before I would leave she would whisper me a question. On her last visit she asked why the Bible she was holding did not have the same number of books as the one in the chapel. I smiled and explained that the Catholic Bible has seventy-three books and a Protestant Bible has sixty-six. Debra had a habit of forgetting to come to adoration some weeks. Since I was the only one there, I would have to stay for two hours, until two in the morning. I would usually get a text message or voice mail from Debra the next day. She would apologize over and over and tell me, "Text me next time!" Toward the end of the quarter, she did not show up again. I texted her. She did not respond. I smirked and figured I would get a frantic phone call the next day with her apologies. Instead, I got a phone call the following week from the lady who came in after her. She wanted to let me know that we would have to split Debra's shift for the rest of the quarter because Debra had died.

Life is short. It is a gift—do not waste the time you have been given. The next time you go to a funeral, think about the story of that life, and what it says to you. Visit a cemetery and take a slow walk. Look at those names and dates etched in stone. I often think of a line from the movie *Gladiator*: "What we do in life echoes in eternity!"

As Christians, we give our brothers and sisters proper burials. The prayers of the Mass are absolutely beautiful. They are a sending forth, a celebration of life. They are also a message to all those still living. People will come to your funeral. What lessons will they leave with? What story will your tombstone tell?

I have to be honest. This section on the corporal works of mercy was one of the most challenging for me to write. I am not an expert on doing these works, and I have discovered that I need to step things up a notch. I have visited some prisons and nursing homes (outside of my regular job) and brought food to some food pantries. My wife has volunteered at the food pantry. But mostly I sought these opportunities out so I would be able to write about them—not a good motivation, but at least a beginning. Writing this book has opened new doors for me in social justice. Performing the corporal works cannot be a one-time action just to have a learning experience. My motivation cannot be fear of being a hypocrite—it must be love for the poor, a real genuine love. If you and I meet someday at a conference or event, you should ask me if I am continuing to visit the prisons and the nursing homes and the homeless shelters. I have sent checks overseas, but almost anybody can write a check. I want to get to know the children I am supporting, and not just send money but send love as well. Pope Francis has been an effective wake-up call for me and for all of us. He said we must always lead with love. The poor have a special right to the Gospel and should have opportunities to encounter Jesus Christ through His hands and feet, through us. It is part of our own journey and transformation. In speaking to a group of wealthy business owners, one bishop told them bluntly, "The poor need you to keep them out of poverty...and you need the poor to keep you out of hell."[10] Let us hold each other accountable for performing the corporal works of mercy.

The Spiritual Works of Mercy

Instruct the Ignorant

Instructing the ignorant is the spiritual equivalent of giving food to the hungry. How often do we hear people say they left the Church because they "were not being fed"?

---

[10] Francis Cardinal George quoted in Joseph Paprocki, 7 *Keys to Spiritual Wellness* (Chicago: Loyola, 2012), 58.

We cannot just brush them aside and say, "If they really knew what they were receiving in the Eucharist, then they wouldn't say they weren't being fed." This is true; but if they do not know what they are receiving in the Eucharist, it is because they do not know their faith and they have never encountered Jesus in the Eucharist. We do not rely on a spiritual method of teaching called "holy-osmosis". We cannot expect all Catholics to learn and fall in love with their faith by sitting in Church on Sunday or in a classroom for an hour during the week.

We do not have an obligation to entertain people, but we do have an obligation to engage them, to give them reasons to believe and make the faith come alive so it is relevant to their everyday lives. It is bad parenting to answer every question a child asks with the words "Because I said so." And it is bad catechesis to answer every question about our faith with the words "Because the Church says so." That will not work with this generation, and it should not. That form of catechesis is based on the image of a God who is a tyrant or a master. God is a Father, and everything we do in Catholicism is done for a reason, and the reasons are beautiful. The New Evangelization is about finding new ways to teach an ageless truth. We do not change the truth in any way, but we do change the method of teaching it as the times change.

I once read an article about "spiritual inoculation". I recognized this phenomenon instantly. Our young people have been inoculated with Catholicism. They have been vaccinated. A vaccine is used to prevent the infection of a certain virus. Scientists take a small sample of the virus and use it in the vaccine. It works because the sample is not enough to make somebody sick, but it is enough for the body to begin to recognize and destroy that virus. The vaccine builds immunity against the virus, so whenever that virus comes around, the body destroys it before it can do any damage. This is what has happened with young people in America in regard to their Catholic faith. They have received bits and pieces growing up but never anything appealing enough to actually "infect" them with Catholicism. They have never been on fire for their faith and have never had a true encounter with Jesus Christ. In many cases, they have simply sat in a classroom as a teacher, who was dragged in as a "volunteer", was forced to teach a class he never wanted to teach. These young people have read outdated textbooks, watched videotapes from the 1970s, and memorized some prayers. That is not instructing the ignorant—that is vaccinating them against Catholicism.

Whenever they hear the word "religion", their defenses go up. They cross their arms, and their spiritual antibodies raise their wall, crying out, "Boring, boring, boring." It is important to find new ways to invite people to events and classes, to read books and to listen to talks. However, if you convince them to come and do not engage them in an attractive way, you can do more harm than good. First, you have to help them encounter Jesus in a real way, which is why Eucharistic adoration has to be a foundational part of the New Evangelization.

Pope Francis emphasizes this in his encyclical *Evangelii Gaudium*. Something powerful must break through the defenses of spiritual inoculation. There is only one force in the world powerful enough to do it—love. We need to be infused with the love of God and the joy of the Gospel so that we cannot help but want to share that joy with others. Apathy is contagious, but holiness is more contagious. We need to break through and "infect" others with the love of Jesus Christ and let the "virus" spread like wildfire to epidemic levels.

Everywhere I have been, directors of religious education struggle to find people to teach the faith to our young people. This should not be happening. We have a duty to teach young people the faith, and it should be a primary task. Volunteers should be lining up to teach them, finding ways to engage them and revealing the genius of Catholicism in an attractive way. Many people have the personality, energy, talent, and knowledge to do it, or at least the ability to gain that knowledge. They need to step up. Why not you? If you do not volunteer, the church staff will call random parishioners and twist their arms. Those people will do it out of guilt or a sense of obligation, but they do not want to do it. If they do not really want to do it, they will not have passion and zeal. If they do not have passion and zeal, they will inoculate those kids, who are forced to miss their sports, or TV shows, or whatever else they would rather be doing to sit in a classroom and be bored.

Learn the faith so you can teach the faith in an attractive way. This does not mean you are going to be perfect, or need to be perfect, or entertaining, or funny, even to consider teaching. Do not let fear stop you. You will not be able to reach all your students; trust me. Teaching teenagers especially has been one of the most challenging tasks in my life, and I am constantly seeking new ways to attract their attention and engage them. What they need more than anything else is authenticity. We have plenty of great resources available now that we did not have before, thanks to great new initiatives like the Dynamic Catholic Institute, Lighthouse Catholic Media, and the Augustine Institute: powerful video presentations, books, and audio recordings, along with other technological offerings. Teenagers can tell if you care or if you do not. Simply care. Care about them and care about the faith with a burning passion. We need a revival in catechesis for a generation (or two) that has lost its faith, but catechesis begins with relationship and love. Thirst for souls, and remember to lead with love. If you do that, you will win your students' respect, and you will make a huge impact on future generations of Catholics. We are all teachers of the faith and instructors of the ignorant.

You never know what opportunities God may give you to instruct the ignorant if you are willing. Not long ago my older brother asked me to pray for his friend Gwynn's grandmother, who had passed away. My brother told me something that day that he had never mentioned before. When he was in college, he and his friend Carl decided that Catholicism was not the true faith, and they were ready to leave and join another church. One day Gwynn invited them over to her grandmother's house. That old lady sat down with those two teenagers and went toe-to-toe with them, answering every question and objection they had about the Catholic faith. After several hours, she had convinced them of the truth of the faith. Carl is now a Catholic priest, and my brother was the one who taught me the genius of Catholicism when I was at my lowest point in life. If it were not for my brother, I would have never become a Catholic author and speaker. If it were not for that old lady, my brother would not even be Catholic. Do you know what that means? It means that that old lady did not just reach two lost teenagers—she reached everyone they reached, including me. If this book has reached you, then that old lady reached you. Again, the movie quote "What we do in life echoes in eternity" holds true. Many good things happened because she knew her faith and was prepared when God sent those two boys her way, even in the fall of her life.

As important as good catechists and teachers are, nobody can replace a child's parents. Remember, as we stated in the beginning of this book, parents are always called to be the primary educators of the faith. My children might grow up and decide to leave the Catholic Church, as my brother almost did. Many good and faithful parents live through this heartbreak, and I have spoken with many of them everywhere I have been. Sometimes good parents raise wayward children, and sometimes wayward parents raise great saints. We all have to choose and make the faith our own. It cannot be forced.

Having said that, if my children do not know their faith; if they do not know that the Eucharist is the body, blood, soul, and divinity of Jesus Christ; if they do not know they need to go to Mass every Sunday, not because it is a rule but because they need it like they need air to breathe; if they do not know the story of salvation history or stories of the great saints; if they do not know how to pray—that is on me. I am their father. Fathers especially need to step it up in this regard. Studies show that when a father is active in his faith, his children are much more likely to continue on in the faith. It is obvious almost everywhere I go that women are the ones working very hard to keep faith alive in their families and parishes. We are indebted to them and we need them to continue with their passion, patience, and hard work. But the Scriptures are pretty clear—men, you are supposed to be spiritual leaders in your family and your neighborhoods.

We live in a "fatherless" nation where the role of father has been drastically downplayed and often mocked. Men, your role is extremely important and irreplaceable. We need to take action. The number-one reason for crime in this country is fatherless children. The number-one reason for poverty in this country is fatherless children. And I propose to you that the number-one reason why 85 percent of confirmation students end up leaving the Catholic faith within ten years of receiving the sacrament is also fatherless children (see p. 15). Fathers are a big part of the problem but also a big part of the solution. Be a spiritual leader—be a man!

Counsel the Doubtful

The most dominant emotion in the United States is fear. When you do not know who you are, or where you are going, or what you were made for, fear will rule your life. I know this well. I was consumed by fear for much of my life—always afraid of letting somebody down, not being good enough, or giving up in the middle of the "race" when things got hard. Sometimes, the fear of failure was so great that I avoided the race all together.

There is a comfortable little place we like to retreat to when things are challenging. It is called mediocrity. I love this place and I hate it. The comfortable world of mediocrity keeps you safe from risk, heartache, and disappointment. It is a place where you cannot lose, but you also cannot win. Mediocrity is not having a favorite team because they are probably going to lose. It is not having any dreams because you might not reach them. It is not having true love because somebody might break your heart. It is not having any goals because you might not reach them. It is not taking any risks because you might disappoint somebody, or yourself. It is safe and comfortable—and lonely. It is a prison cell. We like our captivity because freedom carries a price and a responsibility. Freedom means we are the authors of our own destiny; freedom leaves us with no excuses, and that is frightening. It is a simple choice. You have before you life and death, joy and misery, freedom and slavery—choose life, joy, and freedom. You think making the choice against mediocrity is about being able to trust yourself, but it really is about being able to trust God. Jesus came to show us that we can trust God.

Most people do not know Jesus. They know *about* Him, but they do not *know* Him. Because they do not know Jesus, they do not know God and His infinite love for His children. If they do not know God, they do not know who they are, why they are here, and where they are going—hence fear. This is what counseling the doubtful is all about: helping people realize that God did not create them because He "needed" to create them. God does not need you. He created you out of pure love. This is good news. It means that life is not about what you do; it is about who you are in God's eyes. God can accomplish everything at the snap of a finger. The fate of the world does not rest on what you accomplish. The only failure is not to try. Remember, God gives you challenges and trials and tests not because He needs something from you but because He loves you and wants you to *be* something great—the saint He created you to be. He does the work. You just have to cooperate with Him and trust Him. Everyone needs to rediscover this love of the Father. Jesus is not walking the earth in the same manner that He did two thousand years ago; *you* are His instrument to accomplish His works.

Most people are desperate for just a little word of encouragement. Give them that word. Build people up; do not tear them down. Always seek the good in others. This is especially true for parents in regard to their children. Parents have the duty and the obligation to correct bad behavior and teach their children right from wrong. Because of this, parents have to spend much of the day telling children what they are doing wrong and asking them to fix it. It is extremely important that you take some time each day to praise your children. Tell them their strengths, their value, and how much they are loved by you and by

God. Tell them who they are, why they are here, and for what they are created.

A couple of years ago I heard Father John Riccardo suggest the powerful habit of assigning each family member a certain day of the week so that everyone knows to say extra prayers for that person on that day. I decided to implement this idea into my own family. For example, my oldest daughter has Monday, and she knows that every Monday we are all praying especially for her. Since there are six members in our family, we use Monday through Saturday. It has been very beneficial for all of us, and I recommend every family do this, no matter how old your children are.

Do not just pray privately for your family members. Pray together. At night, everybody says something he likes or appreciates about the person for whom he is praying. At mealtimes, in addition to asking a blessing for our food, I pray for that person. As fathers, it is important that we give our children praise. The prayer at mealtime is not a litany of things they need to work on. For example, I do not say, "Help Isabelle get better at doing her chores." It is simply a time for praise. It can sound something like this:

Heavenly Father, we thank you for Isabelle and all the joy she has brought to our life. Thank you for her talent and how beautiful she is inside and out. Thank you for her willingness to learn new things, and we appreciate how she helped her brother with his homework the other day. Help her piano lessons to go well this week. Keep her safe from dragons and let her know how much You love her. Always guide her so she knows Your will for her, and give her the courage to follow Your loving plan for her life. If it is her vocation to be married, please be with the young man who will one day be her spouse, and guide him to holiness. Help her to be a strong and faithful Catholic her whole life, and help her to become the saint You created her to be.

Now, I know what many of you men are thinking: "I can't do that." Trust me, I know how you feel. Until I started doing this a couple of years ago, I had never said a spontaneous prayer out loud in my entire life. As I was growing up, our family prayers were always memorized prayers, except perhaps when my mom added something. My brothers and I and my dad certainly never said spontaneous prayers. Plus, I am shy and introverted. It just does not fit my personality to say that kind of prayer. Was it awkward the first time I tried it? You bet. Is it still awkward? Actually, it is still a little awkward, but I am getting better.

I understand how difficult it is for many men to pray out loud spontaneously. My advice is the same as it was for the last work of mercy we talked about: Be a man. A real man prays with and for his family. I have to believe that those prayers are having a deep impact on my children. It is a powerful way to help them have confidence and self-worth and overcome the many doubts they will face. To know that their daddy loves them, prays for them, has a dream for them to be saints, and believes in them is a priceless gift.

Admonish Sinners

As an eye doctor, I sometimes have to give patients bad news or challenge them to change habits. For example, diabetes is a leading cause of blindness, and smoking is a leading risk factor for macular degeneration. I ask you: Would you choose me as your eye doctor if I refused to tell you what your problems were for the sake of "keeping the peace"? I would be a terrible doctor if I refused to tell people which of their habits were leading to their own destruction. It is not compassionate just to "live and let live", as the motto goes. Do we use that philosophy with our children and the people we love? Do we say things like "Well, I'd rather my children didn't play on the street, but I don't want to be judgmental, so I am not going to say anything"? As a doctor, I have to tell the truth. It is my job to treat disease and keep people healthy.

In fact, it is an act of mercy to tell somebody that what he is doing is wrong. We cannot judge people's hearts, but we can and should judge certain actions. It is a very challenging thing to do, especially in this day and in this culture that does not seem to believe in right and wrong. As a doctor, if I do not tell my patients what will harm them, I am responsible if they get harmed. The same applies in the spiritual world. Sin is not an arbitrary list of things we should not do. The Church challenges us to warn others against sin because our sins can cause harm emotionally, physically, intellectually, socially, and spiritually. If you do not tell others the truth, then you are responsible for their moral degradation, especially as parents and catechists and priests.

It is important to admonish the sinner, but it is just as important to do it in a compassionate way. Remember, there are two aspects to being a doctor. I should be able to cure disease, but I also need to have a good bedside manner. Some of the smartest doctors in the world can be absolute jerks, and patients simply do not like being around them or asking them for help. It does not do much good to have the medicine if people refuse to come to you for treatment. Always remember: When admonishing the sinner, lead with love. Our motivation must always be to help the other person, and not to win arguments, put people down, or prove we are right. We should always try to avoid gossiping about people or pointing out their faults and weaknesses around others. Listen to the advice of Saint Paul, and begin by talking to the person privately: "If your brother sins against you, go and tell him his fault, between you and him alone. If he listens to you, you have gained your brother. But if he does not listen, take one or two others along with you, that every word may be confirmed by the evidence of two or three witnesses. If he refuses to listen to them, tell it to the Church; and if he refuses to listen even to the Church, let him be to you as a Gentile and a tax collector" (Mt 18:15–17).

Later in this chapter we will talk about forgiveness and bearing wrongs patiently, but it is worth pointing out that directly following this conversation in the Gospel of Matthew, Peter goes on to ask Jesus how often he should forgive his brother. Of course, we know Jesus' reply: "I do not say to you seven times, but seventy times seven" (Mt 18:21). In other words, treating your brother "as a Gentile and a tax collector" does not mean you just write him off at that point and tell the whole world he is evil. Jesus had mercy, compassion, and patience even with the Gentiles and tax collectors. Do not forget that it was a former tax collector (Matthew) who wrote this Gospel.

Saint John Bosco can be a great intercessor in admonishing the sinner. He was a priest in Italy in the 1800s who gathered street youths to minister to them. He built them residences, workshops, schools, and churches. His method of correcting their faults was very much based on a father-son mentality. This is what he said, which we should take to heart:

> It is more fitting to be persistent in punishing our own impatience and pride than to correct the boys. We must be firm but kind and patient with them. I give you as a

model the charity of Paul which he showed to his new converts. They often reduced him to tears and entreaties when he found them lacking docility and even opposing his loving efforts. See that no one finds you motivated by impetuosity or willfulness. It is difficult to keep calm when administering punishment, but this must be done if we are to keep ourselves from ... spilling out our anger. Let us regard those boys ... as our own sons.... Let us not rule over them except for the purpose of serving them better. This was the method of Jesus used with the apostles. He put up with their ignorance and roughness and even their infidelity. He treated sinners with a kindness and affection that caused some to be shocked, others to be scandalized, and still others to hope for God's mercy. And so he bade us to be "gentle and humble of heart." They are our sons, and so in correcting their mistakes we must lay aside all anger and restrain it so firmly that it is extinguished entirely. There must be no hostility in our minds, no contempt in our eyes, and no insult on our lips. We must use mercy for the present and have hope for the future, as is fitting for true fathers who are eager for real correction and improvement.[11]

Bear Wrongs Patiently

The Church is a mother. Pope Francis reminded me of this when he said we must remember the feminine nature of the Church.[12] I thought about this and could not help but see the difference between my and my wife's reactions to our children's faults. I am a doctor, but when my children get hurt, they go to my wife. If one falls off a chair

---

[11] *Office of Readings According to the Roman Rite* (Boston: Daughters of St. Paul, 1983).

[12] Press Conference of Pope Francis during the Return Flight, July 28, 2013, https://w2.vatican.va/content/francesco/en/speeches/2013/july/documents/papa-francesco_20130728_gmg-conferenza-stampa.html.

and bumps his head, my first reaction is anger. "I told you not to stand on the chair! Why won't you listen to me! I'm not paying for those stitches." OK, maybe I am not that bad; I would pay for the stitches. But my reflex reaction is certainly one of anger. I am angry that their disobedience caused them to get hurt, because I love them and I do not want them to be hurt. My wife, on the other hand, has a different reflex reaction. She consoles them, cleans them up, and speaks calmly and gently to them.

Pope Francis used the analogy of a field hospital.[13] First, we must treat the person's wounds. In other words, if somebody is dying from a heart attack, we do not lecture him about blood pressure and diabetes. First we treat the mortal "wound". We care for him, console him, and assure him of our love. No matter how many times people continue to self-destruct and refuse to listen to our advice, we always lead with love and compassion. Remember our conversation about love? Sometimes that means not giving people what they want, but it means always giving them what they need, even if they do not deserve it.

Our doors must always be open to everyone. That is what "catholic" means—universal. Catholicism is for everyone—even the people who anger you or wrong you, even the people who annoy you. Yes, I know, there are a lot of annoying people out there, but those annoying people are an opportunity for you to grow in virtue. They give you occasion to practice patience and to master that virtue.

Most of my patients in the nursing homes are the kindest, nicest people in the world. However, some are really challenging. Some patients have severe dementia or

---

[13] Pope Francis, *The Name of God Is Mercy*, trans. Oonagh Stransky (New York: Random House, 2016), 52–53.

Alzheimer's disease and ask the same questions over and over again. Some are just plain cranky. One patient in particular was really challenging for me. Mrs. Smith, as we will call her, was a ninety-six-year-old lady who wanted to complain about everything. Last time I saw her coming, I was having a bad day, and I was not sure I could handle dealing with her. She came into the room and immediately started to complain. "I can't see anything—I'm blind! These glasses aren't right!"

I replied, "What do you mean, you are blind? Can you see any letters on the chart over there?"

She replied, "Well, the bottom row is E V O T Z 2, but they are fuzzy. Do you know what you are doing? Are you even old enough to be a doctor?"

Do you know what I felt like saying to her? "Do you know why the bottom row is fuzzy? It is because you are old! You are ninety-six years old! Do you know why I look too young to be a doctor? Because you are old! Everybody looks young when you are old." That is what I wanted to say, but of course I did not. I remembered how Mother Teresa described the poor people she was treating as "Jesus in disguise". I realized that the same could be said of the people who test our patience, and we are called to see Jesus in everyone we meet. Mrs. Smith was Jesus in disguise! The point is, if something is important to the King, it is important to you, and every human soul is important to the King. We should want to help get others to heaven, and we should remember this when we choose how to react to other people. We should treat them as we would treat Jesus. So, with all my strength, I tried to ask her *kindly* what she was having trouble seeing. At that point she pulled out her book, which was *Ordinary Lives, Extraordinary Mission* by John R. Wood.

Surprised at seeing my book, I exclaimed, "That's my book!"

She then pulled the book away from me and retorted, "No, it isn't. It's my book!"

I calmly explained to her that I was the author of the book that she was holding in her hands, and showed her my name tag. Her demeanor did a complete 180-degree turn. She was so excited. She even called her friend right then and there and made me talk to her friend on the phone. It was such a humbling turn of events that I would have totally missed had I reacted with impatience.

Mother Teresa had a reflection by Kent Keith hanging on her wall entitled "Do It Anyway". If you have never read that reflection, the main point is that when you try to help people, they might not appreciate you, or may accuse you of false motives, or may even persecute you. Help them anyway.

Patience has always been one of the most challenging virtues for me. My pastor once recommended using the "love chapter" from 1 Corinthians to help me with this. Starting in 13:4, it describes love, beginning with the words "Love is patient and kind." Understanding how repetition is powerful, and to help me learn patience, I recite that chapter over and over, but instead of using the word "love", I use my own name. It sounds like this: "John is patient and kind; John is not jealous or boastful; John is not arrogant or rude. John does not insist on his own way; he is not irritable or resentful; John does not rejoice at wrong, but rejoices in the right. John bears all things, believes all things, hopes all things, endures all things."

This sounded pretty awkward for me the first time I said it, and it still does. But if I repeat this often enough so I am conscious of the virtue I am striving for, then my thoughts can help determine my actions. With perseverance, I can become a more patient person. Try it in your own life and I think you will find it useful, especially when dealing with others who test your patience.

Forgive Offenses Willingly

When I think of forgiveness, I cannot help but recall John Paul II's ultimate witness. In 1981 he survived an attempted assassination. He was shot multiple times by Mehmet Ali Ağca when entering Saint Peter's Square among a crowd of people. What happened is miraculous. One of the bullets that wounded the pope came within a fraction of an inch of a major artery. The shooting occurred on May 13, the anniversary of the first apparition of Our Lady of Fatima. On May 13, 1917, Mary appeared to three shepherd children. Mary would later reveal three secrets to the children, the last of which was not shared publicly for many years. In 2000 John Paul II released the third secret of Fatima, which involved the image of a man dressed in white being shot down. John Paul II believed the secret involved him, and he credited Mary for saving his life. John Paul II actually took the bullet to Fatima and had it placed in the crown of Mary's statue, where it can still be found today.

In 1983 John Paul II visited the man who shot him, in his prison cell. Ağca was a professional assassin firing bullets at close range. His question for the pope when he arrived was, "Why aren't you dead?" Knowing that John Paul II should certainly be dead and knowing that the pope credited Mary for saving his life, Ağca actually feared the Virgin Mary. John Paul II calmed his fears, telling Ağca that Mary loved him. In that prison cell, John Paul II offered the man who tried to kill him his total forgiveness.

Ağca developed a deep respect for John Paul II and even requested to attend his funeral in 2005.

Forgiveness is powerful. Anger toward others can be a poison raging inside of us. We have to let that anger go and forgive willingly. Forgiving somebody does not mean the feelings are going to go away or the damage the person caused you will hurt any less. Forgiving involves making a conscious choice, regardless of how we feel or what the other person deserves. We must remember that none of us deserves forgiveness for our sins, and yet we have all been forgiven. Because of this, we have the power to forgive. This is summed up beautifully in Colossians 3:12–13: "Put on then, as God's chosen ones, holy and beloved, compassion, kindness, lowliness, meekness, and patience, forbearing one another and, if one has a complaint against another, forgiving each other; as the Lord has forgiven you, so you also must forgive."

Forgiveness is a powerful form of evangelization. We simply follow the lead of Jesus, who, while enduring the greatest injustice and evil in the history of the world, prayed in response to all of our sins, "Father, forgive them; for they know not what they do" (Lk 23:34). You have to wonder how the first Christians were so successful at spreading the faith, even in pagan lands. One reason has to be the witness of their people, and especially their martyrs. Saint Stephen, the first martyr after the Resurrection, died while praying for his persecutors. His final words were "Lord, do not hold this sin against them" (Acts 7:60). This kind of forgiveness was something the world had never seen before, and it was highly attractive.

For more modern-day stories of forgiveness, I recommend Allen Hunt's book *Everybody Needs to Forgive Somebody*.[14]

---

[14] *Everybody Needs to Forgive Somebody* (North Palm Beach, Fla.: Beacon, 2016).

Comfort the Afflicted

Suffering is inevitable in this life. You cannot avoid suffering in a fallen world. However, this does not mean we should go looking for suffering, and it does not mean we should not try to relieve the suffering of others. Indeed, the suffering of others is Jesus calling us into action. Even if we cannot relieve suffering, we are called to "take on the odour of the sheep",[15] as Pope Francis said. Taking on the smell of the sheep refers to compassion, which means "the act of suffering with".

I will never forget the final week of my father's life. My family was all home with him so we could spend his final days together. We wanted somebody to be with him twenty-four hours a day as he went through the dying process, so my two older brothers and I did the night shift, staying up with him until about five in the morning, when my mother awoke. What we expected to be just a night or two turned into almost a week. My father's body had been strong and active just months earlier and would just not shut down that quickly.

Those final nights with my father and my brothers left a deep impression on me. My brother suggested we pray a Divine Mercy chaplet each night, and this was my first experience with the chaplet. I had never heard of it before. Those words struck a chord with me: "For the sake of His sorrowful passion, have mercy on us and on the whole world. Holy God, Holy Mighty One, Holy Immortal One, have mercy on us and on the whole world."

My father occasionally wanted to get out of his bed and move to his rocking chair. Being too weak to walk on his

[15] Homily of Pope Francis, Chrism Mass, St. Peter's Basilica, March 28, 2013, http://w2.vatican.va/content/francesco/en/homilies/2013/documents/papa-francesco_20130328_messa-crismale.html.

own, he needed us to help him. With one of us on his right, and another on his left, he put his arms around our shoulders, and we bore his weight as he walked just a few steps. Doing this one night, I pictured in my mind Simon of Cyrene, one of the bystanders when Jesus was carrying His Cross. Seeing that Jesus was unable to go further on His own, the soldiers forced Simon into action. The Gospels simply say that Simon was a passerby "compelled ... to carry his [Jesus'] cross" (Mk 15:21). The movie *The Passion of the Christ* portrays a transformation of Simon of Cyrene. At first, he does not want to help and resists. However, as he walks beside the suffering Jesus, his heart is changed, so much so that by the time they reach the top of the hill, the soldiers have to push him away. We see a man who encourages Jesus, protects Jesus from the blows of the soldiers, and does not want to leave His side when their journey is complete. He encountered the most powerful force in the universe in the humble form of a weak and vulnerable man. One thing is certain—he was never the same.

Helping my father walk that night and staying with him in his suffering, I realized I am Simon. We are all Simon. Sometimes we are called to help the sorrowful and the afflicted, and it seems too difficult for us. We do not want to get involved. However, if you spend time with the poor, the suffering, and the lonely, you begin to feel drawn to them. You find strength you did not know you had. You begin to suffer with them, hoping to relieve the weight of their burden. You begin to be inspired by the way they carry their crosses, and cannot help but get involved.

My father was a man who won at everything, and his endurance and persistence in hanging on in his final days was agonizing to the point where we were begging him just to let go because we did not want him to suffer anymore. However, this endurance was perhaps one of the greatest gifts that my father gave me before he died, and a great lesson that Jesus gave all of us in His passion. By enduring His suffering to the end, Jesus allowed Simon to serve Him—and not just Simon but all of us. He allows us to console His broken heart while He endures the pain and agony of the Cross. Again, we see why "mercy killing" is not merciful or compassionate. It denies the opportunity for compassion (the act of suffering with someone) and denies an opportunity to learn to love. Watching those we love suffer is often more difficult than our own suffering, but through our brothers and sisters who are hurting, we all have the opportunity to answer the call of Jesus in the agony in the garden: "My soul is very sorrowful, even to death; remain here, and watch with me" (Mt 26:38).

Pray for the Living and the Dead

Prayer is one of the most powerful forces in the universe. This is why we pray for one another. This is why we offer petitions at Mass. This is why we pray for conversion and why we pray for our enemies. Jesus taught us the importance of prayer and how to pray and revealed how prayer changes things and can work miracles. I know I have benefited in my life from many prayers. After my grandma Agnes died, somebody told me that she used to walk laps around the church praying rosaries for her children and grandchildren. I know I have benefited from the many prayers of my own mother, since a mother's prayers are powerful.

Working in nursing homes most days, I have discovered a hidden treasure of prayers. The prayers of those who are sick or suffering or lonely are very powerful. In fact, I believe the prayers of these people are sustaining our Church. Visiting my patients who I know have strong prayer lives, the first thing I do is ask them if they would be willing to pray for me and my family. This accomplishes two things. First, the elderly need to know how much they are needed. They need to know the potential they have to help get souls to heaven. Second, I really do need and want those prayers! After that, I can proceed to ask them what I can do for them, not because they are helpless, but because they have offered me such a great gift and I would like to help them in some way as well.

Saint Paul tells us we should "pray constantly" (1 Thess 5:17). One way to do this is to offer up the day for another person. We can offer our sacrifices and sufferings as a form of prayer to help other souls get to heaven. God allows us to participate in salvation history by allowing us to unite our comparatively small sacrifices to His great sacrifice at Calvary. When we wake up in the morning, we can simply pray, "Lord, I offer my day for ..." You can offer it up for a family member, a friend, the lady at the grocery store, that annoying person at work, that person who wronged you—anybody! When people say they need prayers, put them on your list. Actually pray for them. Offer your day for them.

One example of the power of offering sacrifices and suffering as a form of prayer is Servant of God Elisabeth Leseur. She was married to an atheist doctor who often ridiculed her faith. Elisabeth had a difficult life and developed many health problems. After acquiring hepatitis, she developed a painful form of cancer. During all of her suffering, she decided to keep a spiritual journal, in which she wrote about redemptive suffering and how she had decided to offer her own suffering for the conversion of her husband. She died at the young age of forty-eight. After her death, her atheist husband found her writings and discovered her offerings for him. She even predicted that one day her husband would become a priest. When he saw this, he was infuriated. He saw it as nonsense and decided that as a doctor he was going to travel to Lourdes, France, to prove that all the so-called miraculous healings were hoaxes.

He traveled to Lourdes, but instead of proving that the miracles were phony, he was converted to the faith. As his wife had predicted, he went on to become a Dominican priest, and he often spoke about the spiritual writings of his wife and the power of redemptive prayers and suffering. He opened up the cause for the canonization of his wife, whose prayers converted him from atheist to priest.

Not only can we offer prayers and sacrifices for those who are still with us in this life, but we can also offer prayers for those who have gone before us. If you have ever been to a Catholic funeral, you know that the prayers of the Mass do not assume that the person who has died is in heaven. The prayers are all requests to take the soul into heaven. The only people who we are certain are in heaven are the canonized saints, whom the Church has declared to be in heaven through the canonization process. It is our goal to go straight to heaven after death, but unless we make the journey from sinner to saint perfectly in this life, we must finish that journey in the next. If we die in the state of grace but have not yet been fully purified and transformed into the saint we were created to be, then we finish that process in what the Church calls purgatory. The souls in purgatory are guaranteed heaven but only after a final purification. I know it is a challenging and difficult teaching for some people, but perhaps the following analogy will help.

I went through eight years of college to become an eye doctor. It was an extremely expensive process, which left me with a debt that I will be paying off for much of my life. Let us imagine that the debt is so big that I could never pay it off on my own. However, somebody decides to pay the debt for me as a free gift. Now my debt is paid off, but that does not mean I am a great doctor. Becoming a great doctor and being free from debt are two separate things. I have to work hard, study, and pass the proper tests to make sure I have the skills to be a doctor. In much the same way, our human nature has to be purified, even if the guilt of sin is forgiven. We still have to become fully alive, fully loving, and fully the people God created us to be. While somebody can pay my debt, he cannot take the tests for me or help me obtain the proper skills without my effort.

Life is a journey, not a destination. Heaven is the destination; this life is the journey. There are indeed trials, tests, failures, and success. Becoming a doctor is a long process that takes time and commitment and perseverance. You have to go through the process, even if you have a free ride. God is not going to snap His fingers and take care of all our problems and turn us into perfect people. If He did that, we would not be saints—we would be robots. He does not want robots. That is why God gave us each a free will.

Without the process of transforming your heart and your will to conform to the will of God, you do not become the saint God created you to be here in this life; and then you have to finish that journey in the next. It is a choice, and we must use our free will to choose to allow God to transform us. God does the transforming, but we have to cooperate and go through the process. It is not about what you do; it is about who you become. Thank God for purgatory. Aim for heaven with the hopes of going straight there, and if you need a little final purification, then be thankful for purgatory. However, if you aim for purgatory and miss, then you are in trouble.

The good news is that we have many classmates making the journey with us. We are pilgrims, not tourists. The Church that Jesus built on the rock of Peter is like the new ark that replaces the one Noah built, saving us from death and taking us to a new life. But it is not a Carnival cruise ship. It is more like the *Mayflower*. We are going somewhere, and we can help each other reach our destination. Death does not separate us. The saints in heaven are constantly praying and interceding for us, and we can pray and intercede for the souls in purgatory to help them in their purification.

You should get in the habit of praying for the souls in purgatory. There is a very common and well-known prayer that I think works well: "May the souls of the faithful departed, through the mercy of God, rest in peace. Amen." My family often says this after our meal prayer, but I would suggest that every time you drive past a cemetery or walk through a cemetery, you make the sign of the cross and say this short prayer. You will be amazed at how many cemeteries you pass on any given day and how much opportunity you have to help your brothers and sisters by this simple habit.

For all the recommended resources for "Sacrifice and Service", go to the website: www.saintsinthemaking.com /sacrifice-and-service-resources.html.

CONCLUSION

*I long so much to make beautiful things. But beautiful
things require effort and disappointment and perseverance.*

—Vincent van Gogh

Great Cathedrals

The Church has a rich history of beautiful art and music.
Music and art are the language of the soul and proof of its
existence. They are weapons of spiritual warfare employed
by both God and the devil, with the power to lead souls
to corruption or to sanctification. By means of the human
senses, they lead people to encounter the transcendent.

There are two young ladies who sing at most of my
events. They are former students of mine, and I have tried
to be a good teacher for them. It has been one of the
greatest blessings for me to see them grow in their faith
and use their amazing gift of music for the glory of God.
I used to be their teacher, but they have become mine. I
have the ability to speak to people's minds, and I hope at
times to tug at their hearts, but those young ladies have the
ability to move people deeply by the beauty of their songs.
Every cathedral and every song that rises to the heavens
has the ability to help people experience the spiritual and
the divine in a way that mere words cannot.

The great cathedrals of Europe inspire awe and wonder among those who encounter them. I have seen only

pictures, but the visitors say that photos cannot do justice to the magnitude of those cathedrals. I can only imagine the sound of the music that echoes through them. The cathedrals here in the United States always create a deep sense of awe in me. I cannot help but wonder how much time and effort went into creating those masterpieces, with radiant stained glass windows, endless stories told in the form of art, and the beauty and reverence of the golden tabernacle holding the God of the universe. It simply takes your breath away.

Some people say that buildings like that are a waste of time and money and accuse the Church of ulterior motives for building such places. I wholeheartedly disagree. Read the Old Testament and you will see a grand temple filled with gold and cherubim, requested by God to reveal His beauty through awe and wonder to those who approach Him.

Those cathedrals transcend time and for centuries have spoken to mankind about God in a way that words simply cannot. They were built not for instant gratification but with what Matthew Kelly calls the "long view".[1] Hundreds of years later, they still serve the same purpose they were created for. Many people spent their whole lives building these great structures, some knowing they would never live to see their completion. Yet, their work still affects the world today, hundreds of years later. Nobody may truly know the sacrifice it took to build them, but the sacrifice was well worth the effort. The paradox of a cathedral is that is does not point to itself. It points to a greater reality. It teaches us more than anything that the Church is not a building but the family of a loving Creator, and that each of us was made for love. Like a stained glass window, we

[1] *The Long View* (North Palm Beach, Fla.: Beacon, 2014).

are each tiny pieces of a puzzle that, when put together, produce a radiant spectacle of color and design.

In the movie *Field of Dreams*, Kevin Costner's character hears a voice: "If you build it, they will come." Perhaps that is the voice of God in our lives. If you build His Church, people will come. They will see the truth and beauty radiating from your witness, and they will want what you have. There is nothing more attractive than holiness.

The Catholic Church is the spotless and radiant Bride of Christ, preparing herself for the Bridegroom in that moment in the book of Revelation where it says, "For the marriage of the Lamb has come, and his Bride has made herself ready" (Rev 19:7). I love her. She is worth fighting for, worth living for, and worth dying for.

It is worth building this Church one soul at a time. Just like the great cathedrals, those souls reveal the beauty and the mystery of God's love to the world. I am asking you to build. When you pass the faith on to others by your words and witness, you are building great cathedrals. Even if you do not live to see the completion of your great sacrifice, it is worth building. Even if nobody on earth sees your sacrifice, God sees. He has the stopwatch of your life, and He will not let your efforts go to waste. All things in time. One day you will see perfectly how your witness was an essential link in the chain of salvation history.

Hearts on Fire

A couple of summers ago, a huge storm came through our neighborhood and knocked down our best apple tree. It broke at the bottom of the trunk, leaving the roots in the ground. I cut up the tree the best I could with my little, old electric chainsaw, but the trunk was simply too large and fat to cut up. It was also too heavy to pick up. So I rolled it to the backyard and into our burn pile and placed many of the branches on top.

A year later, my children wanted to have a campout in the backyard and start a big bonfire with the dead tree. I do not know a whole lot about starting fires, so it was a bit of a challenge for me to get the fire going. The old, dead leaves caught fire very easily, but the flames quickly died out. I brought out a bunch of old utility and electric bills that I had paid and started them on fire, which was quite enjoyable, but those flames too petered out very quickly. I could not figure out how to get the large branches and the huge trunk to start burning. I have seen people throw gasoline on fires, and while that makes quite an initial outburst of flames, it is not safe, and the initial burst fades once the gasoline is consumed. What is started quickly is often lost quickly.

Finally I found some small wooden fire starters and many smaller pieces of cardboard and wood. I strategically placed them all around the woodpile and lit them on fire one by one. As little fires began to start, I added larger pieces of wood to keep them burning until the small fires came together to form one big fire. Still, the trunk was stubborn and thick, and it took quite a long time of keeping that fire hot before the trunk even seemed to be affected by the flames. Eventually, with enough heat and persistence, that trunk began to glow a bright orange. It did not create a giant flame, but it burned hot from within and produced a huge amount of heat.

I was pretty proud of myself for getting that fire started, and I sat nearby late into the night, until all the branches and limbs had burned away, leaving only the glowing-red tree trunk. The fire looked to be pretty much out since no flames were coming from the trunk, so I went to our tent and fell asleep. The next morning, I noticed smoke still rising from the burn pile and figured it was steam coming from the ashes in the cool morning air. The next day I went off to work and forgot about it. It rained the following day, and two days later I went out to mow the lawn. Suddenly, I noticed smoke rising from the burn pile. I was intrigued, and walked over to find that tree trunk still glowing.

After two days and even a rain shower, the trunk was still being consumed by the fire burning within. It hit me immediately. That is the key to the New Evangelization—setting hearts on fire. The trunk of a tree is the heart of the tree. It is the connection between the roots and the branches. Strong roots do no good without a heart to carry the nutrients from those roots. Branches will surely bear no fruit if the trunk of the tree does not anchor them and pump life-giving nutrients to the extremities like the heart of a body.

This is how we reengage disengaged Catholics. Many have strong roots, but their hearts have gone cold. Many possess great talents and abilities that would bear much fruit if only their hearts were not cold. The question is, How do we set their hearts on fire? Or maybe the first question is, How do we set our own hearts on fire? You cannot give what you do not have, so you can spread a fire only if you have fire.

It is important to remember that what is gained quickly is lost quickly; it takes patient perseverance to retain what we gain. It takes more than a moment—it takes a movement. We have many "honeymoon" moments—an inspiring talk, a good book, a powerful song, a beautiful sunset—and such experiences are essential to get the fire started, but real love begins when the honeymoon is over. Our faith and love for God must be based not on warm fuzzy feelings but on an internal burning love that will persevere in the hardest of times, the greatest of trials, the biggest of storms, and the darkest of nights.

Another lesson I learned from starting that bonfire was that many small fires coming together can make a big fire. It will take all the small fires of each parish and each soul coming together to make a heat so united and powerful that it can set hearts ablaze and keep the flame of faith alive. We are one Church, and we must work together as one—many parts, *one* body.

We all have our roles to play to form the mystical body of Christ, and no role is unimportant:

> And his gifts were that some should be apostles, some prophets, some evangelists, some pastors and teachers, to equip the saints for the work of ministry, for building up the body of Christ, until we all attain to the unity of the faith and of the knowledge of the Son of God, to mature manhood, to the measure of the stature of the fulness of Christ; so that we may no longer be children, tossed back and forth and carried about with every wind of doctrine, by the cunning of men, by their craftiness in deceitful wiles. Rather, speaking the truth in love, we are to grow up in every way into him who is the head, into Christ, from whom the whole body, joined and knit together by every joint with which it is supplied, when each part is working properly, makes bodily growth and upbuilds itself in love. (Eph 4:11–16)

When I think of the importance of unity and working together with our unique talents, I am reminded of a classic scene in the movie *Miracle*, about the 1980 U.S. Olympic men's ice hockey team that won the gold medal. Coach Herb Brooks is mercilessly punishing the team after a poorly played exhibition game in their preparation for the Olympics. He has them skate "suicides" across the ice after the game, over and over. It is almost hard to watch as he keeps saying, "Again, again, again." The players begin to wonder if they will ever get to leave the ice; all of them have legs of Jell-O and lungs on fire. Finally, the man who would later become captain of the team and the hero of the big game against Russia screams his own name with all the breath he has left: "Mike Eruzione!" Coach Brooks then asks Mike, "Who do you play for?", as he had been asking the men throughout their training. Up to this point in the movie, the men had always replied with the name of the college they had attended. "I play for Boston College", "I play for the UMD Bulldogs", etc. As Mike gasps for air, he shouts, "I play for ... the United States of America!" With that, Coach Brooks is satisfied that the men have learned their lesson, and replies, "That is all, gentlemen." He wants them to understand that the name on the front of the jersey (the team) is more important than the name on the back (the player).

Perhaps we need a Coach Herb Brooks to unify us. We often cling to our own buildings and our own customs and our own comfortable routines. We do not play just for Saint Peter's, or Saint Paul's, or Saint Matthew's parish. We play for the *Catholic* Church—the *universal* Church founded by Jesus Christ. We are one! To rebuild this Church, we must work together as one in truth and love. Each parish is a small fire that alone will peter out, but together those fires can burn persistently as the mystical body of Jesus Christ.

I can hear the words that God spoke to Saint Francis more than eight hundred years ago: "Rebuild My Church." Let us work together to set the world ablaze and spread our faith and the love of Jesus Christ to the ends of the earth. You cannot give what you do not have. Learn your faith so you can live your faith and share it with the whole world. You have been given the saving grace ("Saving Grace", chap. 1) necessary to run the good race ("Athletics", chap. 2). You are part of the greatest story ever told ("Instructor's Manual", chap. 3), and you can share that story with the whole world. You can fully experience the love of God ("Need to Know Him", chap. 4), image that love through your body ("Theology of the Body", chap. 5), and be the hands and feet of Jesus Christ ("Sacrifice and Service", chap. 6). Remember, you are not the sum of your fears and failures and past regrets, but you are a child of God—a son or a daughter of the Most High King, an heir to the kingdom of heaven. You are a saint in the making!

ACKNOWLEDGMENTS

Special gratitude to the following individuals who helped make this book a reality:

My wife, Kristin Wood, and my children, Isabelle, Hannah, Isaiah, and Moriah, for their love, support, patience, motivation, and inspiration.

My mother, Kathy Wood, for providing me with a strong foundation and being an authentic witness to the Catholic faith.

My brother Kevin Wood, for sharing his knowledge of the faith; my brother Brian Wood, for being my greatest supporter and encourager; and my brother Father Eric Wood, for his powerful intercession and witness as a priest of almighty God.

Bishop Daniel Thomas, for all his support and for being a great shepherd and a bold leader in the New Evangelization. His holiness, joy, and zeal are contagious.

Father Joseph Poggemeyer, STD, for helping me make sure this manuscript was theologically sound in accordance with the teachings of the Catholic Church.

My spiritual director, Father Paul Fahrbach, for sharing his love for our faith and always giving me a spiritual jolt of enthusiasm.

Father John Riccardo, Father Michael Schmitz, Matthew Kelly, Brant Pitre, Jeff Cavins, Scott Hahn, Jason Evert, Christopher West, Peter Herbeck, Ralph Martin, Jon Leonetti, Allen Hunt, Father Michael Gaitley, and countless other authors and theologians, for teaching me through books, radio, and audio recordings.

Rachel Ann Snyder and Cassandra Acree, for sharing their youthful insight and their musical talent, and for traveling with me across the country to share this message in a much more powerful way than words alone can.

Dennis Erford and Matt Kettinger, for sharing their time, talent, and expertise in helping me with the Theology of the Body chapter.

Beth Church, Carol Kurivial, and Jim Schroeder, for donating their editing talents.

My father, Jack Wood, for introducing me to God the Father. Dad, you continue to be my greatest inspiration. I will keep my promise to you, and always strive to become the saint God created me to be, and inspire millions of others to do the same.

My God, for using ordinary me to do His extraordinary work. God, I thank You for creating me, loving me, and blessing me abundantly in this life. I am Yours. Do with me what You will.

ABOUT THE AUTHOR

Dr. John R. Wood is the author of *Ordinary Lives, Extraordinary Mission: 5 Steps to Winning the War Within* (North Palm Beach, Fla.: Beacon, 2012). It has been one of Dynamic Catholic's best-selling books, with more than 220,000 copies distributed. Since the release of the book in December 2012, John has spoken at more than one hundred parishes and schools across the country, inspiring thousands to embrace the message of the universal call to holiness and help reawaken the sleeping giant called the Catholic Church.

John is very active in his faith and in his local parish. John and his wife Kristin's dedication to the faith earned them the 2011 Centurion Award from the Diocese of Toledo, given for outstanding service to their parish.

John and Kristin currently reside in northwest Ohio with their four children. John is a mobile eye doctor, and he travels to more than forty nursing homes and developmental disability facilities to provide eye care through his business, Mobile Eyes, which he started in 2007.